Pre-Columbian World Systems

Edited by
Peter N. Peregrine *and*
Gary M. Feinman

Monographs in World Archaeology No. 26

PREHISTORY PRESS
Madison Wisconsin

Prehistory Press
2712 Marshall Court
Madison, Wisconsin 53705

James A. Knight, Publisher

ISBN 1-881094-16-2
ISSN 1055-2316

Library of Congress Cataloging-in-Publication Data

Peregrine, Peter N. (Peter Neal), 1963-
Pre-Columbian world systems / Peter N. Peregrine, Gary M. Feinman; contributors, Christopher Chase-Dunn ... [et al.].
p. cm. -- (Monographs in world archaeology, ISSN 1055-2316 ; no. 26)
Includes bibliographical references.
ISBN 1-881094-16-2 (alk. paper)
1. Indians of North America--Antiquities. 2. Mississippian culture. 3. Indians of Mexico--Mexico--Oaxaca--Antiquities. 4. Mayas--Antiquities. 5. Economic history. 6. Economic development. I. Feinman, Gary M. II. Chase-Dunn, Christopher K. III. Title. IV. Series.
E77.9.P428 1996
330.97'00111--dc20 95-49694
CIP

Contents

Preface

Peter N. Peregrine
Gary M. Feinman

This volume was born at the 1992 meetings of the Society for American Archaeology in Pittsburgh, Pennsylvania. Two half-day symposia, one organized by Christopher Chase-Dunn and Thomas Jackson, the other by Peter Peregrine, brought together twenty one scholars to debate the potential of world-systems theory for analyzing pre-Columbian North American societies. The participants found the discussions stimulating, and suggested that the organizers attempt to bring them to a larger audience by pulling the papers together into an edited volume. Peregrine was given the initial task of organizing and editing the papers, and Gary Feinman later offered his editorial experience and skill to make them more focused and coherent. Along the way a number of the original papers fell out of the collection either because their authors had other commitments or because they did not integrate well with the remainder of the volume. The editors would like to thank those scholars whose papers are included here for their continuing interest in the volume. We would also like to thank the three anonymous reviewers who commented on earlier drafts, and whose critiques have certainly made both the individual chapters and the volume as a whole better. Finally, we would like to extend our graditude to Jay Knight of Prehistory Press for his patience and support in bringing this volume into print.

Chapter 1

Introduction: World-Systems Theory and Archaeology

Peter N. Peregrine
Lawrence University

In a seminal paper on pre-capitalist world-systems Jane Schneider (1977:20; reprinted in Chase-Dunn and Hall 1991a) argued that Immanuel Wallerstein's (1974a; 1974b) world-system perspective has tremendous potential for theory building in the social sciences because it is able to provide a single theoretical framework in which to analyze both Western and non-Western societies. Schneider (1977:26) suggested that the world-system perspective "pushes social science toward an understanding of change in which Western and non-Western, traditional and modern, peoples are subject, if not to similar outcomes, then at least to similar laws." This idea has been heeded by a number of archaeologists who in recent years have produced a series of valuable studies of prehistoric world-systems (for reviews see Chase-Dunn and Hall 1991b:36-37; Sanderson 1991:173-175; Hall and Chase-Dunn 1993, 1994; Schortman and Urban 1992b). Volumes by Rowlands, Larsen and Kristiansen (1987), Champion (1989), Chase-Dunn (1992); Chase-Dunn and Hall (1991a) and Schortman and Urban (1992a) provide both theoretical discussions and detailed examinations of prehistoric world-systems.

Despite the important contribution these and other authors have made to archaeology, most archaeologists still only marginally accept the world-system perspective. Rarely does one find an article written from an explicitly world-systems perspective in any of the widely-read archaeological journals, particularly in the Americas. I suggest that part of the reason for this lack of interest in world-systems stems from a basic confusion over two separate concepts: the world-system perspective and world-systems theory. The world-system perspective is a research program, or perhaps more simply, a way of viewing the world. It allows one to perceive the world as a set of autonomous political units linked into a larger functioning unit through economic interdependence. World-systems theory defines the nature of the economic interdependence. So while there are many world-system theories defining many different types of world-systems, there is only one world-system perspective. Unfortunately, the perspective seems to have been dismissed by many archaeologists because of valid arguments against particular theories, especially as applied to situations they were not developed for (see Schortman and Urban 1987:58-59). The purpose of this volume is to direct attention once again to the world-system perspective and to argue that equipped with proper theory, it can, as Schneider suggested and the archaeologists mentioned above have demonstrated, be a powerful perspective for theory building and analysis in archaeology (also see Kohl 1987:2-7).

The World-System Perspective

Wallerstein's (1974a, 1974b) world-system perspective is rooted in the idea that the social sciences have been hindered by unilineal or developmentalist theory building. Wallerstein (1976:344) argues that developmentalists assume individual societies are the basic unit of analysis despite the fact that economic and political reality contradicts that notion. As Wallerstein (1976:345) explains:

> The key difference between a developmentalist and a world-system perspective is the point of departure, the unit of analysis. A developmentalist perspective assumes that the unit within which social action principally occurs is a politico-cultural unit—the state, or nation, or people—and seeks to explain differences between these units, including why their economies are different. A world-system perspective assumes, by contrast, that social action take place in an entity within which there is an ongoing division of labour, and seeks to discover *empirically* whether such an entity is or is not unified politically or culturally, asking *theoretically* what are the consequences of the existence or non-existence of such unity.

The entity within which social action takes place is the world-system. The "world" of a world-system is defined by an economic interdependence, and not by any specific geographical, political, or cultural units (for a more detailed discussion of how world-systems are bounded see Chase-Dunn and Hall 1991a; Hall and Chase-Dunn, this volume). Individual world-systems, however, are more than just the sum of their constituent polities or cultures, but possess properties of their own (Bach 1980:294). These properties, again, are not traits, but processes:

> If there is one thing which distinguishes a world-system perspective from any other, it is its insistence that the unit of analysis is a *world*-system defined in terms of *economic* processes and links, and not any units defined in terms of judicial, political, cultural, geographical, etc., criteria. (Hopkins and Wallerstein 1977:123)

This idea is perhaps best summed up by Bach (1980:295): "For the world-system perspective, then, the whole consists of singular economic processes which *form* and *reform* the relations that express patterns or structures."

The world-system perspective, therefore, begins "with the elementary premise that everything is process" (Wallerstein 1982:91) and that "acting units or agencies can only be thought of as *formed*, and continually reformed, by the relations between them" (Hopkins 1982:149). There are, however, two other premises basic to this perspective. The first is that any world-system will contain within it a geographic (core/periphery) differentiation "according to which particular populations come to play particular roles, their economic, political, and cultural institutions changing to meet the demands of specialization" (Schneider 1977:20). The second is that there will be continuous competition between these geographically differentiated areas. In this way the world-system perspective "hinges on two overlapping processes—one of competition between various geographically localized populations of unequal power; the other of differentiation, division of labor, and interdependence among these same units" (Schneider 1977:20).

World-Systems Archaeology

There are three primary reasons why this world-system perspective is a particularly useful one for theory-building in archaeology. First, the world-system perspective is inherently spatial, focusing attention on cores and peripheries and on the geographical relationships between them, including access to resources, transportation, population, and the like. Archaeology is also fundamentally spatial in orientation, focusing on the search for patterns in spatial data and relating them to the world of social, economic, and political behavior. It is precisely this kind of socio-spatial analysis that the world-system perspective allows one to do (see Agnew 1982; Knox and Agnew 1989; Taylor 1985, 1988).

Second, the world-system perspective is multi-leveled. As Wallerstein (1982:98) explains, one of the things that both complicates and strengthens the world-system perspective is its acceptance of "layers within layers within layers" of economic, social, and political relationships. At one level these relationships exist within a society, but are also seen to extend outward to inter-societal relationships, and inward to intra-family ones. This kind of multi-leveled analysis also occurs in archaeological work. Archaeologists are often primarily concerned with a site or a component of a site, yet that site or component is known to exist in an environmental setting of great importance to its interpretation, as well as in a social and political setting with surrounding sites that, in the rubric of Willey and Phillips (1958), one might term a "phase". Archaeologists also understand that these inter-site social and temporal units exist in larger clusters that one might term macro-regions, "traditions", or "cultures". In short, archaeologists always view sites as only one level in larger social and temporal structures, although theory-building in archaeology has often not taken into account this complicating fact. The world-system perspective not only accepts but demands the kind of multi-leveled reality implicit in all archaeological work.

Third, the world-system perspective is evolutionary. That is, it allows one to propose a typology of socio-political forms among which there is a strong probability a given society will move under an hypothesized set of conditions (see Sanderson 1990:5-7, 210-211, 1991).[1] This is, of course, exactly what archaeologists attempt to do in developing theory (at least "high-level" or "grand" theory).

The world-system perspective, therefore, appears to be a uniquely useful one for theory-building in archaeology (Kohl [1987] and Schortman and Urban [1987] offer a different set of reasons for supporting this conclusion). The question remains why it is not being used more extensively. A large part of the answer stems from the failure to recognize the distinction between the world-system perspective and specific theories of world-system process, and, given that indistinction, concern over valid criticisms of existing world-system theories as applied to archaeological cases.

World-Systems Theory

Given the world-system perspective just described, world-systems theory attempts to define the specific economic processes of different types of world-systems (for some examples see the papers in Chase-Dunn [1992] Chase-Dunn and Hall [1991a] and Rowlands, Larson and Kristiansen [1987]). Wallerstein offers some limited theories of world-system process that define three types of world-systems: (1) world-economies; (2) world-empires; and (3) mini-systems. Despite the impact his theories of world-system process have had in sociology and economic history, Wallerstein shows a lack of understanding when it comes to simple and non-Western economic systems of the kind most frequently studied by archaeologists (Abu-Lughod 1990). As Schortman and Urban (1987:59) put it "anthropological concepts and units of analysis have little part in world-systems theory as formulated by Wallerstein."

This limitation in Wallerstein's theories of world-system process appears more acute when we consider that simple and non-Western economic systems are not included in any of his discussions even though we would expect them to be if, as Wallerstein himself claims, the world-system is the only appropriate unit of analysis for the social sciences. The closest Wallerstein (1976:345-346) comes to a theory of world-system process for simple and non-Western economies is in defining what he calls a "reciprocal-lineage" economy, the processes of which form "mini-systems". The most basic definition of mini-system given by Wallerstein (1974a:390) is "an entity that has within it a complete division of labor and a single cultural framework." Anthropologists have rightly questioned whether any such society exists or has ever existed (Wolf 1982). Regardless of this problem, Wallerstein's definition of mini-systems relies on the reification of a culture as the boundary of the system, and this is contrary to the world-system perspective itself, which says economic processes, not cultures, define the "world" of a world-system. And although Wallerstein (1974a:348) implies that mini-systems are not actually world-systems, but rather some other kind of social system, this implication still contradicts the idea that world-systems are the only appropriate unit of analysis for the social sciences.

The current body of world-systems theory is, therefore, not particularly useful for archaeology because existing theories are focused on capitalism or historic Western civilizations, not on simple or non-Western economic systems (Kohl 1987:29). McGuire (1987:123) expressed this idea succinctly when he said "Wallerstein directs us to the right questions but his work does not provide us the conceptual tools to answer those questions in non-capitalist world-systems." However, as McGuire's statement suggests, this does not mean that the world-system perspective itself is not useful. Indeed, it appears that the world-system perspective both directs archaeology towards interesting questions and provides the framework for constructing interesting answers. What are needed to fit into this framework are new theories of world-system process, theories that are applicable to the kinds of economic systems archaeologists typically study.

Reshaping World-Systems Theory

A number of archaeologists and other social scientists have begun the process of reshaping world-systems theory to make it more applicable to non-capitalist and non-Western economic systems. This reformulation has been proceeding along two general lines: (1) redefining the nature of geographic differentiation within world-systems; and (2) redefining the nature of economic interdependence.

Redefining Core/Periphery Relations

Under the first of these two research agendas, most work has proceeded by rethinking the specific roles or functions of cores and peripheries. As originally conceived by Wallerstein (1974b:401, 1974a:101-102, 354-355; also Shannon 1989:28-30), cores have three primary attributes: (1) they accumulate surplus; (2) they produce items for trade using skilled labor and sophisticated technology; and (3) they have a strong political organization. Peripheries, in Wallerstein's (1974a:392, 1974b:100, 302, 349; also Shannon 1989:28-31) conception, are defined as: (1) being suppliers of raw materials produced using unskilled labor and simple technology; (2) having a weak political organization and (3) being consumers of products manufactured in the core. Wallerstein (1974a:392, 401-403, 1974b:350) understands this relationship (following Frank [1967]) as fundamentally hierarchical. The core dominates the periphery and exploits it by dictating the trade relationship (cheap raw materials for expensive finished products) through which the core constantly accumulates surplus, and by limiting the periphery's access to technology (by which it could, conceivably, produce its own finished products). Wallerstein (1974a:403-405, 1974b:106-107, 349-350; also Shannon 1989:32) also defines a semi-periphery that (1) acts as a "middle man" in trade between the core and the periphery; (2) acts as a political buffer zone, limiting conflict between the core and the periphery and effectively obscuring the nature of the core's domination; and (3) produces some items using older technology imported from the core.

Ekholm and Friedman (1985 [originally 1980]) suggest that anthropologists should consider all societies, whether capitalist or non-capitalist, as part of "global systems" based on both modes of production and modes of social reproduction, rather than part of world-systems based solely on production. Within the concept of global systems, Ekholm and Friedman (1985:113-114) define cores ("centers" in their terminology) and peripheries in a way very similar to Wallerstein, but add to his hierarchy two additional structures: (1) dependent structures, which are dependent on interaction with the global system for their reproduction, but which are neither cores nor peripheries (and which they admit can be similar to semi-peripheries as defined by Wallerstein); and (2) independent structures, which can reproduce themselves outside of the global system, but whose reproduction can affect or be affected by the system. Independent structures may include "predatory" groups such as militaristic nomads (Hall 1991) or groups of "refugee" peoples surviving, untouched, in remote areas of the system (Ekholm and Friedman 1985:114-115).[2] Since all societies should be seen as existing in global systems, this model of core/periphery relations should be applicable to prehistoric societies as well.

Kristiansen (1987) employed Ekholm and Friedman's conception of independent structures in world-systems to conduct a more substantial redefinition of core/periphery relations. Through his analysis of the world-system in Bronze Age Scandinavia he suggests a two-tiered hierarchy of core/periphery relations may exist in some prehistoric world-systems: (1) at the higher level based on organization at a regional scale, but lacking formal exploitive relationships; and (2) at the lower level based on organization at a local scale between centers and attached communities, with formal exploitive relationships (Kristiansen 1987:82). In this model, the independent structures are themselves small world-systems, with local cores exploiting local peripheries. However, these independent world-systems also exist within a larger world-system based on the dependent, but not necessarily exploitive, trade of elite symbols between independent polities. The independent world-systems could physically survive without linkage to the larger system, but elites could not socially reproduce without this connection.

In a further extension of the general concept of independent structures in prehistoric world-systems, Kohl (1987:20-21) argued that peripheries themselves may not be dependent on cores in some prehistoric world-systems. He explains that for Near Eastern Bronze Age societies "peripheries situated between cores were far from helpless in dictating the terms of exchange; they could develop or terminate relations depending upon whether or not these relations were perceived to be in their best interest" (Kohl 1987:20). Kohl (1987:21-23) also argues that, in situations where technology is fairly simple and transportable, peripheries can be technologically sophisticated and even innovative. He concludes that "relations between ancient cores and peripheries were not...analogous to those that underdevelopment theorists postulate are characteristic... today" (Kohl 1987:21), but that comparing prehistoric core/periphery relations with historic ones is important, since it leads us to ask why and in what way those relations are different (Kohl 1987:29).

Chase-Dunn and Hall (1991b, 1991c, 1992, 1993, 1994; Hall and Chase-Dunn 1993, 1994, this volume) have spent considerable effort attempting to answer questions similar to Kohl's; why and in what way were prehistoric, pre-capitalist core/periphery relations different from modern ones? They explain that in order to answer these kinds of questions "What is needed is an explicit effort to formulate competing notions of coreness and peripherality with an eye to a comparative study of intersocietal inequalities" (Chase-Dunn and Hall 1991b:7). As a first step towards the comparative study of world-systems, they have developed a number of guiding principles for examining prehistoric and pre-capitalist cores and peripheries. First, they argue that there is a fundamental difference between core/periphery differentiation and core/periphery hierarchy. All world-systems have differentiated cores and peripheries, they argue, but not all have a hierarchical or exploitive relationship between them (Chase-Dunn and Hall 1991b:18-19), and it is actually important to understand how and why exploitive relationships develop. With this in mind, Chase-Dunn and Hall (1991b:21-32) develop a "typology" of world-systems: kin-based, tributary, and capitalist, and provide hypotheses for the kinds of core/periphery relations present in each under different socio-political conditions. They suggest these are useful categories through which we can begin the comparative study of world-systems, both prehistoric and historic, capitalist and non-capitalist (Chase-Dunn and Hall 1991b:33).

What all these redefinitions of core/periphery relations seem to have in common is the notion that world-systems did exist in prehistoric, pre-capitalist situations, but that Wallerstein's definitions of core/periphery relations are too strict to be directly applied to them (Chase-Dunn and Hall 1992:88-89). Most of the scholars discussed have argued in one way or another that dependency or exploitation is a basic characteristic of the capitalist world-system, but may not have been for pre-capitalist world-systems.[3] Models of core/periphery relations in the absence of this dependency open the world-system perspective to a wide variety of pre-capitalist and non-capitalist situations, precisely the kinds of situations which most archaeologists are primarily concerned with.[4]

Redefining Economic Interdependence

Under the second of the two research agendas discussed above, work has generally proceeded by rethinking the nature of the goods involved in trade within world-systems, and particularly by considering the possibility of an economic interdependence based on luxury goods. Wallerstein (1974a:398) insists that world-systems must be based on trade in staples rather than luxury goods. He tells us bluntly that "In the long run, staples account for more of men's economic thrusts than luxuries" (Wallerstein 1974b:42). The distinction between luxuries and staples is never clearly defined by Wallerstein, although he indicates that within trade relations luxuries are goods that are highly valued by one society but not by another, creating "rich trades" rather than the systemic interdependence of a world-system (Wallerstein 1982:100, 1989:130-132), and that staples are goods valued by all and used by individuals to maintain and reproduce themselves both physically and socially (Wallerstein 1974b:302). The idea that social reproduction can require access to certain goods, goods valued by all members of a trade relation, has been the basis for a wide-ranging critique of Wallerstein's exclusion of luxury goods from the processes of world-systems.

Schneider (1977), very soon after the release of *The Modern World-System*, argued Wallerstein's insistence that staples and staples alone could create a systemic interdependence between polities contradicted the reality of many non-capitalist economic systems. As she (Schneider 1977:21) plainly states,

> Before the emergence of the capitalist world-system...most exchanges between distant places involved the movement of luxuries...For many authorities...[luxuries and staples] are implicitly categorized as opposites: preciosities *versus* essentials or utilities. I suggest that this dichotomy is a false one which obscures the systemic properties of the luxury trade.

Schneider (1977:23-27) goes on to consider a variety of prehistoric and historic cases which support her proposition that luxury trade can have systemic properties. She (Schneider 1977:25) concludes that, for Europe and Asia, "it is possible to hypothesize a *pre-capitalist* world-system, in which core areas accumulated precious metals while exporting manufactures, whereas peripheral areas gave up these metals...against an inflow of finished goods."

Much theoretical work in world-systems archaeology has followed Schneider's lead, predicting and modeling prehistoric situations in which luxury trade is a systemic process. Blanton and Feinman (1984), for example, examine luxury trade in pre-Columbian Mesoamerica. They (Blanton and Feinman 1984:676-677) tell us that the exchange and consumption of particular categories of luxury goods was vital to the maintenance of political power in many pre-Columbian Mesoamerican polities, so vital that it was a major source of both internal conflict and external conquest. Indeed, they (Blanton and Feinman 1984:678) argue that "a consequence of the growth of powerful core states in ancient Mesoamerica was a widespread stimulation of trade, a reorienting of priorities in many places toward production and exchange in the world-system arena." They (Blanton and Feinman 1984:678-679) argue further that, through the demands of tribute in the form of labor-intensive luxury goods that could be exchanged in the world-system, cores actively peripheralized outlying regions in ancient Mesoamerica.

Schneider's argument that luxury trade can have systemic impact in prehistoric worlds has been more directly tied to the idea of social reproduction through the concept of prestige-good systems. As defined in two seminal papers by Friedman and Rowlands (1977) and Frankenstein and Rowlands (1978), prestige-good systems exist when important aspects of political alliance or social reproduction are tied to the consumption or exchange of specific exotic preciosities that can only be obtained through foreign trade. Frankenstein and Rowlands (1978:76) lucidly explain the economic logic of prestige-good systems:

> The specific economic characteristics of a prestige-goods system are dominated by the political advantage gained through exercising control over access to resources that can only be obtained through external trade. However, these are not the resources required for general material well-being or for the manufacture of tools and other utilitarian items. Instead, emphasis is placed on controlling the acquisition of wealth objects needed in social transactions, and the payment of social debts. Groups are linked to each other through the competitive exchange of wealth objects as gifts and feasting in continuous cycles of status rivalry. Descent groups reproduce them-

> selves in opposition to each other as their leaders compete for dominance through differential access to resources and labour power.

While never explicitly linked to world-systems theory, it is clear that there is economic interdependence, geographic differentiation, and competition between independent polities, so it is reasonable to conceive of prestige-good systems as world-systems (Peregrine 1991a, 1992:5-6). Indeed Frankenstein and Rowlands (1978:80-81) discuss economic interdependence in terms of core/periphery relations, and in terms of cores dominating peripheries by controlling their access to prestige-goods.

A number of scholars have applied the concept of prestige-good systems to prehistory in an explicitly world-system perspective. Kristiansen (1987) employed the concept in the paper on Bronze Age Scandinavia discussed above, where he argued that much of the interdependence at the higher level of the world-system, the level of dependent structures, was based on the exchange of prestige-goods needed by political leaders to display and maintain their power. Friedman (1982) applied the idea of prestige-good systems in an attempt to explain the different evolutionary trajectories evident in Oceanic prehistory. He argued that different social and political strategies of control over access and distribution of prestige-goods led to different patterns of political centralization and de-centralization. McGuire (1987) used the idea to examine core/periphery relations the Southwestern United States. He argued that a systemic interdependence existed between elites in the Phoenix Basin, who needed shell from the western Papagueria to produce prestige-goods for their social reproduction, and the peoples of the Papagueria, who relied on the Phoenix Basin core for agricultural products when their unreliable method of obtaining irrigation water from rainfall runoff failed.

In my own work on prehistoric world-systems (Peregrine 1991a, 1991b, 1992, 1995), I have attempted to reformulate the idea of prestige-good systems into a broadly applicable model of pre-capitalist world-systems. I have specifically defined the nature of prestige-goods themselves, and demonstrated that the character of these goods changes as societies become more politically centralized (Peregrine 1991b, 1992:47-67). I have also demonstrated that prestige-good systems can exist in a variety of socio-political contexts, from simple, egalitarian societies to states, and that core/periphery relations in prestige-good systems can also range from simple differentiation to domination (Peregrine 1992:9-26). In addition, I developed a model of social evolution in prestige-good systems that predicts the conditions under which political centralization will change (Peregrine 1992:27-46), and conducted an initial evaluation of the model by using it to examine the evolution of chiefdoms in midcontinental North America (Peregrine 1991a, 1992:69-101).

It seems apparent that work under this second research agenda seems is more limited in scope than under the first. Most research has focused on the single problem of demonstrating that trade in luxury goods can have a systemic impact, and on creating models that explore the impact of luxury trade. More specifically, most of this work has been focused on a single kind of systemic luxury trade, that taking place in prestige-good systems. Few scholars have considered other potential reformulations of the nature of trade (but see Kowalewski, this volume), and many questions remain. Are there other systemic forms of luxury trade outside of prestige-good systems? Can the exchange of information or ritual create a systemic interdependence?

The two research agendas discussed in this section are not as disparate as they may seem. Both attempt to expand the realm of world-systems theory from a focus on a mode of production (particularly capitalism) to one that includes or focuses on a mode of reproduction (see Chase-Dunn and Hall 1992:101-105). In prehistoric worlds most societies appear to be largely self-sufficient in terms of subsistence production, but they often rely on interaction with other societies for social reproduction. Reshaping our conceptions about world-systems to accept the idea that core/periphery relations often involve social reproduction, not subsistence, seems to be a focal point of both agendas. In reformulating world-systems theory to make it more applicable to non-Western and non-capitalist economies, both agendas are, in their own way, focusing on interdependence necessary for social reproduction rather than physical reproduction. Certainly social reproduction may be more vital to survival in the kinds of group-oriented and kin-based societies archaeologists typically study than in our individualistic society, but I suggest the examination of social reproduction and its systemic impact should not be limited to non-Western, non-capitalist societies, but should also be integrated into the study of the capitalist world-system.

World-Systems Analysis in Contemporary Archaeology

As I have been discussing, theory-building is a vital focus of research in contemporary world-systems archaeology, and the contribution by Thomas Hall and Christopher Chase-Dunn (Chapter 2) outlines a theoretical approach to the comparative study of world-systems that updates and significantly refines their earlier work, and which forms a conceptual and analytical base for the other papers in this volume. They explore the issues of conceptualization and theory construction which are raised by the analysis of prehistoric world-systems. Hall and Chase-Dunn suggest that the major differences between different types of world-systems cluster around problems of (1) how social labor is mobilized and (2) how surplus accumulation is accomplished. They argue that what is needed to examine these differences in prehistoric world-systems is a looser set of assumptions for what constitutes a world-system. They also argue that key problems in loosening these assumptions arise in defining the boundaries of world-systems, both geographically and temporally, and suggest the need for analytical methods that can shift levels.

Arguing along similar lines, Stephen Kowalewski (Chapter 3) makes the basic point that we have defined world-systems too rigidly. He argues (along the lines of Ekholm and Friedman [1985]) that all peoples live in world-systems which can be maximally defined in terms of ecological macro-regions. Within these macro-regions are smaller regions of interdependence where matter, energy, and information are transferred among societies. Kowalewski also challenges the idea that prestige-goods are the structuring exchange items in many prehistoric world-systems. He suggests that prestige-good exchanges, rather than structuring relations in prehistoric world-systems, are simply a reflection of those relations, and while they may be a good analytical tool for examining relations in a world-system, they are not a useful theoretical tool for explaining why those relations exist.

In my contribution to the volume (Chapter 4), I argue that part of the difficulty archaeologists have in employing a world-systems perspective is that we are too tightly wedded to the idea of the site as the basic unit of analysis. I examine one of the most vocal debates in contemporary archaeological research in eastern North American , a debate centered on the application of world-systems theory to Iroquoian prehistory. I argue that both sides in the debate are lead astray by their implicit rejection of a basic tenet of the world-systems perspective: that it is a world-system which should be the basic unit of analysis. I attempt to show how this debate might be informed if world-systems were employed as the basic analytical unit.

There are, of course, many ongoing debates in contemporary archaeology (and, indeed, in the social sciences in general, as comprehensively reviewed by Shannon [1989:137-179]) over the utility and validity of research conducted within a world-system perspective, and the paper by Randall McGuire (Chapter 5) lucidly voices some of these critiques. McGuire argues that prehistoric cases do not often match expectations drawn from world-systems theory. He uses the Hohokam cultures of southern Arizona to demonstrate this problem, arguing that while this is precisely the kind of situation in which world-systems theory would appear to be most useful (see the discussion of his previous work above), one cannot demonstrate that the area was ever economically or politically integrated. Therefore, world-systems theory tends to greatly overestimate large-scale processes at the expense of more significant small-scale processes and local social relations. He suggests this gross overemphasis on system-level process is a general problem with the use of world-systems theory in archaeology.

Gary Feinman, Linda Nicholas, and Steadman Upham (Chapter 6) explore the implications of shifting levels or scales in world-system analysis. Through their examination of the later prehistory of the American Southwest and highland Mesoamerica, they suggest that these two regions can be seen as either participants in a single macro-regional world-system or as independent, regional world-systems. Feinman, Nicholas and Upham argue that while both regions did regularly interact with one another, it is more useful to consider them separately, although analysis, they suggest, should be flexible enough to move between these two levels. The reason they argue in this way is because their comparison of the two regions demonstrates that the two differed significantly in the extent of prestige-goods exchanges, in the diversity of cultures, and in the size and stability of political units, all of which appear greater in Mesoamerica. They suggest these differences, while perhaps related to a macro-regional core/ periphery relationship, are more easily explained through the process of state formation in the Mesoamerican world-system, a process which apparently tended to solidify social and cultural barriers rather than unify them.

Cores are a focus of most contemporary research in world-systems archaeology. This is not surprising, as archaeologists' research efforts are, in general, focused on the larger, more complex, and more impressive sites in their areas. Laura Finsten's contribution to the volume (Chapter 7) is an unusual one as she specifically examines a peripheral region, the mountainous area west of the Valley of Oaxaca, Mexico. Through her analysis of architecture and ceramics, Finsten shows how the region developed into an independent polity that was incorporated into the Oaxaca-centered world-system during the Classic period (ca. A.D. 400-900). In addition, she finds two major patterns in the prehistory of the region: (1) that there was a small-scale polity present throughout most of prehistory; but (2) that this polity never achieved the hierarchical development present in the adjacent valley polities. She argues that this is consistent with the traditional world-systems model of peripheral political structure, and that the region's continuous position on the periphery may explain the long-term continuity of the region's polity.

Finally, Edward Schortman and Patricia Urban (Chapter 8) demonstrate the utility (*contra* Kowalewski) of employing the idea of prestige-good systems in their analysis of the prehistory of the Naco Valley in northwestern Honduras. They describe the nature of prehistoric prestige-good exchange and explain how it was the basis for a world-system; however, they also recognize that there are problems inherent in investigating prehistoric prestige-good systems. Through their examination of both artifactual and architectural data, Schortman and Urban demonstrate that powerful rulers of the La Sierra polity monopolized the production and distribution of at least two kinds of prestige-goods: obsidian blades and marine shell ornaments. They conclude that the extensive archaeological record of the La Sierra polity clearly demonstrates that the concept of prestige-good systems can be fruitfully applied to prehistoric situations.

Although the volume is roughly organized by geographical focus, it should be obvious from this brief summary of its contents that this division is somewhat arbitrary. All of the papers transcend their geographical focus to provide new theoretical insights and specific concerns about world-systems theory, while also demonstrating its use in a particular archaeological context. The papers not only demonstrate the potential the world-system perspective has for archaeology, but demonstrate its pitfalls, and offer suggestions for how those pitfalls can be avoided. Through their diverse voices, the eleven authors in this volume leave us with an understanding of the world-system perspective as a self-critical, informative, and powerful theoretical framework for archaeological research.

Notes

1. This idea certainly does not imply that there is any unilineal evolutionary trajectory. Societies move among these forms, but their movement is not necessarily in any one direction, nor do the forms themselves necessarily imply an evolutionary hierarchy.

2. These independent structures may be related to Upham's (1992) idea of "empty spaces" within world-systems. He defines these spaces simply as "those areas between major populations centers: areas without obtrusive or distinctive evidence of population" (Upham 1992:141). While empty spaces may seem devoid of population, Upham (1992:149) argues that they profoundly affect world-systems by posing "significant obstacles to travel, trade, and communication." More importantly (and perhaps in more direct relation to the idea of independent structures), Upham (1992:150) explains that empty spaces provide living areas for people whose social, political, and economic organization is different than those in other areas of the system. Maintaining access or control over empty spaces requires societies in both the core and the periphery to develop mechanisms for interrelating with these peoples, mechanisms that are often maintained with difficulty (the need for interrelation with peoples of different socio-political organization seems to be related, in turn, with Hall's [1989] conception of contact peripheries in the capitalist world-system).

3. A very different conception of core/periphery relations, and indeed of world-systems, has been put forward recently by Frank (1993; Frank and Gills 1993). He argues that there has only been one world system (without the hyphen) in world history, that has been continuously developing for 5000 years. Wallerstein's modern world-system (with the hyphen) is only the most recent transformation of the ancient one. The logic of cores and peripheries in Frank's conception is simple: cores are constant accumulators of goods, information, capital, or whatever, and peripheries are constant suppliers (Gills and Frank 1991:84-93). This is an intriguing idea that Frank and others are already beginning to formulate into a provocative model of world history. However, there are problems with the articulation of this model to the Americas. Since the core of world system began in Mesopotamia and spread from there, it is unclear how pre-Columbian world-systems in the Americas (of the kind examined in this book) fit into Frank's conception of a singular world system (Chase-Dunn and Hall 1991c:280).

4. I am, of course, leaving out the varied and important work of historic archaeologists examining capitalist societies in a world-system perspective (see Paynter 1989 for a review).

References

Abu-Lughod, Janet
1990 *Before European Hegemony: The World System A.D. 1250-1350.* Oxford University Press, New York.

Agnew, John
1982 Sociologizing the Geographical Imagination: Spatial Concepts in the World-System Perspective. *Political Geography Quarterly* 1:159-166.

Bach, Robert
1980 On the Holism of a World-Systems Perspective. In *Processes of the World-System*, edited by T.K. Hopkins and I. Wallerstein, pp. 289-318. Sage, Beverly Hills.

Blanton, Richard and Gary Feinman
1984 The Mesoamerican World-System. *American Anthropologist* 86:673-682.

Champion, Timothy
1989 *Centre and Periphery: Comparative Studies in Archaeology.* Unwin Hyman, London.
Chase-Dunn, Christopher
1992 *Comparing World-Systems.* Special issue of *Review* (Volume 15, Number 3).
Chase-Dunn, Christopher and Thomas Hall
1991a *Core/Periphery Relations in Precapitalist Worlds.* Westview, Boulder.
1991b Conceptualizing Core/Periphery Hierarchies for Comparative Study. In *Core/Periphery Relations in Precapitalist Worlds*, edited by C. Chase-Dunn and T. Hall, pp. 5-44. Westview, Boulder.
1991c Epilogue. In *Core/Periphery Relations in Precapitalist Worlds*, edited by C. Chase-Dunn and T. Hall, pp. 277-290. Westview, Boulder.
1992 World-Systems and Modes of Production: Toward the Comparative Study of Transformations. *Humbolt Journal of Social Relations* 18:81-117
1993 Comparing World-Systems: Concepts and Working Hypotheses. *Social Forces* 71:851-886.
1994 The Historical Evolution of World-Systems. *Sociological Inquiry* 64:257-280.
Ekholm, Kasja and Jonathan Friedman
1985 Towards a Global Anthropology. *Critique of Anthropology* 5:97-119.
Frank, Andre Gunder
1967 *Capitalism and Underdevelopment in Latin America.* Monthy Review Press, New York
1993 Bronze Age World-System Cycles. *Current Anthropology* 34:383-430.
Frank, Andre Gunder and Barry Gills
1993 *The World System: Five Hundred Years or Five Thousand?* Routledge, London.
Frankenstein, Susan and Michael Rowlands
1978 The Internal Structure and Regional Context of Early Iron Age Society in South-Western Germany. *Bulletin of the Institute of Archaeology of London* 15:73-112.
Friedman, Jonathan
1982 Catastrophe and Continuity in Social Evolution. In *Theory and Explanation in Archaeology*, edited by C. Renfrew, M. Rowlands, and B. Segraves, pp.175-196. Academic Press, New York.
Friedman, Jonathan and Michael Rowlands
1977 Notes Towards an Epigenetic Model of the Evolution of "Civilisation". In *The Evolution of Social Systems*, edited by J. Friedman and M. Rowlands, pp. 201-276. Duckworth, London.
Gills, Barry and Andre Gunder Frank
1991 5000 Years of World System History: The Cumulation of Accumulation. In *Core/Periphery Relations in Precapitalist Worlds*, edited by C. Chase-Dunn and T. Hall, pp. 67-112. Westview, Boulder.
Hall, Thomas
1989 *Social Change in the Southwest, 1350-1880.* University of Kansas Press, Lawrence.
1991 The Role of Nomads in Core/Periphery Relations. In *Core/Periphery Relations in Precapitalist Worlds*, edited by C. Chase-Dunn and T. Hall, pp. 212-239. Westview, Boulder.
Hall, Thomas and Christopher Chase-Dunn.
1993 World-Systems Perspective and Archaeology: Forward into the Past. *Journal of Archaeological Research* 1:121-143.
1994 Forward into the Past: World-Systems Before 1500. *Sociological Forum* 9:295-306.
Hopkins, Terence
1982 World-Systems Analysis: Methodological Issues. In *World-Systems Analysis: Theory and Methodology*, edited by T.K. Hopkins and I. Wallerstein, pp 145-158. Sage, Beverly Hills.
Hopkins, Terence and Immanuel Wallerstein
1977 Patterns of World-System Development: A Research Proposal. *Review* 1:111-145.
Knox, Paul and John Agnew
1989 *The Geography of the World Economy.* Edward Arnold, London.
Kohl, Philip
1987 The Use and Abuse of World-Systems Theory: The Case of the Pristine West Asian State. In *Advances in Archaeological Method and Theory,* Volume 11, edited by M. B. Schiffer, pp. 1-36. Academic Press, San Diego.

Kristiansen, Kristian
1987 Centre and Periphery in Bronze Age Scandinavia. In *Centre and Periphery in the Ancient World*, edited by M. Rowlands, M. Larsen, and K. Kristiansen, pp. 74-85. Cambridge University Press, Cambridge.
McGuire, Randall
1987 The Papaguerian Periphery: Uneven Development in the Prehistoric U.S. Southwest. In *Polities and Partitions: Human Boundaries and the Growth of Complex Societies*, edited by K.M. Trinkaus, pp. 123-139. Arizona State University, Anthropological Research Papers, Number 37.
Paynter, Robert
1989 The Archaeology of Inequality. *Annual Review of Anthropology* 18:369-399.
Peregrine, Peter
1991a Prehistoric Chiefdoms on the American Midcontinent: A World-System Based on Prestige Goods. In *Core/Periphery Relations in Precapitalist Worlds*, edited by C. Chase-Dunn and T. Hall, pp. 193-211. Westview, Boulder.
1991b Some Political Aspects of Craft Specialization. *World Archaeology* 23:1-11.
1992 *Mississippian Evolution: A World-System Perspective.* Prehistory Press, Madision.
1995 Networks of Power: The Mississippian World-System. In *Native American Interactions*, edited by M. Nassaney and K. Sassaman, pp. 247-265. University of Tennessee Press, Knoxville.
Rowlands, Michael, Mogens Larsen, and Kristian Kristiansen
1987 *Centre and Periphery in the Ancient World*. Cambridge University Press, Cambridge.
Sanderson, Stephen
1990 *Social Evolutionism: A Critical History.* Basil Blackwell, London.
1991 The Evolution of Societies and World-Systems. In *Core/Periphery Relations in Precapitalist Worlds*, edited by C. Chase-Dunn and T. Hall, pp. 167-192. Westview, Boulder.
Schneider, Jane
1977 Was There a "Pre-Capitalist" World-System? *Peasant Studies* 6:20-29.
Schortman, Edward and Patricia Urban
1987 Modeling Interregional Interaction in Prehistory. In *Advances in Archaeological Method and Theory*, Volume 11, edited by M. B. Schiffer, pp. 37-95. Academic Press, San Diego.
1992a *Resources, Power, and Interregional Interaction.* Plenum, New York.
1992b The Ancient World-System. In *Resources, Power, and Interregional Interaction*, edited by E. Schortman and P. Urban, pp. 17-21. Plenum, New York.
Shannon, Thomas
1989 *An Introduction to the World-System Perspective.* Westview, Boulder.
Taylor, Peter
1985 *Political Geography: World-Economy, Nation-State, and Locality.* Longman, London.
1988 World-Systems Analysis and Regional Geography. *The Professional Geographer* 40:259-265.
Upham, Steadman
1992 Interaction and Isolation: The Empty Spaces in Panregional Political and Economic Systems. In *Resources, Power, and Interregional Interaction*, edited by E. Schortman and P. Urban, pp. 139-152. Plenum, New York.
Wallerstein, Immanuel
1974a The Rise and Future Demise of the Capitalist World-System: Concepts for Comparative Analysis. *Comparative Studies in Society and History* 16:387-415.
1974b *The Modern World-System I.* Academic Press, New York.
1976 A World-System Perspective on the Social Sciences. *British Journal of Sociology* 27:343-352.
1982 World-Systems Analysis: Theoretical and Interpretive Issues. In *World-Systems Analysis: Theory and Methodology*, edited by T.K. Hopkins and I. Wallerstein, pp 91-103. Sage, Beverly Hills.
1989 *The Modern World-System III.* Academic Press, New York.
Willey, Gordon and Philip Phillips
1958 *Method and Theory in American Archaeology.* University of Chicago Press, Chicago.
Wolf, Eric
1982 *Europe and the People Without History.* University of California Press, Berkeley.

Chapter 2

Comparing World-Systems: Concepts and Hypotheses

Thomas D. Hall
DePauw University

Christopher Chase-Dunn
Johns Hopkins University

The use of theories of social evolution for understanding, predicting, or influencing social changes has a long, if tawdry, history (Nisbet 1969; Lenski 1976; Granovetter 1979; Sanderson 1990, 1995b inter alii). Ever since world-system theory first appeared in social science discourse (Wallerstein 1974a, 1974b) archaeologists have seen in it potential for analyzing interregional interactions. However, after closer inspection they typically walked away muttering, "close, but no cigar!" This reaction runs from one of the earliest such attempts (Pailes and Whitecotton 1975, published in 1979) through Blanton and Feinman's *American Anthropologist* note (1984) and appeared recently in Ferguson and Whitehead's (1992:4-8) book on war, in Christopher Edens's (1992) discussion of the Mesopotamian "world system," and Schortman and Urban's (1992) collection on interregional interaction, especially in the contribution by Santley and Alexander (1992). The entire January 1977 issue of *Journal of Peasant Studies* was devoted to critical reviews of world-system theory. Jane Schneider's critique of Wallerstein's concentration on trade in bulk goods to the exclusion of trade in preciosities, or luxury goods, is the most frequently cited article in that issue (1977).

In this essay we argue that while these reactions were, no doubt, appropriate, to maintain them is to ignore recent developments in what Peregrine in the introduction to this volume has properly called the "world-systems perspective." Those who would dismiss the utility of world-system theory in addressing archaeological problems solely on the basis of the works of Immanuel Wallerstein are poorly informed, indeed. In this chapter we will recapitulate briefly work we have conducted since our two earlier summaries (Hall and Chase-Dunn 1993, 1994) and present our version of an expanded and revised world-system approach intended to facilitate analysis of precapitalist settings. We will end with a brief recitation of some of the attempts to use this approach in actual field investigations.

We hasten to add that we do not see our work, including this chapter, as the final or definitive word. Rather, we see this as part of a larger dialog that refines our understanding by refining concepts and theories, then uses those refined concepts to study empirical cases, which in turn will be used to further refine and develop concepts and theories. What we present are the results of a few such iterations. This collection adds further material for further refinements.

Following Wallerstein's analysis of the modern world-system (1974a, 1974b, 1980, 1989), we claim that the fundamental unit of social change is the world-system, not the society. We contend that it is necessary to comprehend whole intersocietal systems in order to explain why social structures change or remain the same.

Relevance of a World-Systems Perspective to Archaeological Issues

Some archaeologists have recognized the utility of world-system concepts for explaining changes in ancient societies. Phil Kohl (1978:489) notes:

> ...even the earliest "pristine" example of state formation cannot be explained entirely as an internal process of social differentiation but must be viewed partly as the product of a "world-economy" at different levels of development...

But he also specifies what was different:

> ...the development of underdevelopment in the Bronze Age was sharply constrained or itself underdeveloped. Critical technologies, such as metal working, could diffuse relatively easily and new means of transportation and sources of power, such as horses, could be raised in peripheral zones and radically restructure this ancient world system.

Anthropologists have been at the forefront of the examination of the incorporation of peoples and cultures into the modern world-system (e.g., Wolf 1982; Blanton et al, 1996). Sociologists Michael Mann (1986), John A. Hall (1986, 1987), and Ronald Glassman (1986) use Weberian perspectives to study historical development. Janet Abu-Lughod (1989, 1990, 1993), Andre Gunder Frank and Barry K. Gills (1993), and Samir Amin (1991) have pushed world-system theory into precapitalist settings. World historians and civilizationists have turned serious attention to the world-system perspective (Sanderson 1995a; Wilkinson 1995).

Comparisons between the contemporary global political economy and earlier intersocietal systems have stimulated renewed interest in the logics of social development. Do human societies sometimes change their basic modes of social reproduction, or do they simply alternate between different forms of basically the same logic? Is social change cyclical or transformational? These are old questions, but questions which are only now being addressed from a world-systems perspective.

An explicitly comparative approach has great theoretical and methodological advantages. The basic structural features of the modern world-system, for example the interstate system of competing states, are often taken for granted. In order to understand the reproduction of basic structural features it is desirable to be able to compare intersocietal networks which are structurally different. In order to know how systemic structure and logic changes it is necessary to study how world-systems have become transformed in the past. The comparative study of world-systems will make it possible to examine hypotheses about differences in structure by comparing cases.

It is our claim that, although all world-systems share some broad features, there are important differences between different types of world-systems. The most important differences cluster around the problems of how social labor is mobilized and how accumulation is accomplished. Thus, the Wallersteinian notion of an intersocietal division of labor in the production of basic goods and the idea of a core/periphery structure have broad utility. However, they cannot simply be imported wholesale into precapitalist settings. Doing so would cavalierly impose the present on the past. Rather, Wallerstein's concepts must be modified.

We convert many of Wallerstein's original concepts into working hypotheses in need of empirical investigation and conceptual elaboration. We draw current knowledge of precapitalist settings to rethink the concept of a world-system. In doing so we rethink core/periphery relations, develop a working typology of core/periphery structures, and present a few working hypotheses for empirical investigation. In this way we intend to make world-system ideas more useful to archaeologists. As noted, we see this exercise as the first step in an iterative process that moves from theory construction to empirical investigation, and then back to theory construction.

We begin with an examination of alternative concepts of world-systems.

Contending Definitions of World-Systems

Immanuel Wallerstein (1974a, 1974b, 1979) defines a world-system as a single division of labor which contains multiple cultures. He distinguishes between two types of world-systems: world-empires and world-economies. A world-empire is an intersocietal division of labor which is encompassed by a single overarching imperial polity. A world-economy is an intersocietal division of labor which is politically organized as an interstate system, a multicentric system of unequal and competing states. Wallerstein (1984) excludes stateless societies from the category of world-systems. He calls them "mini-systems" in which production of basic subsistence goods is supposedly accomplished within a single cultural entity.

We (Chase-Dunn and Hall 1991a, 1991b, 1993:855, 1996:Chap.2) developed a somewhat more general definition of world-systems: "intersocietal networks in which the interactions (e.g., trade, warfare, intermarriage, [information, etc.]) are important for the reproduction of the internal structures of the composite units and importantly affect changes which occur in these local structures." (Material in brackets added for 1996).

We use "core/periphery structures" in place of world-system because of the unfortunate confusion between "world" as "self-contained system" (Wallersteinian usage) and "world" as global. Several studies challenge Wallerstein's sharp distinction between mini-systems and world-systems because there are important cross-cultural interactions (including exchange of basic foodstuffs) which affect the reproduction and historical development of constituent groups (e.g. Sahlins 1972; Collins 1992).

The empirical universe for comparisons consists of all the sedentary small, medium-sized, and large core/periphery structures which have existed on Earth over the last ten thousand years. Only by studying very different core/periphery structures can we formulate a theory of structural transformations. Since basic transformations are few, it is desirable to study as many as possible in order to develop a theory of transformational processes. Furthermore, at this stage of theorizing we argue that a variation maximizing strategy is preferable to more limited sampling strategies.

We seek to avoid the mistake of simply imposing vocabularies developed to explain the modern system on earlier systems. For instance, we avoid the assumption that all world-systems are hierarchical. We can imagine core/periphery structures without intersocietal inequalities or exploitation. The existence of exploitation, domination, or unequal exchange should not be assumed, but rather investigated empirically. We expect to find that many stateless intersocietal systems did not have core/periphery structures, while others had only mild and episodic ones. In order to understand the conditions which generate intersocietal inequalities it is useful to examine cases in which they are absent.

To facilitate this discussion we begin by briefly reviewing the analysis and categorization of productive systems.

Modes of Production

The world-system perspective has stimulated a new understanding of capitalism which emphasizes the necessity of peripheral forms of capitalism, the importance of the interstate system, and variety in the forms and degrees of the commodification of labor within the capitalist world-economy (Chase-Dunn 1989). Extending this perspective to precapitalist systems raises new questions and reopens old debates about other modes of production and their transformations. We use "mode of production" to refer to the deep structural logic of production, distribution, exchange, and accumulation, not necessarily restricted to the point of production.

This approach renews the "substantivist-formalist" debate (Polanyi 1944; Polanyi et al., 1957) and the debate among "primitivists" and "modernists" about commodification processes (see Chase-Dunn and Hall 1993, 1996 for reviews). Scholars such as Ekholm and Friedman (1982) and Frank and Gills (1993) emphasize the latter positions, whereas we emphasize the former positions. We do this both because we think they provide a more accurate understanding of the past, and because comparative studies should show us wrong, if we are.

In order to clarify the terms of the renewed debate we will adopt some heuristic distinctions among modes of production based on the work of Amin (1980, 1991) and Wolf (1982), and supplemented by Polanyi (1977). We distinguish among four classes of systemic logics which are designated as:

1. kin-based modes of production, in which social labor, distribution, and collective accumulation is mobilized by means of normative integration based on consensual definitions of value, obligations and rules of conduct — a moral order;
2. tributary modes, in which accumulation of surplus product is mobilized by means of politically institutionalized coercion based on codified law and formally organized military power;
3. capitalist modes, in which land, labor, wealth and goods are commodified and strongly exposed to the forces of price setting markets[1] and accumulation occurs primarily through the production of commodities using commodified labor; and
4. possible socialist modes, a potential class of logics in which major policy, investment and allocation decisions are controlled democratically by the people they affect according to a logic of collective rationality.

We stress that these distinctions are heuristic, intended to facilitate comparisons. In order to study world-systems comparatively we must conceptualize the spatial boundaries of such systems in ways which allow comparisons among very different kinds of intersocietal networks.

Spatial World-System Boundaries: A Multicriteria Approach

We (Chase-Dunn and Hall 1991b:8-15, 1993:858-862) review and critique the proposals of several scholars regarding criteria for spatially bounding intersocietal interaction networks. We conclude that it is presumptuous to argue that some forms of interaction are always causally more important than others, especially in studies of very different world-systems. The relative importance of different types of interaction probably varies among different types of core/periphery structures. We argue that statements about relative importance of types of interaction should be the result of research rather than initial assumptions. We propose an approach to spatial bounding which is inclusive enough to make broad comparisons possible.

Both economic and political forms of interaction are important features of all world-system networks. We agree with Wallerstein (1974b, 1979) that bulk-goods exchanges are very important and constitutive forms of interconnection. However, we also agree with Jane Schneider (1977) and Janet Abu-Lughod (1989) that prestige or luxury goods exchanges are often vital for the reproduction of power structures. In short, all regularized material exchanges should be included as criteria of system boundedness. Thus, it is necessary to consider how relatively localized networks of bulk-goods exchange are nested within much larger networks of prestige-goods exchange in any system.

We also agree with Tilly (1984:62) and Wilkinson (1987) that political interconnections are important. We use the criterion of regularized political-military conflict interaction proposed by Wilkinson as a possible bounding mechanism of a system. This will often produce yet a different network boundary from the bulk-goods and prestige-goods networks.

Since developing these criteria, we have added a fourth criteria, information exchanges (1996:Chap. 2). Based on work by Schortman and Urban (1987), discussions of civilizationists (Melko and Scott 1987; Melko 1995), Jerry Bentley's (1993) masterful survey of cross-cultural encounters in Eurasia, and critical comments by William H. McNeill (1995), we argue that networks of information in a variety of forms, including, but not limited to, ideology, religion, technical information, and culture must also be included as a bounding mechanism. We do not expect the information network will necessarily coincide with any of the other networks.

The use of multiple boundary criteria often will result in nested levels of system boundedness. Generally, bulk goods will compose the smallest regional interaction net. Political/military interaction will compose a larger net which may include more than one bulk-goods net. Prestige-goods exchanges will link even larger regions composed of smaller conflict nets (see Figure 2.1). The information net will be of the same order of size as the prestige-goods net: sometimes larger, sometimes smaller.

At first it may seem counter intuitive to have the information boundary inside the prestige-goods exchange, since exchange of goods typically implies some exchange of information. There are, however, well known mechanisms by which goods can be exchanged beyond the range of information. First, is down-the-line trade. When trade goes from partner to partner the physical objects may move along unaltered, but information typically will become garbled and lost. Anyone who has observed the transformations of a phrase whispered from person to person recognizes how quickly the information may be lost. Occasionally, when warfare is severe the political/military boundary may cut the flow of information, even while prestige-goods may effectively cross the boundary via circuitous down-the-line exchanges.

Rather than applying the term world-system to one of these types of linkage and using other words for the others, we propose that whole world-systems are constituted by all four forms of linkage. We do not claim that the networks will always be nested in the fashion shown in Figure 2.1. Indeed, the relative scopes of these four boundary criteria remain a theoretical and empirical problem. Occasionally as in both the modern global world-system and some earlier geographically isolated systems the four networks may converge. This convergence may be an important characteristic which differentiates some core/periphery structures from others. We also recognize that the boundaries of all four networks are empirically and theoretically fuzzy. That is, how much interaction in any of these four types constitutes a connection remains problematic. Furthermore, different sets of factors may shape changes in boundaries, so that all four do not necessarily shift simultaneously, nor even in the same direction. Here, again, further empirical research will guide further theoretical development.

We now turn to a discussion of social relations within core/periphery structures.

Core/Periphery Relations

Considerable controversy still exists about the best way to conceptualize and measure coreness and peripherality in the modern global political economy (e.g., Arrighi and Drangel 1986; Chase-Dunn 1989:Chap. 10). The issues are somewhat different when we consider the comparative study of core/periphery structures across very different kinds of world-systems. Here we need a more general conceptualization which can accommodate greater variation. We also need to allow for the possibility that some world-systems may not have core/periphery hierarchies.

Applying the notion of a core/periphery hierarchy to other than the modern world-system is itself somewhat controversial. The economic historian Paul Bairoch (1986) argued that premodern core/periphery

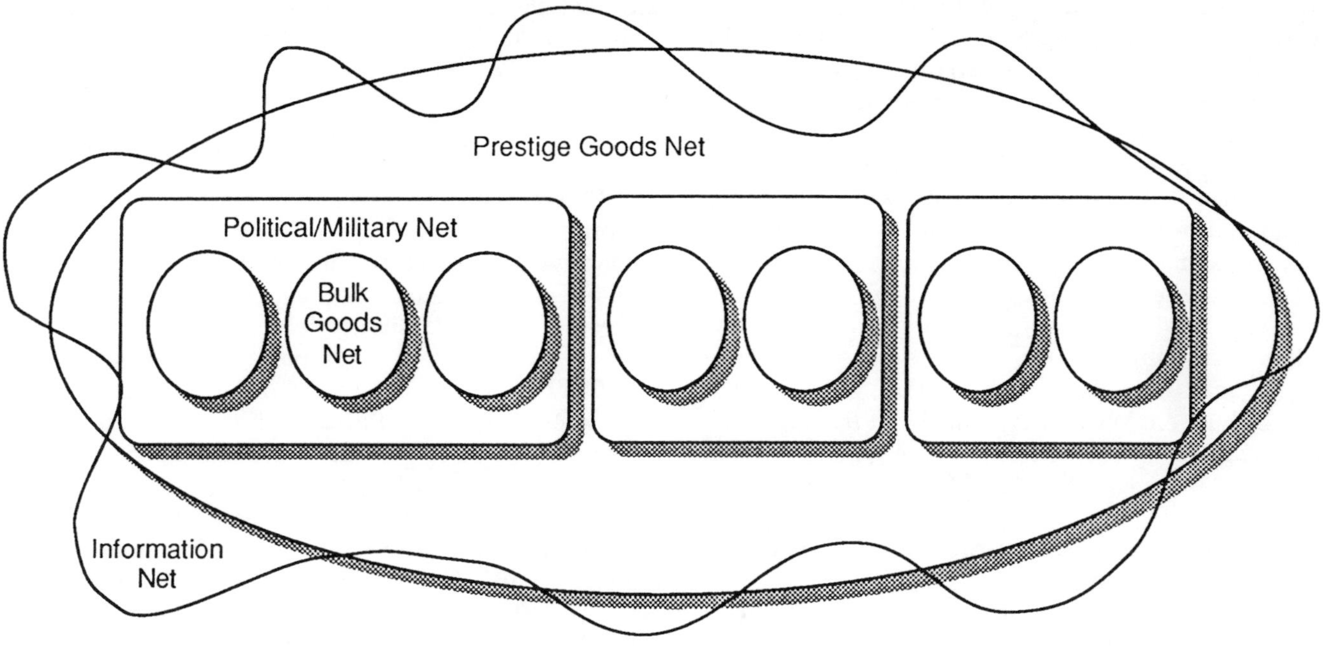

Figure 2.1 Model of a world-system.

relations were relatively unimportant because there were no significant differences in the level of living between the populations of core and peripheral areas. Most historians of the ancient empires would disagree with his assessment.

Degree of stratification in core and peripheral areas may be an important difference between the modern and earlier world-systems. In the modern world-system income inequality is typically less among core societies than among peripheral societies. This may have been the reverse in many of the ancient world-systems where the core was urbanized and class-stratified, while peripheral areas contained less stratified groups of pastoralists and horticulturalists.

Based on this probability we define two types of core/periphery relations. First is core/periphery differentiation, in which societies at different levels of complexity and population density interact within one world-system. Second is core/periphery hierarchy, in which political, economic, or ideological domination exists among different societies within the same core/periphery structure. This includes political domination and unequal exchange as well as extraction of resources through raiding, taxation, and tribute. We are also interested in cultural definitions of superiority/inferiority, and how these may interact with more objective forms of exploitation and domination.

We distinguish between differentiation and hierarchy because we think it is mistaken to assume that all relations among "more developed" and "less developed" societies involve exploitation and/or processes of the development of underdevelopment (Frank 1966). We need not assume that the "more developed" society always exploits the "less developed." We seek to analyze how differences within societies such as size, complexity, technological productivity, and internal stratification are related to intersocietal domination. Comparative study should reveal the nature, longevity, and consequences differing degrees of hierarchy for social change in both core and peripheral areas.

We intentionally omit consideration of the nature of what is produced and traded between cores and peripheries. The notion that coreness and peripherality in the modern world-system are essentially constituted around a division of labor in which the core produces manufactured goods and the periphery produces raw materials is itself quite controversial (Chase-Dunn 1989:Chap. 10). Furthermore, important reversals of this relationship sometimes occurred within ancient world-systems (e.g., Lamberg-Karlovsky 1975; Kohl 1987). This issue is best resolved by empirical investigations of the linkages between core/periphery differentiation and core/periphery domination.

The intersection between the problem of world-system boundaries and core/periphery hierarchy is especially salient at the edge of the periphery. Wallerstein (1989:Chap. 3) argues that even though an area has been plundered by a core power, it is not yet incorporated and peripheralized until local production has become integrally linked into the "commodity chains" of the larger world-system. Plunder often preceded the development of coerced production in both ancient empires and the Europe-centered world-system. Indeed, there may have been systems, such as the Nuer-Dinka (Kelly 1985) in which plunder was the sole form of core/periphery interaction. It is better to consider the dynamics of such cases rather than ruling them out a priori.

If we use Wilkinson's definition, which includes regularized plunder as a form of linkage defining the boundaries of a world-system, West Africa was incorporated into the Europe-centered world-system when slave raiding became regularized, rather than, as Wallerstein would have it, after the development of colonial agriculture in Africa. If we use the criteria of trade in bullion, West Africa has been linked to the Mediterranean and Near Eastern core regions since at least AD 800 (Curtin 1990:32). Most of the gold coins minted in Byzantium and Egypt of which Janet Abu-Lughod (1989) writes, were struck from West African gold (see Moseley 1992).

Economic exploitation is a more stable form of exploitation than plunder because it does not decimate the peripheral society to the same extent that plunder does, nor typically does it exhaust resources as rapidly. It is not the case, however, that precapitalist cores only extracted tribute and left production processes untouched. The Inkas completely reorganized production in incorporated territories and relocated populations to new regions in which intensified horticulture was feasible (La Lone and La Lone 1987; La Lone 1991). Similarly, the fur trade in North America produced major changes in indigenous social organization (Kardulias 1990, Dunaway 1994, 1996). Finally, Hall (1989:Chap. 2) suggests that incorporation is far more complex and subtle than Wallerstein indicates.

In addition to reconceptualization of core and periphery we need to rethink the idea of the semiperiphery for the purposes of comparing world-systems. As with coreness and peripherality, the definition of the semiperiphery remains controversial even within the modern world-system (see Chase-Dunn 1989:Chap. 10). At this point we suggest that a semiperipheral region:

1. may mix both core and peripheral forms of organization;
2. may be located spatially between core and peripheral regions;
3. may mediate activities between core and peripheral areas;
4. may have institutional features which are intermediate between those found in core and periphery.

Sorting these different types of semiperipheries remains an empirical as well as theoretical problem. We also think it is premature to assume that all core/periphery hierarchies have three distinct tiers. Until more detailed comparisons among different kinds of world-systems are completed it would be premature to define the semiperiphery concept more narrowly.

A Typology of World-Systems

Based on our discussion we propose a typology of world-systems or core/periphery structures. We do not conceive of these categories as fixed boxes into which all intersocietal networks must be stuffed. Rather, they are a set of general sign-posts for sorting types so as to maximize diversity for comparative purposes.

Our central distinction in studying systemic logic is the mode of accumulation, which we define as the structural logic of production, distribution, exchange, and accumulation (Chase-Dunn and Hall 1992). We prefer mode of accumulation over mode of production to avoid becoming mired in essentially scholastic arguments about "what Marx really meant."

We define kin-based relations as normative regulation based on consensual definitions of what exists and what is good. No societies are exclusively structured around this kind of social control, but in some societies, those without classes or states or markets, kin-based mechanisms of control and distribution are the dominant sources of social cohesion. Two points are salient. First, kinship is the dominant mode of organizing society. This is not to say that other relations, relative wealth, power, prestige, ability, etc., do not enter into day to day interactions, or do not shape social processes and social relations. Rather, we emphasize the primary and determinative role of kin relations—including age and gender. Second, in all other modes of accumulation other factors take the dominant and determinative role in shaping social relations. This, however, does not mean that kinship, age, and gender, cease to have social importance. Rather, it is to emphasize that these factors become secondary in shaping social relations. How this transition occurred, how many times it occurred, and the range of flexibility of the transformation remain important problems.

The tributary mode of accumulation entails the use of physical coercion to mobilize labor. A ruling class establishes control over some essential social resource and then uses this control to extract "surplus product" from direct producers. There are many different institutional forms by which this is accomplished (taxation, tribute, serfdom, slavery, etc.). Most historical societies mix a variety of these forms of coercion.

The capitalist mode of accumulation is based on the commodity form, the mediation of human interaction by pricesetting markets, and market-like institutions. The commodification of goods, land, wealth, and labor are never complete within capitalist systems, but markets play a much greater role than in other modes.

Aspects of other modes continue to be found, but they are complementary with the reproduction of commodified relations. Thus we distinguish between world-systems in which kin-based, state-based, and capitalist modes of accumulation are predominant.

By utilizing these distinctions we are in no way endorsing a unilinear model of evolution. Historical development is open-ended and path dependent. That is, it must operate on a social structure provided by historical legacy within the confines of the current context. Important bifurcations and discontinuities of development, rapid transformations, and instances of devolution are normal characteristics of the historical processes of social change (see Sanderson 1990, 1995b). While we seek to evaluate the idea that the core/periphery relation rather than the society is the focal unit of analysis for understanding these processes, we do not mean to ignore the characteristics or processes which operate within societies.

In order to study the processes and patterns by which modes of accumulation are transformed we propose a working typology of world-systems based the preceding distinctions. This typology of core/ periphery relations indicates the level of complexity characteristic for the most complex societies within each world-system (Chase-Dunn and Hall 1993, 1996:Chaps. 1-4):

I. Kin-based mode dominant
- A. Stateless, classless
  1. Sedentary foragers, horticulturalists, pastoralists
  2. Big man systems
- B. Chiefdoms (classes but not states)

II. Tributary modes dominant (states, cities)
- A. Primary state-based world-systems (Lower Mesopotamia, Egypt, Indus Valley, Ganges Valley, China, Mexico, Peru)
- B. Primary empires in which a number of previously autonomous states have been unified by conquest (Akkad, Old Kingdom Egypt, Magahda, Chou, Teotihuacan, Huari)
- C. Multicentered world-systems composed of empires, states and peripheral regions (Near East, India, China, Mesoamerica, Peru)
- D. Commercializing state-based world-system in which important aspects of commodification have developed but the system is still dominated by the logic of the tributary modes (Afroeurasian world-system)

III. Capitalist mode dominant
- A. The Europe-centered subsystem since the sixteenth century
- B. The global modern world-system

Within category II (tributary mode) there are a number of distinctions which need to be explained. Primary or pristine states are those which develop without contact with existing states. States developing in interaction with existing states are termed secondary or reactive. The same distinction can, of course, be applied to empires and we do so in category IIB.[2] We suggest that most primary state-based core/periphery relations were politically structured as interstate systems of competing city-states within a core region. Secondary multicentric empires are distinguished from primary empires by the prior existence of empires and often by the larger size of the constituent empires.

Within empires the degree of commodification increased, but unevenly and not in the same way in each area. There were spurts ahead and then either devolution to subsistence feudalism or reassertion of imperial control of the economy. The rise to predominance of capitalism in a core region was a tipping point which occurred first in Europe, and then spread to the rest of the world. Thus, we are not strict substantivists. We recognize that markets, capitalist production, and commodity exchange took place within tributary empires. Our substantivism is more subtle. These capitalist activities were always embedded in a larger tributary structure and subordinate to it.

We do not want this typology to generate a lot of dispute about which cases go into which categories. Obviously there are many borderline cases. Our point is to define a set of types which allow us and others to investigate the problem of processual similarities and differences. While analyses of very long sequences of change would contribute to the same goal, we argue that it makes sense to focus first on the structural patterns of world-systems. After these are mapped we can attend to the causal nature of processes of reproduction and transformation.

We now present a few working hypotheses that emerge from this discussion.

Working Hypotheses

The most general questions for a comparative study of core/periphery relations are:

1. Do all world-systems have core/periphery differentiation and/or core/periphery hierarchies?
2. Do the stability, magnitude, and nature of core/periphery relations vary systemically with the types of societies that compose world-systems?
3. What is the relationship between core/ periphery differentiation and core/ periphery hierarchy within single world-systems and over the range of world-system types?

4. What are the relationships between core/periphery structures and processes and the reproduction/transformation of basic systemic logics?
5. What are the similarities and differences between sequences of political centralization and decentralization across different kinds of world-systems?

Obviously intersocietal networks in which the constituent societies are all at about the same level of complexity do not have core/periphery differentiation as defined above, but they may nevertheless have core/periphery hierarchy. Of greater interest is the matter of core/periphery hierarchies. Do all core/periphery structures have relatively stable core/periphery hierarchies in the sense that some societies exploit or dominate others over extended periods of time? This involves consideration of the nature, degree, and longevity of intersocietal exploitation and domination. In addition it is desirable to consider differential rates of development, co-evolution, the development of underdevelopment, and processes affecting these. Also of interest will be the relative size of core, peripheral, and semiperipheral areas, and the nature of relations among core societies and among peripheral societies.

In consideration of the preceding discussion we propose the following hypotheses for investigation:

Hypothesis 1

Our first hypothesis is that stable relations of intersocietal domination are difficult to create and reproduce in the absence of hierarchical social institutions within the societies involved. The development of internal stratification and forms of the state are quite important in the stabilization and reproduction of core/periphery exploitation. Thus we predict that kin-based intersocietal systems will tend to have only minimal and short-lived core/periphery hierarchies. Those world-systems composed of chiefless sedentary foragers will not have any regularized intersocietal domination or exploitation.

We expect that intersocietal exploitation among most sedentary foraging groups is limited to episodic raiding and competition over favorable natural sites. War-captive slavery found among some of the more hierarchical hunter-gatherers (e.g. the Yurok) and some pastoralists (e.g. the Nuer) is likely to be of a relatively mild. This is because slaves must be incorporated into existing kinship networks in order to mobilize their labor. However, incorporation into kinship networks usually bestow rights as well as obligations (Patterson 1982).

Kristiansen (1987) has studied local and regional hierarchical relations among Bronze Age stateless peoples in Scandinavia. Although he uses the terms core and periphery to describe these relations, he characterizes them as based on the "ritual superiority" of local centers over hinterlands based on the control of prestige-goods. Friedman and Rowlands (1977) have argued that core/periphery structures based solely on prestige-goods economies are unstable and ephemeral. Peripheries are able to adopt core-like characteristics rather quickly because the ideological nature of intersocietal stratification is not backed up by military coercion or more stringent dependencies on non-replaceable goods. Prestige-goods and religious hierarchies are more subject to redefinition by oppressed groups, while military advantages and monopolies of basic foods or raw materials are less easily outmaneuvered.

We suggest that the terms "spread effects" and "backwash effects" following Myrdal (1971) be employed to differentiate consequences of core/periphery interaction. Under some circumstances such interaction causes peripheral areas to develop in directions which are more core-like (spread effects) whereas other sorts of interaction cause peripheral areas to become underdeveloped (backwash effects).

Hypothesis 2

Our second hypothesis is that the stability and exploitativeness of core/periphery hierarchies increases with the degree of stratification within core societies and with the development of "techniques of power," (Mann 1986) which enable centralized empires to extract taxes and tribute from peripheral regions. Specialized military organization, logistics, strategy, and weaponry, as well as organizational techniques for ruling distant provinces and extracting tribute and taxes are key institutions which make core domination work.

We hypothesize that the very first "pristine" states were more successful at extracting resources from peripheral areas than kin-based cores, but not as successful as later, more centralized, empires. Also the "co-evolutionary" spread effects of development (Schortman and Urban 1987; Renfrew and Cherry 1986) by which new centers emerge as a result of interaction with the original core areas, will be relatively strong compared to "underdeveloping" effects because the techniques for concentrating and sustaining resources in the core are less developed than in later empires.

Thus, we predict that core/periphery hierarchies will be relatively more stable, more hierarchical, and more underdevelopmental for peripheral regions once centralized empires have emerged. The decentralizing phase of the process of the rise and fall of empire-centers will reverse this trend somewhat, as increased local autonomy for controllers of land slows the concentration of resources in the center.

Hypothesis 3

Our third hypothesis is that the growth of market forms of exchange, monetary systems, local and long-distance market trade, etc. will again increase "spread" effects relative to "backwash" effects — that is, peripheral regions will more quickly adopt the social and technological features of core regions. More sophisticated empires, in which the state-based mode of accumulation remains dominant, learn to extract surplus from market trade without smothering it. In these instances central empires which provide pacification and protect trade routes will strengthen spread effects.[3] Commercialized states also learn to control the disruptive aspects of market relations and to deal effectively with potentially threatening peripheries.

Ancient core/periphery hierarchies were often central to the reproduction of centralized state apparati. Keith Hopkins (1978) contends that the Roman empire was a system which, like capitalism, needed to expand in order to survive. But, unlike the capitalist world-economy, its expansion was based almost exclusively on conquest, the importation of booty and slaves, and the distribution of land and dependent laborers to a growing class of non-producers. When the empire reached a zero rate of return in terms of spatial expansion it was no longer able to provide the resources necessary to sustain its growing overhead costs. It then began to turn in upon itself, and eventually it crumbled.

In other cases, such as China, the mode of accumulation was "tributary" in the sense that coercive power was used to mobilize labor and accumulation, but this accumulation was primarily accomplished without exploitation of peripheral regions. In many of these cases the periphery did importantly affect the core by threatening border regions or by occasionally conquering the core (see Barfield 1989, 1991; Hall 1991a, 1991b). Whether as a source of exploitable resources or military threats, peripheral regions were often important to the reproduction and transformation of social structures within cores.

Hypothesis 4

Many semiperipheral regions have also played important roles in large scale social change. We hypothesize that this is because of the organizational opportunities available to groups "in the middle" of core/periphery hierarchies. Semiperipheral regions, we argue, are unusually fertile zones for social innovation because they can combine peripheral and core elements in new ways, they are less constrained by core domination than are peripheral areas, and are less committed than older core regions to the institutional baggage which comes along with core status. We expect that the particular techniques used by upwardly mobile semiperipheries vary depending on the nature of the world-system in which they are operating (see Chase-Dunn 1988; Chase-Dunn and Hall 1996:Chap. 5):

1. conquest by semiperipheral marcher chiefdoms;
2. conquest by semiperipheral marcher states;
3. extensive and intensive commodification by semiperipheral capitalist city-states;
4. the rise of European hegemony;
5. the rise and fall of hegemonic core states within the Europe-centered world-system; and
6. the emergence of revolutionary challenges to capitalism in the semiperiphery of the contemporary world-system.

Discussion and Conclusions

In a theoretical and conceptual paper like this, the word "conclusion" is inappropriate. Still, we argue that by redefining world-systems more generally as core/periphery structures researchers will be able to sort out the important similarities and differences which ought to be the explicit backdrop for understanding past and possible future transformations.

In our view the next order of business should be a series of exploratory case studies which explicitly address the problems of concept formation and comparable measurement which we have raised. Ultimately we think that it would be desirable to be able to compare more core/periphery structures rather than use limited case studies to gain greater certitude and refinement with respect to these working hypotheses about core/periphery structures. We continue to recognize, however, that this strategy needs to be supplemented with long-term case studies. Comparisons over both time and space must be combined. We are not proposing a "cross-sectional" design, but rather systematic comparisons among a number of long-term (at least 500 years) case studies of specific core/periphery structures.

Some progress has already been made along these lines. Schortman and Urban (1994, Chapter 8 this volume) have used this approach to study Southeastern Mesoamerica, and have already elaborated some of the distinctions drawn here. Similarly, Andre Gunder Frank (1993) has reanalyzed the entire Bronze Age in similar terms. Guillermo Algaze (1993a, 1993b) has even begun comparative work. Darrell La Lone (1994) has re-examined Inka development in this light. Peter Peregrine has used a similar approach to the study of pre-Columbian Mississippian cultures (1992, 1995, Chapter 4 this volume). Andrew Bosworth (1995) and Chase-Dunn and Hall (1995) have studied ancient urbanism comparatively. Mitchell Allen (1992, 1995) looks at ancient Mesopotamian peripheries in insightful ways. All of these studies indicate that there is yet much to mined from using a world-system perspective to study archaeological problems—despite Immanuel Wallerstein's demurrers (1993, 1995).

Probably the most striking confirmation is in recent works of Andrew Sherratt (1993a, 1993b, 1993c) [see Hall 1995, Hall and Chase-Dunn 1995]. His study of Bronze Age Europe uses world-system analytic techniques modified in accord with Jane Schneider's (1977) critiques of Wallerstein in ways that are remarkably close to what we propose here. In those accounts he found many of the sorts of processes we have suggested should be occurring.[4] Sherratt's papers also suggest some practical ways in which archaeologists can operationalize some of the concepts discussed here.

While these confirmations are encouraging, they are far from definitive. We argue only that these studies, and those that follow in this volume, are sufficient evidence to warrant further work in a precapitalist world-system perspective. There is a great deal of empirical work to be done. As this work is completed much of what we present here will need to be rethought and reformulated. But this is how good science is done. Theories and conceptualizations are merely stopping points in a continuous process of empirical investigation.

Notes

1. Price-setting markets are those in which the competitive buying and selling of goods by actors operating to maximize their own returns largely determines the rates of exchange (prices) among traded goods. Many forms of exchange which look like markets, are not price-setting markets. In no societies are all social objects commodified, but market societies are those in which the provision of substantial elements of the daily life of the average member is mediated by market forces.

2. This distinction can also be applied to tribes and chiefdoms. Reactive or secondary social change implies that interactions between various social structures induce changes in some of them toward increased similarity. For example, a state system interacting with a big man system may induce the formation of a tribe with appointed leaders, and may even induce the formation of a chiefdom (Hall 1989).

3. Mann (1986:Chap. 5) stresses the beneficial effects on economic development of "compulsory cooperation" and pacification of large areas organized by the early conquest empires, while other scholars (e.g. Diakonoff 1973) emphasize the exploitative and destructive effects which these empires had on peripheral regions. It is undoubtedly the case that some empires had greater beneficial effects than others. These matters need to be sorted out by studies which examine all the regions within a specific world-system and systematically compare world-systems.

4. We have benefited from several exchanges and meeting with Andrew Sherratt at the Lund conference (see Hall and Chase-Dunn 1995). In our conversations the degree of convergence in our approaches was more apparent. This surprised us all—rather pleasantly—given that we had begun our work independent of each other.

References

Abu-Lughod, Janet

1989 *Before European Hegemony: The World System A.D. 1250-1350.* Oxford University Press, New York.

1990 Restructuring the Premodern World-System. *Review* 13:273-286.

1993 Discontinuities and Persistence: One World System or A Succession of World Systems? In *The World System: Five Hundred Years or Five Thousand?*, edited by Andre Gunder Frank and Barry K. Gills, pp. 278-290. Routledge, London.

Algaze, Guillermo

1993a Expansionary Dynamics of Some Early Pristine States. *American Anthropologist* 95:304-333.

1993b *The Uruk World System: The Dynamics of Expansion of Early Mesopotamian Civilization.* University of Chicago Press, Chicago.

Allen, Mitchell

1992 The Mechanisms of Underdevelopment: An Ancient Mesopotamian Example. *Review* 15:453-476.

1995 *Contested Peripheries: Philistia in the Neo-Assyrian World-System.* Unpublished Ph.D. dissertation, Interdepartmental Archaeology Program, UCLA.

Amin, Samir
1980 *Class and Nation, Historically and in the Current Crisis.* Monthly Review Press, New York.
1991 The Ancient World-Systems versus the Modern Capitalist World-System. *Review* 14:349-385.
Arrighi, Giovanni and Jessica Drangel
1986 Stratification of the World-Economy: An Explanation of the Semiperipheral Zone. *Review* 10:9-74.
Bairoch, Paul
1986 Historical Roots of Economic Underdevelopment: Myths and Realities. In *Imperialism After Empire: Continuities and Discontinuities*, edited by Wolfgang J. Mommsen and Jurgen Osterhammerl, pp. 191-216. Allen and Unwin, London.
Barfield, Thomas J.
1989 *The Perilous Frontier: Nomadic Empires and China.* Basil Blackwell, Cambridge, MA.
1991 Inner Asia and Cycles of Power in China's Imperial Dynastic History. In *Rulers from the Steppe: State Formation on the Eurasian Periphery*, edited by Gary Seaman and Daniel Marks, pp. 21-62. Ethnographics Press, Center for Visual Anthropology, University of Southern California, Los Angeles.
Bentley, Jerry H.
1993 *Old World Encounters: Cross-Cultural Contacts and Exchanges in Pre-Modern Times.* Oxford University Press, Oxford.
Blanton, Richard and Gary Feinman
1984 The Mesoamerican World-System. *American Anthropologist* 86:673-92.
Blanton, Richard, Peter Peregrine, Thomas D. Hall, Deborah Winslow
1996 *Economic Analysis Beyond the Local System.* University Press of America, Lanham, MD.
Bosworth, Andrew
1995 World Cities and World Economic Cycles. In *Civilizations and World-Systems: Two Approaches to the Study of World-Historical Change*, edited by Stephen K. Sanderson, pp. 192-213. Altamira Press, Walnut Creek, CA.
Chase-Dunn, Christopher
1988 Comparing World-Systems: Toward a Theory of Semiperipheral Development. *Comparative Civilizations Review* 19:39-66.
1989 *Global Formation: Structures of the World-Economy.* Basil Blackwell, Cambridge, MA.
Chase-Dunn, Christopher and Thomas D. Hall.
1991a *Core/Periphery Relations in Precapitalist Worlds.* Westview, Boulder, CO.
1991b Conceptualizing Core/Periphery Hierarchies for Comparative Study. In *Core/Periphery Relations in Precapitalist Worlds*, edited by Christopher Chase-Dunn and Thomas D. Hall, pp. 5-44. Westview, Boulder, CO.
1992 World-Systems and Modes of Production: Toward the Comparative Study of Transformations. *Humboldt Journal of Social Relations* 18:81-117.
1993 Comparing World-Systems: Concepts and Working Hypotheses. *Social Forces* 71:851-886.
1995 Cross-World-System Comparisons: Similarities and Differences. In *Civilizations and World-Systems: Two Approaches to the Study of World-Historical Change*, edited by Stephen K. Sanderson, pp. 109-121. Altamira Press, Walnut Creek, CA.
1996 *Rise and Demise: Comparing World-Systems.* Westview Press, Boulder, CO.
Collins, Randall
1992 The Geopolitical and Economic World-Systems of Kinship-Based and Agrarian-Coercive Societies. *Review* 15:373-388.
Curtin, Phillip
1990 *The Rise and Fall of the Plantation Complex.* Cambridge University Press, Cambridge.
Diankanoff, Igor M.
1973 The Rise of the Despotic State in Ancient Mesopotamia. In *Ancient Mesopotamia*, edited by I. M. Diakonoff, pp. 173-203. (G. M. Sergheyev, trans.). Dr. Martin Sandig, Walluf bei Weisbaden.

Dunaway, Wilma

1994 The Southern Fur Trade and the Incorporation of Southern Appalachia into the World-Economy, 1690-1763. *Review* 18:215-242.

1996 *The First American Frontier: Transition to Capitalism in Southern Appalachia, 1700-1860.* University of North Carolina Press, Chapel Hill.

Edens, Christopher

1992 Dynamics of Trade in the Ancient Mesopotamian "World System." *American Anthropologist* 94:118-139.

Ekholm, Kasja and Jonathan Friedman

1982 'Capital' Imperialism and Exploitation in the Ancient World-Systems. *Review* 6, 1:87-110.

Ferguson, R. Brian and Neil Whitehead

1992 *War in the Tribal Zone.* School of American Research Press, Santa Fe.

Frank, Andre Gunder

1966 The Development of Underdevelopment. *Monthly Review*, September:17-31.

1993 The Bronze Age World System and its Cycles. *Current Anthropology* 34:383-413.

Frank, Andre Gunder and Barry K. Gills

1993 *The World System: Five Hundred Years or Five Thousand?* Routledge, London.

Friedman, Jonathan and Michael Rowlands

1977 Notes Towards and Epigenetic Model of the Evolution of 'Civilization'. In *The Evolution of Social Systems*, edited by J. Friedman and M. J. Rowlands, pp. 201-278. Duckworth, London.

Glassman, Ronald

1986 *Democracy and Despotism in Primitive Societies: A Neo-Weberian Approach to Political Theory,* 2 Vols. Associated Faculty Press, Millwood, NY.

Granovetter, Mark

1979 The Idea of 'Advancement' in Theories of Social Evolution and Development. *American Journal of Sociology* 85:489-515.

Hall, John A.

1986 *States in History.* Basil Blackwell, London.

1987 *Powers and Liberties: The Causes and Consequences of the Rise of the West.* University of California Press, Berkeley.

Hall, Thomas D.

1989 *Social Change in the Southwest, 1350-1880.* University of Kansas Press, Lawrence.

1991a The Role of Nomads in Core/Periphery Relations. In *Core/Periphery Relations in Precapitalist Worlds*, edited by Christopher Chase-Dunn and Thomas D. Hall, pp. 212-239. Westview, Boulder, CO.

1991b Civilizational Change: The Role of Nomads. *Comparative Civilizations Review* 24:34-57.

1995 Rethinking Spatial Aspects of World-System Theory: A Precapitalist Perspective. Paper presented at American Association of Geographers meeting, Chicago, IL.

Hall, Thomas D. and Christopher Chase-Dunn

1993 The World-Systems Perspective and Archaeology: Forward into the Past. *Journal of Archaeological Research* 1:121-143.

1994 Forward into the Past: World-Systems Before 1500. *Sociological Forum* 9:295-306.

1995 Rethinking Spatial Aspects of Precapitalist World-Systems. Presented at World System History: The Social Science of Long Term change, University of Lund, Sweden.

Hopkins, Keith

1978 *Conquerors and Slaves.* Cambridge University Press, Cambridge.

Kardulias, P. Nick

1990 Fur Production as a Specialized Activity in a World System: Indians in the North American Fur Trade. *American Indian Culture and Research Journal* 14:25-60.

Kelly, Raymond C.
1985 *The Nuer Conquest: The Structure and Development of an Expansionist System.* University of Michigan Press, Ann Arbor.

Kohl, Phillip
1978 The Balance of Trade in Southwestern Asia in the Mid-Third Millennium B.C. *Current Anthropology* 19:463-492.
1987 The Ancient Economy, Transferable Technologies and the Bronze Age World-System: A View from the Northeastern Frontier of the Ancient Near East. In *Centre and Periphery in the Ancient World,* edited by Michael Rowlands, Mogens Larsen, and Kristian Kristiansen, pp. 13-24. Cambridge University Press, Cambridge.

Kristiansen, Kristian
1987 Centre and Periphery in Bronze Age Scandinavia. In *Centre and Periphery in the Ancient World,* edited by Michael Rowlands, Mogens Larsen, and Kristian Kristiansen, pp. 74-86. Cambridge University Press, Cambridge.

La Lone, Darrell E.
1991 The Development of State Production Enclaves in the Inca Empire. Unpublished paper presented at Society for Economic Anthropology, Bloomington, IN.
1994 An Andean World-System: Production Transformations Under the Inka Empire. In *The Economic Anthropology of the State,* edited by Elizabeth M. Brumfiel, pp. 17-41. Mongraphs in Economic Anthropology, No. 11. University Press of America, Lanham, MD.

La Lone, Mary B. and Darrell E. LaLone
1987 The Inka State in the Southern Highlands: State Administrative and Production Enclaves. *Ethnohistory* 34:47-62.

Lamberg-Karlovsky, C. C.
1975 Third Millennium Modes of Exchange and Modes of Production. In *Ancient Civilization and Trade,* J. A. Sabloff and C. C. Lamberg-Karlovsky, pp. 341-368. University of New Mexico Press, Albuquerque.

Lenski, Gerhard
1976 History and Social Change. *American Journal of Sociology* 82:548-564.

McNeill, William H.
1995 *The Rise of the West* After Twenty-Five Years. In *Civilizations and World-Systems: Two Approaches to* the *Study of World-Historical Change,* edited by Stephen K. Sanderson, pp. 303-320. Altamira Press, Walnut Creek, CA.

Mann, Michael
1986 *The Sources of Social Power: A History of Power from the Beginning to A.D. 1760.* University Press, Cambridge.

Melko, Matthew
1995 The Nature of Civilizations. In *Civilizations and World-Systems: Two Approaches to the Study of World-Historical Change,* edited by Stephen K. Sanderson, pp. 27-45. Altamira Press, Walnut Creek, CA.

Melko, Matthew and Leighton, R. Scott, eds.
1987 *The Boundaries of Civilizations in Space and Time.* University Press of America, Lanham, MD.

Moseley, Katherine P.
1992 Caravel and Caravan: West Africa and the World-Economies ca. 900-1900 AD. *Review* 15:523-555.

Myrdal, Gunnar
1971 *Economic Theory and Underdeveloped Regions.* Harper and Row, New York.

Nisbet, Robert
1969 *Social Change and History: Aspects of the Western Theory of Development.* Oxford University Press, New York.

Pailes, Richard A., and Joseph W. Whitecotton
1975 Greater Southwest and Mesoamerican World-Systems. Paper presented at the Southwestern Anthropological Association meeting, Santa Fe, NM.

1979 The Greater Southwest and Mesoamerican World System: An Exploratory Model of Frontier Relationships. In *The Frontier: Comparative Studies*, edited by W. W. Savage and S. I. Thompson, pp. 105-121. University of Oklahoma Press, Norman.

Patterson, Orlando
1982 *Slavery and Social Death: A Comparative Study*. Harvard University Press, Cambridge, MA.

Peregrine, Peter
1992 *Mississippian Evolution: A World-System Perspective*. Monographs in World Archaeology No. 9. Prehistory Press, Madison, WI.
1995 Networks of Power: The Mississippian World-System. In *Native American Interactions*, edited by M. Nassaney and K. Sassaman, pp 247-265. University of Tennessee Press, Knoxville, TN.

Polanyi, Karl
1944 *The Great Transformation: The Political and Economic Origins of Our Time*. Beacon Press, Boston.
1977 *The Livelihood of Man*, edited by Harry W. Pearson. Academic Press, New York.

Polanyi, Karl, Conrad Arensberg and Harry Pearson.
1957 *Trade and Market in the Early Empires*. Regnery, Chicago.

Renfrew, Colin R. and John F. Cherry.
1986 *Peer Polity Interaction and Socio-Political Change*. Cambridge University Press, Cambridge.

Sahlins, Marshall
1972 *Stone Age Economics*. University of Chicago Press, Chicago.

Sanderson, Stephen K.
1990 *Social Evolutionism: A Critical History*. Basil Blackwell, Cambridge, MA.
1995a *Social Transformations: A General Theory of Historical Development*. Basil Blackwell, London.
1995b *Civilizations and World-Systems: Two Approaches to the Study of World-Historical Change*. Altamira Press, Walnut Creek, CA.

Santley, Robert and Rani Alexander
1992 The Political Economy of Core-Periphery Systems. In *Resources, Power, and Interregional Interaction*, edited by Edward M. Schortman and Patricia A. Urban, pp. 23-59. Plenum Press, New York.

Schneider, Jane
1977 Was there a Pre-Capitalist World-System? *Peasant Studies* 6:20-29. (Reprinted in *Core/Periphery Relations in Precapitalist Worlds*, edited by Christopher Chase-Dunn and Thomas D. Hall, pp. 45-64. Westview, Boulder, CO.)

Schortman, Edward M. and Patricia A. Urban
1987 Modeling Interregional Interaction in Prehistory. In *Advances in Archeological Method and Theory*, Vol. 11, pp. 37-95. Academic Press, New York.
1994 Living on the Edge: Core/Periphery Relations in Ancient Southeast Mesoamerica. *Current Anthropology* 35:401-430.
1992 *Resources, Power, and Interregional Interaction*. Plenum Press, New York.

Sherratt, Andrew
1993a What Would a Bronze-Age World System Look Like? Relations Between Temperate Europe and the Mediterranean in Later Prehistory. *Journal of European Archaeology* 1:1-57.
1993b Core, Periphery and Margin: Perspectives on the Bronze Age. In *Development and Decline in the Mediterranean Bronze Age*, edited by C. Mathers and S. Stoddart, pp. 335-345. Sheffield Academic Press, Sheffield.
1993c Who are You Calling Peripheral? Dependence and Independence in European Prehistory. In *Trade and Exchange in Prehistoric Europe*, edited by C. Scarre and F. Healy, pp. 245-255. Oxbow (Prehistoric Society Monograph), Oxford.

Tilly, Charles
1984 *Big Structures, Large Processes, Huge Comparisons*. Russell Sage, New York.

Wallerstein, Immanuel

1974a The Rise and Future Demise of the World Capitalist System: Concepts for Comparative Analysis. *Comparative Studies in Society and History* 16:387-415.

1974b *The Modern World-System I: Capitalist Agriculture and the Origins of the European World-Economy in the Sixteenth Century.* Academic Press, New York.

1979 *The Capitalist World-Economy*. Cambridge University Press, Cambridge.

1980 *The Modern World-System II: Mercantilism and the Consolidation of the European World-economy, 1600-1750.* Academic Press, New York.

1984 *The Politics of the World-Economy*. Cambridge University Press, Cambridge.

1989 *The Modern World-System III: The Second Era of Great Expansion of the Capitalist World-Economy, 1730-1840s.* Academic Press, New York.

1993 World System vs. World-Systems. In *The World System: Five Hundred Years or Five Thousand?*, edited by Andre Gunder Frank and Barry K. Gills, pp. 291-296. Routledge, London.

1995 Hold the Tiller Firm: On Method and the Unit of Analysis. In *Civilizations and World-Systems: Two Approaches to the Study of World-Historical Change*, edited by Stephen K. Sanderson, pp. 239-247. Altamira Press, Walnut Creek, CA.

Wilkinson, David

1987 Central Civilization. *Comparative Civilizations Review* 17:31-59.

1995 Civilizations are World Systems! In *Civilizations and World-Systems: Two Approaches to the Study of World-Historical Change*, edited by Stephen K. Sanderson, pp. 234-246. Altamira Press, Walnut Creek, CA.

Wolf, Eric R.

1982 *Europe and the People Without History.* Berkeley: University of California Press.

Chapter 3

Clout, Corn, Copper, Core-Periphery, Culture Area

Stephen A. Kowalewski
University of Georgia

This chapter contains four main points. First, the North American culture areas of the Northwest, Southwest, and Southeast were world-systems. Their component societies owed their nature and existence to macroregional interactions, in which patterns of labor procurement and warfare figured significantly but differently in each case. Second, I criticize the idea that prestige goods structured these macroregional social systems. Third, we archaeologists tend to favor bottom-up, locality-to-macroregion method and theory, but top-down, macroregion-to-locality method and theory provides its own insights. Fourth is that ecological adjustments are not fundamentally local but are macroregional too.

Culture Areas are World-Systems

Systems

A "world-system" is at least subcontinental in size, and it is a system, meaning that its component societies are integrated such that changes in one will have effects upon the others. All systems have spatial and temporal bounds, and degrees of complexity, meaning numbers of different parts (Blanton et al. 1981). The scale, boundedness, integration, and complexity of component societies are affected by their interactions with other societies, either in complementary relations, such as the domination of core-periphery interactions (Rowlands, Larsen, and Kristiansen 1987), or in "peer-polity" interactions (Renfrew and Cherry 1986) in which the components are approximately alike and there are few lasting relations of domination. In peer-polity situations, various local groups take on similar attributes by virtue of their participation in a common network of interaction, and the latter then is a field of competition in which the players operate by certain rules and symbols. Though they may strive toward domination, no player can succeed, at least for very long. If they do, then we don't have peer-polity interaction.

Systems must be integrated and their components must be interdependent. This means that something must move between the system's parts—matter, energy, or information. I also take concordant change, when the components are transformed together in roughly the same way, as an indication of interdependence, and hence systemness. One might imagine concordant change as the result of a completely exogenous cause such as climate change. But even this might imply systemness if component societies adjust in similar ways. Another, more controversial criterion of systemness is that systems should have emergent properties, meaning that higher-level phenomena cannot always be predicted by or are not simply aggregations of attributes measured in the component parts.

This definition of system and world-system is thus similar to Chase-Dunn and Hall's "intersocietal networks in which the interactions (e.g., trade, warfare, intermarriage) are important for the reproduction of the internal structures of the composite units and importantly affect changes that occur in these local structures" (1993:855; also Hall and Chase-Dunn this volume). Further, this concept of world-system expects core-periphery structure. Core-periphery may be of domination (as in Wallerstein's concept [1974]), or it may simply involve differentiation. This definition of world-systems is useful for comparative purposes and for archaeologists in particular because it is not limited to a particular mode of production, form of accumulation, or societal type. World-systems frameworks provide a conceptual framework for ordering, comparing, and testing models of large-scale to local, local to large-scale interactions. I believe I am correct in saying that since the demise of culture-history and its diffusionist theory and waves of influence, archaeologists have had no other conceptual framework except world-systems for treating macroregional-local interaction.

Culture Areas

The concept of culture areas has been an important one for scholars of indigenous North America since the turn of the twentieth century (Wissler 1926; Kroeber 1939). Wissler and Kroeber defined culture areas on the basis of similarities in culture traits. This is not necessarily a requirement of world-systems or geographers' regions, since component parts of regional systems usually differ functionally depending on their different roles in the system. Joseph Jorgensen's (1980) major cross-cultural study of western North America in the ethnographic present shows many similarities among neighboring societies, especially where technological and economic variables are concerned, and generally a little less coherence with social, political, and ideological variables. This finding may reinforce earlier observations about the coincidence of cultural and natural areas.

Here I offer a somewhat different interpretation of culture area. First I briefly describe the three culture-area cases that are the subjects of this paper—Northwest Coast, Southwest, and Southeast—in terms of their properties as systems and their core-periphery structure.

Northwest Coast

Included within the Northwest Coast boundaries as I define them are the coast proper, Northern California, and interior tribes of the Plateau (Jorgensen 1980; Adams 1981; Mitchell and Donald 1988; Ames 1994). The duration may be for the last 4000 years (Hebda and Mathewes 1984). The traditional culture area is usually defined as the Northwest Coast and perhaps northern California, because of likeness. But raiding to procure labor from interior tribes, and sharing of some social and political institutions, including feasting and ceremonial exchange, suggest integration (interdependence and mutual shaping) of both coastal and Plateau societies.

For support of the idea that the Northwest Coast and the Plateau were linked in functional relationships, we can look at Jorgensen's (1980) seven major cultural variable categories. The coast and the interior are internally similar but differ from each other in technology, subsistence, and economic organization. For the most part they are separate entities, but have some overlap in social, political, ceremonial, and shamanism variables. Raiding as a means of labor recruitment was common in coastal societies, with forays into the interior. Labor supply and recruitment were key organizing features, and to a degree this extended into the Plateau (Jorgensen 1980; Adams 1981). Internal complexity was weak, consisting of a coastal core and an interior periphery.

As I see it, the Northwest Coast was a macroregional system held together by the flows of people. People moved about in patterned, institutional ways of intermarriage, feasting, and warfare. The system had a core that typically needed labor (for fish and sea mammal processing) and a periphery that typically supplied labor. The system was weakly bounded. It became less of a system as one moved north since extra labor was not a requirement of increasingly mobile groups, and it became less of a system in the east with greater distance from the labor-demanding coast.

Southwest

The Southwest as a culture area includes the Colorado Plateau through Hohokam, parts of Sonora and Chihuahua, and occasionally outer regions such as Fremont. It emerges from the wider western macroregion after A.D. 1 (Jorgensen 1980; Spicer 1962; Cordell 1984; Crown and Judge 1991). Concordant change such as the pithouse-to-pueblo transition, and the exchange and raiding relations between nucleated towns and surrounding dispersed populations, suggest broad integration. David Wilcox (1991) describes several bounded, internally differentiated macroregional systems within the prehistoric Southwest. He defines these by their distinctive, macroregionally shared institutions of local and regional integration (e.g., Hohokam ballcourts or Chacoan great houses).

In terms of complexity, the Southwest typically had two types of functionally distinct parts: population clusters and surrounding, much more dispersed populations. One might think of these as cores and peripheries. Within the macroregional-scale systems in the

Southwest there were multiple cores consisting of clusters of aggregated population, and interstitial peripheries of lower density. At this scale core and periphery differentiation and domination are evident. At a larger scale, there were at times structural peripheries or frontiers between the large, macroregional systems, as in the Verde Valley and Mogollon rim country between the Anasazi of the Colorado Plateaus and the Hohokam of the desert. The history of occupation on these frontiers has much to do with the changing power and demographic attraction of distant centers (Redman 1993:12-13, 166-169). In any case, to explain the history of local human settlement one has to look beyond the locality to wider regions, and one has to understand shifting cores and peripheries.

As I did for the Northwest Coast and the Plateau, I looked for complementarities between the Pueblo and the non-Pueblo Southwest in Jorgensen's ethnographic data (1980). Puebloan and non-Puebloan societies separate out on all categories except individual spirits and shamanism, where there is considerable sharing. Puebloan societies were targets of non-Puebloan raids, but in contrast to the semi-sedentary communities of the Northwest Coast, labor recruitment did not have the same significance for the Pueblos. Pueblo and non-Pueblo social and political organizations did not tend to become more alike culturally because of raiding or because of personal shamanistic practices. This is consistent with the low-level movement of individuals, often through marriage, and the strong community-scale, corporate definition of Puebloan societies. Raiding, trading, and boundary maintaining institutions grew out of the interaction between dispersed and aggregated communities (e.g. the Plains-Pueblo interaction discussed in Spielmann 1991, Schaafsma 1992). The strong distinction seen ethnographically between the Puebloan and non-Puebloan niches in the Southwest was not so marked in pre-Athabaskan times, prior to the sixteenth century. There was more integration between core towns and peripheral rural populations prehistorically. As increasingly large, aggregated communities formed in prehistoric times, they developed institutions promoting internal integration and boundedness. But in doing so, integrated and bounded communities had to develop special mechanisms for their relationships with surrounding, more dispersed populations, as with the Chacoan outlier great houses and the surrounding "communities" (Warburton and Graves 1992), Hohokam settlement systems that had centers with ballcourts or platform mounds and often dispersed hinterland populations (Fish and Fish 1994), the modern Havasupai and the tribal land they legally control but do not live on (Manners 1974), or the modern Hopi claims to a greater sphere defined as lands occupied by their ancestors.

Maintaining appropriately bounded communities was the key optimization problem for Southwestern populations. By "appropriately bounded" I mean interdependence of enough people and sufficient resources to sustain life and political viability. Drawing and holding people—their labor—was the critical problem in the arid Southwestern environment. Communities had elaborate institutions to accomplish this. It is no coincidence that these institutions were similar over very large, macroregional areas: ballcourts, platform mound political ceremonialism, kachinas, sodalities, kivas, war societies, etc. (see also Kintigh 1994).

Southeast

The Southeastern culture area includes the Mississippian area, with Plains, Florida, and northern groups such as the Iroquois also affected. The final prehistoric form of the Southeastern macroregion emerges around A.D. 900 from an Eastern North American macroregion of long duration (Hudson 1976; Smith 1978b, 1986, 1990; Tuck 1978). In terms of complexity, the system components included competing regional chiefdoms, paramount chiefdoms, less centrally organized peripheries, and possible gateway-and-periphery combinations (cf. Hirth (1978). The Mississippian-era Southeast, like the Northwest Coast and the Southwest, exhibits core-periphery differentiation, without much evidence of core-periphery domination.

Many archaeologists in the Southeast still refer to "Woodland" or "Mississippian" or "Mississippianized" societies, but I think this terminology is insufficient. In my view using "Woodland" and "Mississippian" to refer to social or cultural forms (in short, for anything other than general time periods) betrays the inadequacies of culture-historical thought. The culture-history concepts imply essentialism, cultural evolutionary teleology, and a Mississippian "modernization theory" in which Woodland folk continued to live in backwardness unfazed (unphased?) by modern chiefly, agricultural life.

A comparative world-system conceptualization has certain advantages over the older culture-history paradigm. I see the Southeast from Late Woodland times on as having core-periphery relations in which the internal organizations of relatively more centralized and relatively decentralized regional societies were partly shaped through mutual, often hostile, interaction. The archaeological reality shows a Southeastern world in Late Woodland and Mississippian times in which core-region experimentation with new, centralized organizations and new modes of production and warfare was matched by equally new (not older, Early or Middle Woodland) forms of organization on a developing periphery.

Organizational flux is one of the central themes of recent comparative studies of Late Woodland societies

(Nassaney and Cobb 1991). Between 800 and 1200 A.D the re-organization and mutual shaping is manifested in Georgia, an area with which I am familiar, by new ceramic complexes distinctive from one another in style. Triangular arrow heads are common, and there is more evidence of warfare. Territorial boundaries were redefined. The Macon Plateau mound center was a striking contemporary contrast in the midst of these new, dispersed, non-centralized settlement systems. All of these exhibited new modes of production and organization; none were simply the perpetuations of older ways of life (Stephenson 1990; Elliott and Wynn 1991; Worth and Duke 1991; Braley 1993; Pluckhahn 1994; Ledbetter 1995).

The Mississippian emergence, resulting in similar chiefly organization across the Southeast, is an example of concordant, macroregional change. I think the mechanism forcing this rapid move toward chiefly organization and reorganized regional societies on the periphery was warfare. Warfare belongs to the intermediate geographical range in Chase-Dunn and Hall's model of different types of flows or spatial interactions (1993). (Saying that warfare shaped Southeastern societies does not imply a particular cause for war, especially not conflict over access to agricultural land due to population pressure, nor does it imply origin and diffusion from a single point.)

Twenty years ago Bruce Smith (1978a:488-491) pointed out that Mississippian settlement patterns extended along a continuum from dispersed to nucleated. The more dispersed forms have a great capacity for potential production; the more nucleated forms may be a response to certain types of warfare (see also, among others, Kowalewski and Hatch 1991). This link between interregional diplomatic-military activity, basic production, and regional and local settlement patterns has a most interesting implication: an obvious way for large-scale interactions to structure behavior at the local and household levels. Such macro-micro linkages are avenues for using commonly found archaeological information to evaluate world-systems models.

These three cases are more than culture areas defined by similarity. The aboriginal culture areas of the Northwest Coast, the Southwest, and the Southeast are large, multisociety, world-systems. For long durations they had degrees of boundedness, complexity, and integration. These world-systems were characterized by core-periphery differentiation rather than domination. In the Northwest Coast world-system, labor procurement by people-hungry coastal "houses" was the key, system-defining interaction. In the Southwest it was the regulation of membership in and boundaries between aggregated and dispersed populations. In the Southeast the system-shaping interdependence in late times was the military competition between chiefdoms. Note that these macroregional social systems changed over time, in their scale, boundaries, complexity, and integration. In each macroregional system there was concordant change. Component societies significantly determined one another's states, in concert. These three cases were more weakly integrated than Postclassic Mesoamerica, imperial China, or early modern Europe (cf. Wallerstein 1974), yet for long periods of time and across thousands of kilometers they maintained the properties of systems. The rest of this paper considers how these systems were integrated.

Critique of the "Prestige Goods Economy"

Figure 2.1 is Hall and Chase-Dunn's model for world-system interaction. Bulk goods—corn, for example—are expected to travel within the most limited sphere, and so the regular, system-defining interaction involving bulk goods has the smallest range. It is easy to see how people may be bound up in relations of interdependency involving the production, exchange, and consumption of bulk goods. This is what Wallerstein (1974) wrote about for Europe and the modern world-system. When Spain regularly obtained wheat from Poland the two regions were closely bound up in a circuit of interdependence and a regional division of labor.

Regular political and military interaction may take place over longer distances, as in raiding, slaving, or marriage alliances. This is clout. Such interaction has logistical and communications limits, but they are wider. It is easy to see how regular political and military interaction can be system-transforming and system-shaping. Bronze Age or Medieval European landscapes without hill forts or castles would be quite different settlement systems. Spores (1967) has described how Mesoamerican royal marriage alliances consolidated political power over long distances, and paved the way for other types of exchange.

At the broadest scale in Figure 2.1 is interaction involving prestige goods, such as copper. This interaction involves real things or people, but what counts is the symbolic content, not the item per se or even the bearer. Long-distance symbolic interaction can operate to transfer value from one point to another. In aboriginal North America, a returned pilgrim, a vision quester, one who acquires a new dance, or one who owns the rights to display a crest could acquire some prestige, power, or wealth useful in internal competition and perhaps useful for external recognition. Symbolic objects convey information about the social relations of givers and receivers. As symbols the stuff is completely arbitrary, except that items should be rare, light, exotic, or crafted. Here we can think of gold in the Old World, or copper bells, crests, or breastplates in

North America; and as Helms (1979) has shown, knowledge itself may be a prestige good.

The informational value of a symbol, what specifically a symbol represents, or what other value it may be translated into may not necessarily be mutually recognized by all parties in exchange. All that may be required is that the parties understand that the symbol is valuable in some way. It is not true that symbolic items will carry the same meanings within or between social groups across space. A wonderful example is the ship's biscuit conveyed from the arriving Hernando Cortis through Indian emissaries to the Aztec king Motecuhzoma. This biscuit was so exotic and valuable-seeming, in the context of Aztec ideology, that, it is said, Motecuhzoma had it buried in the Quetzalcoatl temple at Tula (Duran 1967:510-511; another version has colored glass beads instead of a biscuit [Sahagzn 1975:724-725]). The famous biscuit was unimportant to the Spanish, and rather marvelous to the Aztecs, or so it would seem. The point is that biscuit, beads, copper, or other such preciosities in prestige goods exchange have values so arbitrary that they must be continually reaffirmed by something else, which in my opinion is power. In cross-cultural communication and generally in symbolic interaction, the parties to interchange have differing or contested values and interpretations, ultimately decided in the arena of power. The "negotiated" value may be conveyed by the social context of the exchange—again, people are involved directly and the negotiated value is a function of their relative power. As I argue below, macroregional social and ecological processes are thus mediated through human interactions in which power is never absent.

One may be tempted to see the Hall and Chase-Dunn diagram as the spatial mapping of a bottom-up materialism (Harris 1979), in which the basic economic determinations occur at the local level, with resultant political organization at the regional scale, and ideological categories, being determined by the former, whirring about in macroregional, superstructural space. But, to anticipate arguments I make below, let me put this into ecosystems terms, where it becomes more subtle and more complicated. Interactions at each of these scales, local through macroregional, are informational, energetic, and material, and they have substantial effects on other system components. Major, widespread territorial redefinition, as seen in the Late Woodland in eastern North America, or the thirteenth century in much of the Southwest, must have involved virtually every aspect of cultural systems, from the social relations of production and exchange to demography. And on the local scale to say that the movement of food items in household and local group contexts did not involve ideological categories and the flow of information would be tantamount to ignoring half of the legacy of economic anthropology. Matter, energy, and information flows define human ecosystem scale, boundedness, integration, and complexity at all levels. So "Think Globally, Act Locally" doesn't mean that thought only happens at the world-system scale or that action is only effective locally. Action at home and at a distance involves social exchange, ideas, and movement of all sorts.

Each type of interaction (bulk, political and military, and symbolic) probably has particular time properties, that is, properties of duration, structuration, and storage or maintenance of value. People can move bulk items efficiently only over short distances. Bulk items are in regular use and dependence on them is rather urgent. Most food, fuel, and fiber is consumed fairly soon after production and transfer, so the need is urgent and the cycle is often repeated, establishing a regular rut of interaction. Political and military interaction is the carrying out of human will, it is about power. What moves from point to point is people. In terms of duration, single, short-lived exercises of power may be decisive, but their persistence in time may be only moderate, and continual reminders may have to be sent. I see the effects of such events as potentially lasting longer than a cycle of production and exchange of bulk necessities. Perhaps its common upper limit is the human generation or human life span, but this is a topic needing more study.

The duration and structuration properties of prestige goods and other symbolic interactions are potentially long, but fragile. Being symbols, these items often do not convey exact, complete, or accurate information about the state of receivers and givers. Symbols may be misrepresented, lied about, inflated, deflated, twisted, spun, overvalued, or ignored, and they need constant inputs of human time and energy for their maintenance, renewal, and reinterpretation. So for symbolic, prestige goods interaction to be effective in causing change at a distance, somewhere along the line the symbol must be translated into human action at a more basic level, and that level is the arena of power. Signification is important, but as Eric Wolf reminds us, "power is never external to signification" (1990:593).

In the last decade archaeologists have allowed their latent goody-hunting instincts to conspire hypergamously with high-class Eurostructural idealism, an ill-conceived offspring of which is the North American Prestige Goods Economy, Unlimited. For example, "Elite activities were the interregional contacts that made the Mesoamerican world" (Blanton, Kowalewski, Feinman, and Appel 1981:246). Those just-cited authors did describe in more detail ties between prestige goods interaction, wealth, power, and ordinary economics: "...the prestige system, as a regulator of more basic transactions, played a key role in the functioning and dynamics of ancient Mesoamerica" (p. 250). But others give prestige goods a more causative role: "In Powhatan's world, copper was a key symbol, if not the source, of power and authority in matters secular and sacred" (Hantman 1990:685).

From copper as symbol of power we leap to copper as source of power, and from there it's only a small hop to the proposition that interrupting the flow of preciosities is very upsetting to society:

> If the symbols that legitimize the status and authority of the elite become unavailable, then the legitimacy of the elite inevitably will be called into question. If only a few of the symbols become unavailable, it is probable that substitutes can be introduced. However, if a large number of legitimizing symbols are persistently or chronically unavailable, the system of statuses is likely to break down (Welch 1991:194).

In contrast, I argue that in the Northwest Coast, Southwest, and Southeast, the more prosaic institutions of labor procurement, boundary maintenance, and warfare were the root structures of macroregional integration.

Other common criticisms of prestige goods models include:

1. That sometimes archaeologists establish the "eliteness" of contexts in which preciosities are found only by preciosities and not by other evidence, so that ascriptions of eliteness are tightly circular.
2. That independent archaeological evidence of the connection between symbol-wearing and power wielding is sometimes lacking (see Kowalewski, Feinman, and Finsten 1992 for a discussion of these two points).
3. That the archaeological occurrences of preciosities are spotty, ephemeral, and difficult to link predictably to expected variation in other features, such as settlement patterns. For example, in the Southeast ceremonial exotica are not always or simply coincident with the power or extent of chiefdoms as understood from other data. Note the differences on this issue among the various authors in Galloway (1989) and Smith (1990).

This paper's second main point is that prestige goods are impotent as cause of the origins and reproduction of total regional and macroregional structure. There may be prestige goods subsystems, but not whole prestige goods economies or societies. Ethnographic and archaeological data can support hypotheses that prestige goods sub-systems were reflective of, or helped motivate, or were some of the contested resources of social relations, but to date, claims that prestige goods interactions structured whole economies or societies are in my opinion unconvincing.

Top-Down Structuration

We archaeologists often begin with what we normally think of as the most concrete, artifacts and sites, and then move up by chains of inference and out spatially to catchment area, region, and macroregion. Bottom-to-top seems to us a natural organizing framework (e.g., Flannery 1976) and it has proven productive. But sometimes it helps to break out of what seems natural. For a sharp contrast in analytical approach, compare the multi-scale research strategy of Meentemeyer and Box (1987) with reductionist strategies such as those recommended by Bettinger (1991).

Imagine our normal bottom-up view turned upside down. Macroregions would be prior—after all, the macroregional cultural system is the least mutable, most perduring. In North America, macroregional cultural systems existed from the moment Paleoindians came onto the scene. Paleoindians were not cultureless; they had common cultural institutions from the beginning. There was never a time without macroregional cultural interaction, without world-systems. We recognize broad, unbounded Paleoindian societies, somewhat narrower but still very wide ranging Archaic societies, and it is not until much later in eastern North America that more closed territorial societies emerge. The internal integration, complexity, boundedness, and scale of emergent social groups was partially dependent on the integration, complexity, scale, and boundedness of surrounding social groups.

The crystallization of semi-bounded social groups was a whole-network process. The Hopewellian interaction sphere is to us a more visible moment of the eastern North American world-system, not its birth—that blessed event took place 10,000 years earlier. From the top-down perspective, Hopewellian stylistic behavior is easier to see as a property of a whole, prior network instead of the coincidence of multiple, disparate, autonomous groups (Braun 1986). How do we get similar but contrasting totems, clan names, or prestige statuses employed across disparate environments and disparate language groups? Because they are created within a pre-existing macroregional network. From this top-down perspective regional territories are instances of macroregional structures or symbol sets, franchises of the league as a whole, so to speak. Regions are created out of macroregions, localities are variations, and sites are transient points or limited expressions of a much wider entity.

Top-down, neither the individual decision-maker nor the local community is prior, and macroregional interaction does not come about just every once and a while. Kopytoff (1987:34-35) has a similar argument. The idea that cultures are normally small and discrete may be a product of the nationalisms of our own recent history, and another piece of culture-history baggage. If cultures were only small, then Galton's Problem wouldn't exist. But in reality, cultures drawn from the same macroregion aren't independent samples or independent events. They are dependent, not through mechanical diffusion as older theory had it, but interdependent in a systemic sense.

What is macroregional culture? How would we describe it? Again, macroregional culture should not be described by lists of traits as in older theory. I can think of two ways to describe big culture: in terms of the systematic properties of its regional parts (as in Wallerstein's world division of labor) and in terms of the "emergent properties" of the macroregional whole, which might include boundary institutions and the ways in which values are produced, transferred among its component parts, and consumed.

This paper's third point is that people have always lived in world-systems, that culture is a big thing not a little thing. The researcher ought to view these objects top-down and bottom-up, alternatively giving priority to the one and then the other as an analytical strategy (see Peregrine, this volume).

Big Ecosystems

My fourth point is that the human ecosystem is macroregional too. Ecological adjustments are not firstly or fundamentally local. Human ecosystems have significant determining properties at all levels from the locality to the macroregion. There's more to human ecosystems than getting food in one's local catchment-that you have a catchment to eat in at all has much to do with power, social relations, and biotic and abiotic factors only understandable at regional and macroregional scales.

The human ecosystem undergoes its most dramatic changes, and those that entail the most dramatic consequences for the nonhuman components of the environment, in waves that affect all localities over broad macroregions (such as the pithouse-to-pueblo transition in the Southwest, or the rather sudden adoption of maize as a staple in eastern North America). The eastern North American macroregion changed as a whole from Paleoindian to Early Archaic to Middle Archaic to the Late Archaic. These concordant changes in the North American Archaic are well known, as in the classic work of Coe (1964). Maximal and minimal social groups, settlement systems, mobility strategies, storage, resource strategies, demographic regimes, relations of production, consumption, and exchange, etc., were not arrived at independently at local or regional scales. At any one time decidedly ecological variables like these were mutually adjusted across eastern North America, and they changed concordantly from period to period across quite varying environments, a phenomenon not expected if most features of cultural systems are primarily due to local adaptations.

World-systems or macroregional cultural systems are distinctive ecological regimes. Variation in biotic and abiotic components is often not restricted to localities, but is broad in scope (e.g., frost in the Mexican highlands, drought in the Southwest and Southeast, or the population dynamics of fish). Wissler and Kroeber described correspondences between culture areas and climate, vegetation, and major food sources: the Northwest Coast culture area coincided with the Northwestern Hygrophytic Coniferous Forest (Kroeber 1939:28), and Wissler's "Salmon" food area coincides with his North Pacific Coast and Plateau culture areas (Wissler 1922, cited in Kroeber 1939:7). These early twentieth-century anthropologists thought that culture areas were made by ecological adaptations of local groups and a history of diffusion between local groups, but the top-down approach has local adaptations derivative of or transformations of prior strategies resident at the broadest scale.

What do the macroregional human ecosystems consist of and how should they be described? They consist of particular arrangements of human populations and sub-populations. The flows or interactions defining such broad ecosystems are the movements of people as they interact. One might think of these flows as involving bulk goods, political and military interaction, and symbolic or luxury goods exchange, each having different spatial spheres, as in Figure 2.1. The flows occur through social institutions, hence the main flows in human ecosystems are mediated, meaning they can only take place through, social institutions. One cannot describe the human ecosystem without attending carefully to the key social institutions. Certain social institutions having directly to do with the allocation of people and their labor are the key boxes in the world-system or large-scale human ecosystem flow chart, as I tried to explain in the examples in the first section of this paper. Finally, social institutions are put together, maintained, or brought down by people exercising power. Power structures the human ecosystem and power transforms it.

The premise that large-scale human ecosystems (our world-systems) are socially mediated departs from other theoretical approaches. Localist interpretations will completely miss the extraordinary, extralocal determination of local events. Favorite-variable explanations (take your pick: population pressure, soil exhaustion, firewood exhaustion, climate change, prolonged drought, falling water table, etc.) usually fail to specify the spatial and temporal scales of causes and effects. Worse, those who push favorite-variable explanations fail to run their exogenous inputs through social institutions wherein people with power may radically transform the expected outputs.

How are macroregional ecosystems reproduced and transformed? Here we need to ask how matter, energy, or information operate at a distance in such a way that what happens in one region will affect what happens elsewhere. The movement of people and the playing out of social relations is the main mechanism by which something is transferred from place to place. The ecologist of human systems cannot ignore power and political economy, because it is through this channel of political economy that the determining inputs and outputs flow on the human side of things.

Finally, what makes this interesting and potentially productive in the scientific sense is that macroregional ecosystem structure has direct links to what what most of us study archaeologically every day: local settlement patterns, household activities, production, consumption, and exchange. For example, how people in Mississippian times in the Southeast distributed themselves on the landscape (dispersed, nucleated) and the activities they carried out (e.g., more or less intensive corn production, raiding) are everyday archaeological concerns and the basic stuff of ecology. The same matters—demography, activities—are "outputs" of the social institutions of political economy. And these are the same social institutions that in my interpretation define the Northwest Coast, Southwestern, and Southeastern world-systems. Macroregional structure is composed of rather ordinary materials.

Conclusions

Early twentieth-century anthropologists were on to something when they described "culture areas," but their adherence to diffusionist concept impeded seeing the culture area as the outcome of systematic large-scale social interaction. I argued that the culture areas were world-systems. Aboriginal North America was organized into just a few world-systems with historically defined core-periphery differentiation. These world-systems were also macroregional ecological regimes, because, among other things, the distribution and abundance of the human species was governed by institutions in effect chartered by forces wider than the region or locality. Local adaptations were colored strongly by position in the larger system, for example, position in the core or on the periphery. Matter, energy, and information were transferred and interdependence cemented among component regions largely through the movement of people (clout, energy), as opposed to bulk goods like corn (matter) or preciosities like copper (information). The movement of people and the allocation of their labor was controlled through widely recognized, shared social institutions. Such social institutions were created and maintained by people wielding power. One cannot understand macroregional structure or the workings of large-scale human ecosystems without placing political-economic power at the center of the inquiry.

References Cited

Adams, John W.
1981 Recent Ethnology of the Northwest Coast. *Annual Review of Anthropology* 10: 361-392.

Ames, Kenneth M.
1994 The Northwest Coast: Complex Hunter-Gatherers, Ecology, and Social Evolution. *Annual Review of Anthropology* 23:209-229.

Bettinger, Robert L.
1991 *Hunter-Gatherers: Archaeological and Evolutionary Theory.* Plenum, New York.

Blanton, Richard E., Stephen A. Kowalewski, Gary Feinman, and Jill Appel
1981 *Ancient Mesoamerica: A Comparison of Change in Three Regions.* Cambridge University Press, Cambridge.

Braley, Chad O.
1993 What Are They Doing Here? Late Woodland-Early Mississippi Use of the Upper Coastal Plain in the Savannah and Ogeechee Watersheds. *Early Georgia* 21(2):45-59.

Braun, David P.
1986 Midwestern Hopewellian Exchange and Interregional Interaction. In *Peer Polity Interaction and Sociopolitical Change,* edited by Colin Renfrew and John F. Cherry, pp. 117-126. Cambridge University Press, Cambridge.

Chase-Dunn, Christopher, and Thomas D. Hall
1993 Comparing World-Systems: Concepts and Working Hypotheses. *Social Forces* 71(4):851-886.
Coe, Joffrey L.
1964 The Formative Cultures of the Carolina Piedmont. *Transactions* 54(5), American Philosophical Society, Philadelphia.
Cordell, Linda S.
1984 Southwestern Archaeology. *Annual Review of Anthropology* 13: 301-332.
Crown, Patricia L., and W. James Judge
1991 *Chaco & Hohokam: Prehistoric Regional Systems in the American Southwest.* School of American Research, Santa Fe.
Duran, Fray Diego
1967 *Historia de las Indias de Nueva Espaqa e Islas de la Tierra Firme.* 2 vols, edited by Angel Garibay K. Editorial Porrua, Mexico City.
Elliott, Daniel T., and Jack T. Wynn
1991 The Vining Revival: A Late simple Stamped Phase in the Central Georgia Piedmont. *Early Georgia* 19(1):1-18.
Fish, Suzanne K., and Paul R. Fish
1994 Multisite Communities as Measures of Hohokam Aggregation. In *The Ancient Southwestern Community: Models and Methods for the Study of Prehistoric Social Organization,* edited by W. H. Wills and Robert D. Leonard, pp. 119-129. University of New Mexico Press, Albuquerque.
Flannery, Kent V.
1976 *The Early Mesoamerican Village.* Academic Press, New York.
Galloway, Patricia
1989 *The Southeastern Ceremonial Complex: Artifacts and Analysis - The Cottonlandia Conference.* University of Nebraska Press, Lincoln.
Hantman, Jeffrey L.
1990 Between Powhatan and Quirank: Reconstructing Monacan Culture and History in the Context of Jamestown. *American Anthropologist* 92(3):676-690.
Harris, Marvin
1979 *Cultural Materialism: The Struggle for a Science of Culture.* Vantage, New York.
Hebda, Richard J., and Rolf W. Mathewes
1984 Holocene History of Cedar and Native Indian Cultures of the North American Pacific Coast. *Science* 225(4663):711-713.
Helms, Mary W.
1979 *Ancient Panama: Chiefs in Search of Power.* University of Texas Press, Austin.
Hirth, Kenneth G.
1978 Interregional Trade and the Formation of Prehistoric Gateway Communities. *American Antiquity* 43(1):35-45.
Hudson, Charles
1976 *The Southeastern Indians.* University of Tennessee Press, Knoxville.
Jorgensen, Joseph G.
1980 *Western Indians: Comparative Environments, Languages, and Cultures of 172 Western Indian Tribes.* W. H. Freeman, San Francisco.
Kintigh, Keith W.
1994 Chaco, Communal Architecture, and Cibolan Aggregation. In *The Ancient Southwestern Community: Models and Methods for the Study of Prehistoric Social Organization,* edited by W. H. Wills and Robert D. Leonard, pp. 131-140. University of New Mexico Press, Albuquerque.
Kopytoff, Igor
1987 The Internal African Frontier: The Making of African Political Culture. In *The African Frontier: The Reproduction of Traditional African Societies,* edited by Igor Kopytoff, pp. 3-84. Indiana University Press, Bloomington.

Kowalewski, Stephen A., Gary Feinman, and Laura Finsten
1992 "The Elite" and Assessment of Social Stratification in Mesoamerican Archaeology. In *Mesoamerican Elites: An Archaeological Assessment*, edited by D. Z. Chase and A. F. Chase, pp. 259-277. University of Oklahoma Press, Norman.
Kowalewski, Stephen A., and James W. Hatch
1991 The Sixteenth-Century Expansion of Settlement in the Upper Oconee Watershed, Georgia. *Southeastern Archaeology* 10(1):1-17.
Kroeber, A. L.
1939 Cultural and Natural Areas of Native North America. *Publications in American Archaeology and Ethnology*, vol. 38, University of California, Berkeley.
Ledbetter, R. Jerald
1995 Radiocarbon Dates for the Averett Phase: Early Mississippi Period on the Chattahoochee. *The Profile: Newsletter of the Society for Georgia Archaeology* 86(spring):8-9.
Manners, Robert A.
1974 *Havasupai Indians*. Garland Press, New York.
Meentemeyer, Vernon, and Elgene O. Box
1987 Scale Effects in Landscape Studies. In *Landscape Heterogeneity and Disturbance*, edited by Monica Goigel Turner, pp. 15-34. Springer-Verlag, New York.
Mitchell, Donald, and Leland Donald
1988 Archaeology and the Study of Northwest Coast Economies. In *Research in Economic Anthropology, Supplement 3*, edited by Barry L. Isaac, pp. 293-351. JAI, Greenwich, CT.
Nassaney, Michael S., and Charles R. Cobb
1991 *Stability, Transformation, and Variation: The Late Woodland Southeast.* Plenum Press, New York.
Pluckhahn, Thomas J.
1994 Mississippian Settlement in the Upper Oconee and Middle Broad River Valleys. *Early Georgia* 22(1):1-34.
Redman, Charles L.
1993 *People of the Tonto Rim: Archaeological Discovery in Prehistoric Arizona.* Smithsonian Institution Press, Washington.
Renfrew, Colin, and John F. Cherry
1986 *Peer-Polity Interaction and Socio-Political Change.* Cambridge University Press, Cambridge.
Rowlands, Michael, Mogens Larsen, and Kristian Kristiansen
1987 *Centre and Periphery in the Ancient World.* Cambridge University Press, Cambridge.
Sahagun, Fr. Bernardino de
1975 *Historia General de las Cosas de Nueva España.* Edited by Angel Marma Garibay K. Porrua, Mexico City.
Schaafsma, Polly
1992 Imagery and Magic: Petroglyphs at Comanche Gap, Galisteo Basin, New Mexico. In *Archaeology, Art, and Anthropology: Papers in Honor of J. J. Brody*, ed. by Meliha S. Duran and David T. Kirkpatrick, pp. 157-174. Archaeological Society of New Mexico, Albuquerque.
Smith, Bruce D.
1978a Variation in Mississippian Settlement Patterns. In *Mississippian Settlement Patterns*, edited by Bruce D. Smith, pp. 479-503. Academic Press, New York.
1978b *Mississippian Settlement Patterns*. Academic Press, New York.
1986 The Archaeology of the Eastern United States: From Dalton to de Soto, 10,500 - 500 B.P. *Advances in World Archaeology* 5:1-92.
1990 *The Mississippian Emergence*. Smithsonian Institution Press, Washington.
Spicer, Edward H.
1962 *Cycles of Conquest: The Impact of Spain, Mexico, and United States on the Indians of the Southwest, 1533-1960.* University of Arizona Press, Tucson.

Spielmann, Katherine A.
1991 *Farmerers, Hunters, and Colonists: Interaction Between the Southwest and the Southern Plains.* University of Arizona Press, Tucson.
Spores, Ronald
1967 *The Mixtec Kings and Their People.* University of Oklahoma Press, Norman.
Stephenson, Donald Keith
1990 *Investigation of Ocmulgee Cord Marked Pottery Sites in the Big Bend Region of Georgia.* M.A. thesis, Department of Anthropology, University of Georgia, Athens.
Tuck, James A.
1978 Northern Iroquoian Prehistory. In *Northeast,* edited by Bruce G. Trigger, pp. 322-333. *Handbook of North American Indians,* Vol. 15, William G. Sturtevant, general editor. Smithsonian Institution Press, Washington.
Wallerstein, Immanuel
1974 *The Modern World-System I: Capitalist Agriculture and the Origins of the European World-Economy in the Sixteenth Century.* Academic Press, New York.
Warburton, Miranda, and Donna K. Graves
1992 Navajo Springs, Arizona: Frontier Outlier or Autonomous Great House? *Journal of Field Archaeology* 19(1):51-69.
Welch, Paul D.
1991 *Moundville's Economy.* University of Alabama Press, Tuscaloosa.
Wilcox, David R.
1991 Changing Contexts of Pueblo Adaptations, A.D. 1250-1600. In *Farmerers, Hunters, and Colonists: Interaction Between the Southwest and the Southern Plains,* edited by Katherine A. Spielmann, pp. 128-154. University of Arizona Press, Tucson.
Wissler, Clark
1926 *The Relation of Nature to Man in Aboriginal America.* Oxford University Press, New York.
Wolf, Eric R.
1990 Distinguished Lecture: Facing Power - Old Insights, New Questions. *American Anthropologist* 92(3):586-596.
Worth, John E., and W. Maxwell Duke
1991 Hogcrawl Creek: Early Mississippian Period Occupation in the Middle Flint River Floodplain. *Early Georgia* 19(1):19-42.

Chapter 4

Hyperopia or Hyperbole? The Mississippian World-System

Peter Peregrine
Lawrence University

Archaeology in eastern North America, even in its most radical and "post-processual" forms, has tended to have a myopic focus on sites. My primary argument in this chapter is that it would be beneficial for North American archaeologists to make a break with this myopic focus and develop what I am calling a hyperopic one in which sites blurr into a mass of human interaction and what comes into focus are larger analytical units formed by an interdependence between local populations (see Kowalewski's chapter for a related perspective). In my mind (and as I explained in the introduction to this volume), the world-system perspective is the uniquely well-suited for doing this.

World-Systems Theory and the Problem of Mississippian Origins

Mississippian societies represent the pinnacle of cultural evolution in eastern North America (see Peregrine 1995a for an overview). Beginning about A.D. 900, the Mississippians developed large population centers in the Mississippi River valley and its major tributaries, traded with peoples as distant as the Florida Gulf coast and the Great Plains, and constructed the largest pre-Columbian structures north of Mexico. Mississippian influence spread across eastern North America in the following century, and by A.D. 1100 it was the predominant culture across the Southeast and had fundamentally influenced peoples in the Ohio River region, in the northern Mississippi valley, and west into Iowa, Kansas, and Oklahoma. This influence continued even as some of the earliest Mississippian settlements declined beginning about A.D. 1200. Although altered by time and restricted in their geographical range, Mississippian-like ways of life still existed in parts of the Southeast and the lower Mississippi River valley when Europeans first entered the North American continent.

The evolution of complex societies is one of the most enduring questions in archaeological research, and the question of Mississippian origins is certainly central to research in eastern North America. Humans came to North America from Asia at least 12,000 years ago, and the millennia between their arrival and the origin of Mississippian societies witnessed a series of cultural peaks in eastern North America. The Middle Woodland cultural fluorescence, around A.D. 1 to 300, was in some ways similar to Mississippian. Riverine habitation was common, mound building and long-distance trade of exotic goods were a central part of the culture, maize was in use (although not heavily) by

A.D. 200, and political centralization was greater than earlier periods. However, these Middle Woodland societies changed into less centralized forms, so that the immediate predecessors of the Mississippians were living in comparatively simple societies. Any theory of Mississippian evolution, then, has to explain the relatively rapid evolution of three elements: (1) social stratification; (2) subsistence economies based on maize horticulture; and (3) concentration of population around large riverine centers.

In previous work I have argued that Mississippian societies evolved through the processes of a unique type of world-system which I call a prestige-good system (Peregrine 1991a, 1992a). In prestige-good systems political power is based on the control and manipulation of exotic, imported preciosities. Elites in all social systems display and maintain their status in part through the control of exotic goods and esoteric knowledge (Frankenstein and Rowlands 1978:75; Helms 1979, 1988; Clark 1986), but in prestige-good systems these elite symbols are needed by all members of the society for social reproduction (Ekholm 1972; Friedman and Rowlands 1977; Friedman 1982). Exotic goods in these societies are used to fund social debts, such as bridewealth payments, initiation and funerary fees, and punitive damages, and elites able to control access to these fungible exotic goods gain political power in direct proportion to the demand for them (Frankenstein and Rowlands 1978:76; cf. Kowalewski, this volume).

Prestige-good systems tend to evolve from a corporate lineage structure in situations where lineage elders cannot readily control the means of production (Peregrine 1992a; Friedman and Rowlands 1977). In these situations, elders employ symbols of office and esoteric knowledge about the supernatural to control younger members of the lineage, who must align themselves with an elder in order to socially reproduce (Meillassoux 1978). Elders supply youths with knowledge and ritual insignia so that they can be initiated, get married, take office in the lineage, and the like. It is from the power elders gain through their control of ritual insignia that a prestige-good system first begins.

The theory I developed to explain Mississippian evolution posited that Archaic and Woodland lineage elders, who controlled lineage and other status symbols, fostered the use of these goods in ceremonies of social reproduction. As the goods came to be in greater demand, the lineage elder's power grew in direct proportion, and during the Early Mississippian period they gained enough power to differentiate themselves from other lineage members, becoming an emergent elite.

The mechanisms through which this Mississippian world-system evolved out of Late Woodland societies are not obvious. Prior to the Mississippian emergence burial ceremonialism declined, the territorial, riverine settlement pattern of Middle Woodland societies was replaced by a more dispersed one, and (most importantly from my perspective) the Hopewell Interaction Sphere, through which exotic prestige-goods moved across the midcontinent during the Middle Woodland period, disappeared (although trade in shell and other less exotic prestige-goods continued [Droessler 1981:12]). Despite the arguments of several scholars (particularly Braun 1977; Braun and Plog 1983; Buikstra 1976, and Styles 1981) that there is social continuity between the Middle and Late Woodland periods, the disappearance of elaborate burial ceremonialism, alterations in settlement patterns, and decline of interregional trade in exotic goods are evidence of important social changes taking place.

Joseph Tainter (1975, 1977a, 1977b, 1983) has suggested that these social changes were brought about by the dissolution of the highest level of the Middle Woodland political hierarchy. He argues that Late Woodland societies became organized at a lower hierarchical level, and in so doing, split into smaller social units. These smaller units distributed themselves widely across the landscape, and practiced a different pattern of social interaction than the riverine-based one of Middle Woodland societies.

Changes in household and community patterns during the Woodland-Mississippian transition in the American Bottom tend to support Tainter's view, as they suggest that distinct social and political reorganizations took place between the Middle and the Late Woodland periods (Peregrine 1992b). Late Woodland communities tend to be circular in their layout and houses tend to be small (Peregrine 1992b:135-136). This community pattern appears to be similar to what Flannery (1972:30-31; also Kelly 1990) has defined as a "circular hut compound" and generally relates to an economic system where communities function as autonomous social and economic units, and where political organization is based upon a lineage system.

Late Woodland community patterns are quite different from both Middle Woodland and Mississippian ones. Middle Woodland communities are not well represented, but they appear to be larger than Late Woodland communities and more complex in their layout, containing clusters of large circular houses suggesting they were composed of extended families coordinated into a single economic unit through a political hierarchy (Griffin 1978:244-45). Mississippian communities, in contrast, tended to be linear in their layout, and houses are rectangular (Peregrine 1992b:137-139). Flannery (1972:38-39) argues this type of pattern reflects the presence of economically independent nuclear and extended families. Based on these changes in household and community patterns I have argued that a primary social change taking place in the Woodland-Mississippian transition is the attenuation of the basic social and economic unit, from lineage-focused units in the Late Woodland period to family-focused ones in the Mississippian period (Peregrine 1992b:141-142).

The lineage-focused social organization apparent in Late Woodland settlement patterns may have fostered competition between lineage heads and encouraged further social changes that increased their control over flows of prestige-goods. It is difficult, given the inadequacies of available data, to precisely describe the changes that took place, but I hypothesize that they may have included the development of sumptuary rules restricting consumption of higher-order goods to elders, new mechanisms of labor control for the manufacture and transportation of prestige-goods, and perhaps new forms of political structure or alliance for solidifying the control of trade routes (Peregrine 1991a, 1992a).

These social transformations set the stage for a re-emergence of higher-level political leaders in the Early Mississippian period, and intensification of production necessary to sustain these emergent leaders followed. In prestige-good systems individuals find it necessary to support local (usually lineage) leaders, for they control the goods needed to fulfill social obligations and to maintain an adequate standard of living. The basic idea here is that individuals would have intensified production to support their local leaders in competitive exchanges of prestige-goods so that they would have had better access to these goods, and hence a better opportunity to socially reproduce themselves at acceptable levels (see Renfrew 1982 for an analogous situation).

As leaders competed for goods in the emergent Mississippian prestige-good system, those located at nodal points on trade routes, and who had a supportive population, may have been able to control those routes and the goods flowing through them (Peregrine 1991b). Population would have been attracted to leaders who offered greater access to prestige-goods, and hence better opportunities to socially reproduce (Friedman and Rowlands 1977). In this way social stratification, maize horticulture, and political centers with dense populations could have readily emerged in the central riverine valleys of the midcontinent, where riverine trade could be controlled, and where intensified production was possible.

Evidence to support this theory has been presented in detail elsewhere, and I will only briefly summarize it here (also see Brown, Kerber, and Winters 1990; Peebles 1987; Steponaitis 1991). A study I conducted (Peregrine 1992a) using burial data from the American Bottom and East Tennessee demonstrated that the distribution of prestige-goods, both within and between communities, is consistent with that expected from a prestige-good system. Work in progress (Peregrine, Cunningham, and Stuby n.d.) suggests this is a unique pattern, not found in Late Archaic or Middle Woodland burial populations from the same areas. Further evidence for the existence of a Mississippian prestige-good system comes from a study conducted by Paul Welch (1991), who tested four models of chiefdom political economy against the material record for Moundville and the Black Warrior River region. He found that the model most consistent with the archaeological record is that of a prestige-good system (using Frankenstein and Rowlands (1978), as I do, as the basis for his definition of a prestige-good system).

In recent years I have attempted to present more detailed evidence that Mississippian societies evolved out of and were participants in a prestige-good system. I have demonstrated that Mississippian material culture changed to accomodate the pressures associated with increased demand for prestige-goods (Peregrine 1991c, 1992a), that large Mississippian centers are located where trade in prestige-goods could be readily controlled (Peregrine 1991a, 1992a), and that warfare among Mississippian polities involved only these large centers and was potentially focused on disputes over or conquest of nodal trade locations (Peregrine 1993, 1994a). I have also presented evidence to suggest that Mississippian societies evolved in a way similar to ethnographically-known prestige-good systems (Peregrine 1992a).

Taken together, this evidence seems to reasonably support the idea that Mississippian societies evolved out of and were participants in a world-system based on prestige-goods. Despite this, the idea of a Mississippian world-system has not been widely accepted or even seriously debated. Why? I think the reason stems in part from the general misconceptions about the world-system perspective that I discussed in the volume introduction, but more specifically from the myopic view prevalent in eastern North American archaeology. As evidence of this I would like to explore a single case where the world-system perspective has been applied to another question of central concern in eastern North American archaeology, that of Iroquois origins.

A Case Study: Iroquois "Tribalization" and the Cahokian World-System

One of the more central questions in the archaeology of the northeastern United States is the origin of Iroquoian groups. The historic northern Iroquois existed in an unusual situation: they were settled village horticulturalists with matrilineal descent groups, a ranked form of political organization, and speaking a macro-Siouan language, but they were surrounded by more mobile, patrilineal, and less politically centralized Algonkin speakers. This situation appears to have roots that extend back to at least circa A.D. 1000, when a series of distinct changes in settlement pattern and ceramic technology occurred (Snow 1980:307-319). Once diverse settlement became consolidated in large, upland villages. Houses almost universally transformed to a "longhouse" style containing multiple families, suggesting a transformation towards matrilineal residence (see M. Ember 1973). And ceramic production changed from predominantly coil techniques to predominantly paddle-and-anvil techniques.

In an article that has created considerable criticism (Griffin 1993; Milner 1990; Pauketat 1992; Snow 1995), Dina Dincauze and Robert Hasenstab (1987, 1989) argued that the development of matrilineal descent groups, political centralization, and population nucleation in the Iroquois region of western New York state can be understood as the outcome of interaction with a Cahokia-centered world-system. They argue that the Cahokia polity had a dominating effect on midcontinental North America: "One has to be open to the possibility that the influence of an expanding city-state / religious center / trade nexus could have been felt 950 km to the northeast to begin some productive speculations about processes at the interface between complex societies and village farmers" (Dincause and Hasenstab 1987:3), and that this dominance made Cahokia the core of the Mississippian world-system: "In the language of world-systems theory, Cahokia had many of the attributes of a core" (Dincause and Hasenstab 1987:4).

Cahokia, located in what is today East St. Louis Illinois, was indeed an impressive settlement during the early Mississippian period. The site is thought to cover at least 5 kilometers, it contains over 100 earthen mounds, and almost certainly had a population of more than 10,000. A number of scholars have argued that local resources could not have supported this scale of settlement, and that Cahokians must have acquired hides, meat, timber, and perhaps other resources from external areas (for example, Conrad 1991:131; Tiffany 1991a:190, 1991b). During the Stirling phase (ca. A.D. 1050-1150) Cahokians apparently did migrate from the St. Louis area into central Illinois, southern Wisconsin and Minnesota, and the Kansas City region, among others (for example, Gibbon and Dobbs 1991; O'Brien 1978). This migration, combined with the hypothesized need for additional resources, has suggested to some scholars that Cahokia was, in effect, colonizing the midcontinent, establishing outposts to acquire resources from diverse areas (for example, Conrad 1991).

Dincause and Hasenstab propose that Iroquoia was one of the areas from which Cahokians were acquiring resources. They argue that proto-Iroquois populations provided maize, meat, hides, minerals, and captives (through the Fort Ancient peoples of the Ohio River valley) to Cahokia in return for prestige-goods and calendrical ceremonies and knowledge helpful for raising maize. Their model suggests that the Iroquois region became a classic periphery, a producer of raw materials for the Cahokian core which was rapidly depleting resources within the site's environs (Dincause and Hasenstab formally state that Iroquoia was external to this system and that the Fort Ancient region was the actual periphery; however, I would argue, based on the suggested roles played by these populations, that the Fort Ancient region was in a "middle-man," and hence semiperipheral, role in this system and Iroquoia, as a producer of raw materials and bulk goods, in a peripheral one). It was the pressures of intensification and later of defense within this peripheral position which led proto-Iroquoian groups to develop a more compact and permanent settlements and more centralized political structures.

Dincause and Hasenstab provide a variety of evidence to suggest close contact between peoples living in Iroquoia and Mississippians (although not specifically Cahokians—an important point I shall return to later), including (1) thin-walled pottery, (2) triangular projectile points, (3) wall-trench architecture, and (4) northern flint corn. While there is some debate concerning the Mississippian origin of these traits, it is the proposed connection between Cahokia and proto-Iroquois populations through the Fort Ancient region that has fostered the most criticism.

Critiques of the Dincauze and Hasenstab model have been varied, but James Griffin (1993:11) perhaps summarizes them best when he says "A 'world system' model is no substitute for adequate knowledge of the data," for there do seem to be some substantial data problems. First of all, there is no direct evidence of Cahokian interaction with peoples beyond central Ohio. Second, there is no evidence that Cahokia traded for or was provisioned with maize, meat, or hides, and no clear evidence that they would have needed to be. Third, there are problems in the timing of Cahokian expansion and Iroquoian "tribalization." Cahokia's main period of interaction with others occurs during the Stirling phase (A.D. 1050-1150), while the period of initial "tribalization" seems to begin earlier (perhaps as early as A.D. 900—see Snow 1995), and Dincauze and Hasentab indirectly posit a very late starting date (circa A.D. 1300).

More generally, a fundamental criticism of the Dincause and Hasenstab model is that Cahokia was not as large or politically powerful as has often been suggested. As Griffin (1993:11) put it:

> Most of the modern myths about Cahokia have resulted from a gross overestimate of its population at 30,000 or more, which was

> used to bolster the concept that Cahokia was a "state." To some archaeologists, this, in turn, made Cahokia the primary and most prominent society in Mississippian times, a Rome of the eastern United States, establishing trade controlling centers and dominating much of the east from A.D. 1000-1200, with a ripple effect lasting to the seventeenth century.

Cahokia was certainly a large community, with, as I stated earlier, a population of more than 10,000, but it was likely able to sustain itself within the rich riverine environment of the central Mississippi River valley and likely only held firm political control over an area extending perhaps a few dozen miles in any direction (see Milner 1990 for an excellent discussion).

My problem with this debate, the problem I am trying to highlight here, is that while both sides are attempting to address macro-regional processes, both end up focusing their debate largely on a particular site—Cahokia. Dincause and Hasentab consider socio-political processes taking place at a semi-continental level, but end up discussing interactions stemming only from this one site. Griffin, on the other hand, critiques the idea that macro-regional processes would have influenced cultural evolution in Iroquoia, but supports his critique by examining solely evidence of Cahokian expansion and interaction. It would seem that the site as the basic unit of analysis is so deeply rooted in our minds that even when we attempt to discuss macro-regional processes we end up focusing on sites. What would happen to this particular debate, which is basically over the extent to which Mississippian populations effected non-Mississippians, if we used a region or macro-region as a unit of analysis? In other words, what do we see if we take a hyperopic view?

The Hyperopic View

The hyperopic view is one where we do not concentrate on sites, but rather on interacting and interdependent regions. In this view, Iroquoia may be a periphery of the Mississippian world-system, but is not in any way a periphery of Cahokia or of a Cahokia-centered world-system. It may also be an external area to the Mississippian world-system, but that is an empirical question that cannot be readily answered on the basis of negative evidence (i.e. the lack of Cahokian pottery as in Griffin's agrument against the Dincause and Hasenstab model). We do have some cultural features that suggest the possibility of direct interaction between Mississippian and proto-Iroquois populations (for example, Kapches (1980) suggests that Mississippian influence is evident in wall-trench house construction techniques on some Iroquoian sites), and if Iroquoia was a periphery of the Mississippian world-system, proto-Iroquoian populations may well have been put under pressures to transform. For example, a study of peripheral societies in the contemporary world I recently completed suggests that the evolution of matrilineality is a common transformation in societies encountering world-systems for the first time (Peregrine 1994b).

In a world-wide sample of 87 societies I found that there is a significant tendency for societies initiating contact with the capitalist world-system within the last 100 years to have matrilineal forms of residence and descent (Peregrine 1994b). Why? I posited that lineal descent groups tend to develop on the peripheries of world-systems to provide a larger pool of labor in a new competitive economic situation (Ember, Ember and Pasternak 1974). Matrilineal residence and descent have already been demonstrated to be correlated with situations where males are absent for long periods of time on raids (C. Ember 1974). I posited that new opportunities or trading, laboring, or warring with other populations in the capitalist world-system might similarly foster a desire for larger labor pools and absense of males, and hence might foster matrilineality. In addition, matrilineal residence is also correlated with situations of rapid cultural change, apparently because matrilineal residence tends to create a more stable home base than bilateral or patrilineal forms (Helms 1970).

Given the tendency for matrilineality to be correlated with a peripheral position in the capitalist world-system, it seems reasonable to suggest that matrilineal residence and descent might have evolved among groups on the periphery of the Mississippian world-system for similar reasons, groups like those living in Iroquoia (also see Trigger 1978). This would certainly not be due to direct interaction with Cahokia or any other particular Mississippian polity, but rather would be an outcome of the processes of differentiation and competition within the world-system itself.

One tantalizing piece of evidence to support this idea is found in the historic distribution of societies with matrilineal residence and descent in North America. Figure 4.1 shows the distribution of matrilineal residence among North American societies in the Standard Cross-Cultural Sample (Murdock and White 1969). The circles show the general location of societies with matrilineal residence. There is a clear pattern in the eastern and midcontinental regions of North America, with a zone devoid of matrilineal residence in the general area of the central Mississippi River basin surrounded by a zone predominating in matrilineal residence.

A similar pattern is evident in Figure 4.2, which presents the distribution of matrilineal descent among societies in the Standard Cross-Cultural Sample. The Again, the circles show the general location of societies

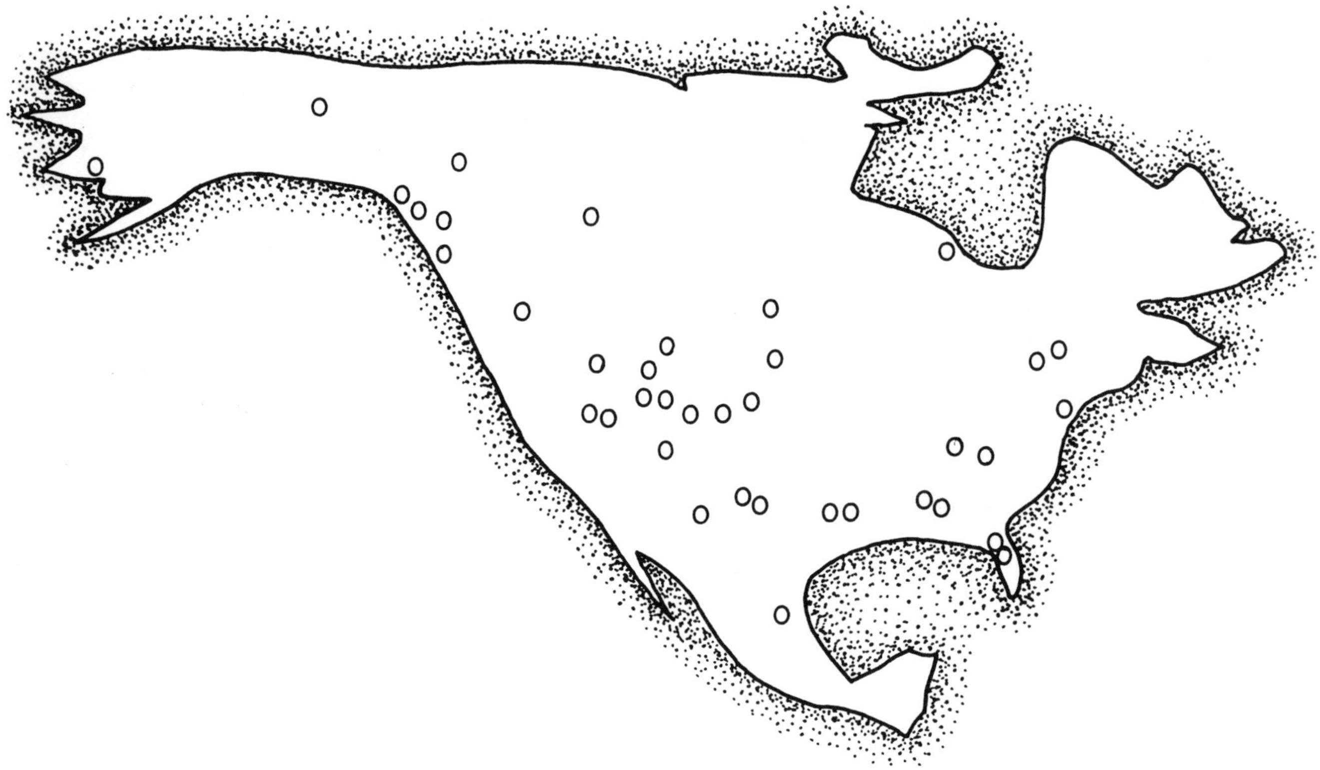

Figure 4.1 Distribution of matrilocal societies in North America.

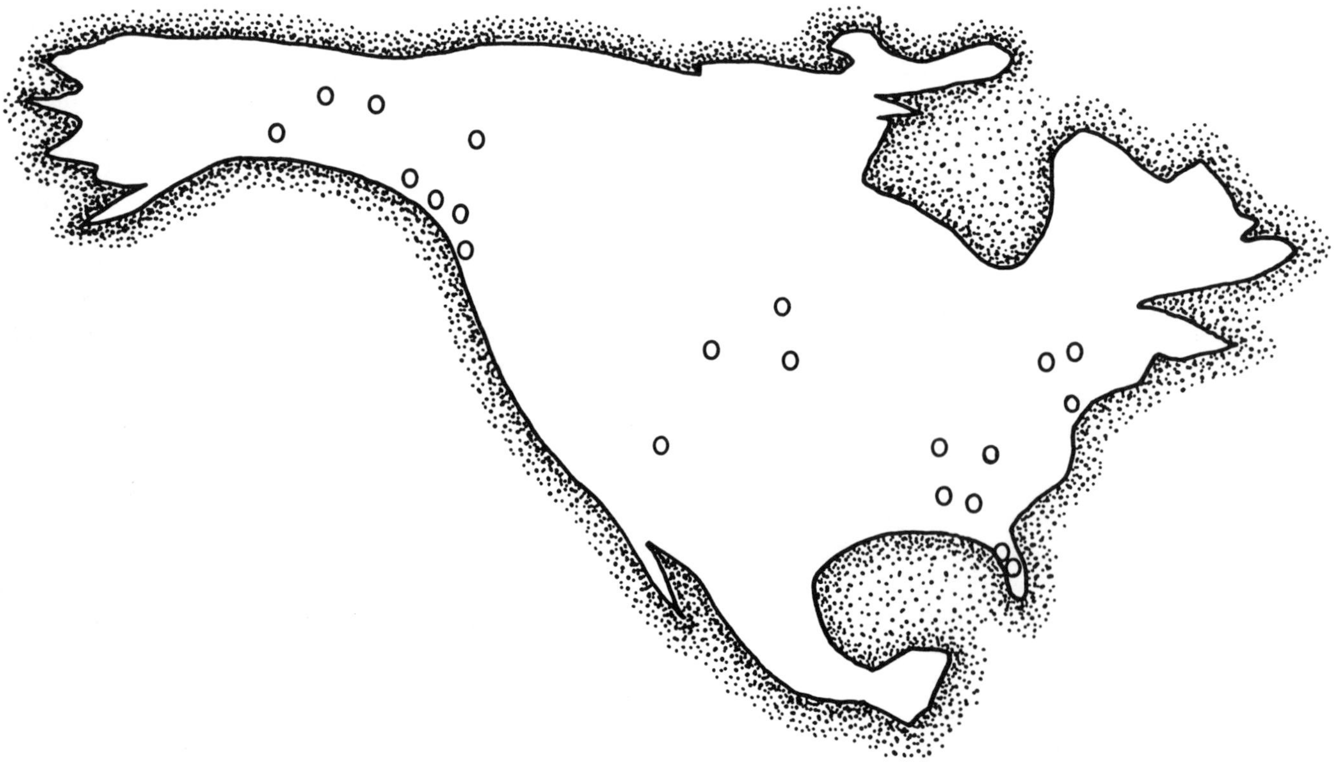

Figure 4.2 Distribution of matrilineal societies in North America.

with matrilineal descent. In both figures, the area lacking matrilineality corresponds generally to the core area of the Mississippian world-system I defined through graph theory (Peregrine 1991c, 1992a) and Thiessen polygons (Peregine 1995b), and, therefore, the area where matrilineality predominates corresponds to what would have been the peripheral area of the Mississippian world-system.

The implication of the historic distribution of matrilineality is that matrilineality tends to be correlated with what would have been peripheral regions in the Mississippian world-system. Correlation does not, of course, necessarily imply a causal relationship, but it is interesting that where we would expect a similar effect to that proposed for Iroquoia, on the western periphery of the Mississippian world-system, we indeed find similar transformations occurring among Middle Missouri tradition groups, and at about the same time as they were occurring among proto-Iroquoian groups (Lehmer 1971). Although we cannot assume that ethnographic data directly corresponds to prehistoric cultural developments—there was far too much cultural disruption in eastern North America for that—I would argue that the historic distribution of matrilineality and the fact that matrilineal groups do appear to evolve prehistorically on both the proposed eastern and western peripheries of the Mississippian world-system does lend some credence to the hyperopic view of Iroquois "tribalization".

I admit that the above discussion is speculative. There are significant problems with the analysis presented, not the least of which is the availability of data to answer the questions that arise from it. When did Iroquoian tribalization begin? What evidence is there of Mississippian contact at this time? What level of contact or interaction is necessary to foster matrilineality? Were Algonkin groups in the Northeast also interacting with Mississippians and if so, why didn't they develop matrilineality?

There is also the problem of the renewed perspective (which had once been the predominant one in Northeastern archaeology but which fell into disfavor two decades ago) that the evolution of Iroquoian lifeways was not an *in situ* event but was caused by the migration of proto-Iroquoian peoples from the south (Snow 1995), making this debate superfluous. I would suggest, however, that the hyperopic view might also benefit this perspective (which is, itself, hyperopic in many ways—see Schortman and Urban 1992 for an excellent discussion). Why would proto-Iroquoian groups move northward? The answer most frequently given is to find suitable agricultural lands, a quest fostered by a new, warmer climatic regime. While this may indeed be an important part of the answer, I posit that more direct access to the midcontinent and the Mississippian groups there via the St. Lawrence and Great Lakes might have been an equally compelling reason for migration.

Finally, the hyperopic perspective creates a very real problem of agency. Cultural change is envisioned as stemming from the processes of the system itself, and not from the actions of individual humans. In a sense, humans are at the mercy of the world-system; its processes determine their society, their world. This is a difficult vision for many social scientists to accept (see Bell 1992:33-38 and Dowling 1984:61-75 for overviews).

Hyperopia or Hyperbole?

The ideas I have just presented must certainly seem hyperbole from a site-focused perspective, but is the hyperopic view reasonable or is it fantastic? The hyperopic view seems fantastic because we cannot deal with such a large system in readily quantifiable terms, so we can't demonstrate statistically (or even scientifically, depending on your definition) if what we are describing is real or make-believe. But is that in itself a reason not to explore prehistory through it, at least some of the time? I think many North American archaeologists would say yes, but in his introduction to *The Modern World-System I* Wallerstein (1974:8) makes a persuasive counter-argument:

> It is a major tragedy of twentieth-century social science that so large a proportion of social scientitsts, facing this dilemma, have thrown in the sponge. [Data at this scale] seemed to them vague and crude, hence unreliable. They felt there was little to be done about it, and that hence it was best to avoid using it. And the best way not to use it was to formulate problems in such a way that its use was not indicated.
>
> Thus the quantifiability of data determined the choice of research problems which then determined the conceptual apparatuses with which one defined and handled empirical data. It should be clear on a moment's reflection that this is an inversion the the scientific process. Conceptualization should determine research tools, at least most of the time, not vice versa.

I argue, with Wallerstein, that it is not valid to dismiss the hyperopic view simply because data limit the precision of the analysis, particularly as the hyperopic view seems reasonable for a number of reasons. First, a hyperopic view, particularly in the form of world-systems theory, has led to profound insights and important debates in other branches of social science, largely because it has made the unit of analysis a primary issue (Shannon 1989:171; also see McGuire, this volume). Second, in archaeology the macro-regional perspective has done the same in the few instances where it has actually been applied, for example, in the Valley of Oaxaca Settlement Pattern Project which Colin Renfrew and Paul Bahn (1991:454) have called "among the most successful in the entire history of archaeology" (see Kowalewski and Fish 1990 for more examples).

In the end, the answer seems really to get down to the view of history one holds—are we seeking the ideal of the past "the way it truly was," progressing towards that true past in incremental steps which, if violated by questioning basic assumptions, seems unreachable; or are we seeking to understand the past for ourselves, and thereby seeking knowledge in any form, discovering it any way that seems to help? If we seek understanding, the hyperopic view and the world-system perspective seem to provide a unique viewpoint offering a unique insights into the past.

Acknowledgements

My thoughts about the "hyperopic" view of eastern North American prehistory and of Mississippian influence on Iroquoian "tribalization" have benefitted from a large number of people. I must specifically thank Gary Feinman, George Milner, and Dean Snow for their detailed and thoughtful comments and criticisms on earlier drafts of this work. Their suggestions were not always heeded, but their efforts are deeply appreciated.

References Cited

Bell, James
1992 Capturing Agency in Theories about Prehistory. In *Representations in Archaeology*, edited by J. Gardin and C. Peebles, pp. 30-55. Indiana University Press, Bloomington.

Braun, David
1977 *Middle Woodland-(Early) Late Woodland Social Change in the Prehistoric Central Midwestern United States.* Ph.D. dissertation, University of Michigan, Ann Arbor.

Braun, David and Stephen Plog
1982 Evolution of "Tribal" Social Networks: Theory and Prehistoric North American Evidence. *American Antiquity* 47:504-25

Brown, James, Richard Kerber and Howard Winters
1990 Trade and the Evolution of Exchange Relations at the Beginning of the Mississippian Period. In *The Mississippian Emergence*, edited by Bruce Smith, pp. 251-280. Smithsonian Institution, Washington, D.C.

Buikstra, Jane
1976 *Hopewell in the Lower Illinois River Valley*. Northwestern Archaeological Program, Scientific Papers, Number 2, Evanston.

Clark, Graham
1986 *Symbols of Excellence: Precious Metals as Expression of Status.* Cambridge University Press, London.

Conrad, Lawrence
1991 The Middle Mississippi Cultures of the Central Illinois River Valley. In *Cahokia and the Hinterlands*, edited by T.E. Emerson and K.G. Farnsworth, pp. 119-156. University of Illinois Press, Urbana.

Dincauze, Dena F., and Robert J. Hasenstab
1987 Explaining the Iroquois: Tribalization on a Prehistoric Periphery. In *Comparative Studies in the Development of Complex Societies, Part 4, Centre-Periphery Relations*, edited by Timothy C. Champion, pp. 1-17. Deparment of Archaeology, University of Southampton, Southampton, UK.
1989 Explaining the Iroquois: Tribalization on a Prehistoric Periphery. In *Centre and Periphery: Comparative Studies in Archaeology*, edited by Timothy C. Champion, pp. 67-87. Unwin Hyman, London.

Dowling, William C.
1984 *Jameson, Althusser, Marx.* Cornell University Press, Ithaca.

Droessler, Judith
1981 *Craniometry and Biological Distance.* Center For American Archaeology, Evanston.

Ekholm, Kajsa
1972 *Power and Prestige: The Rise and Fall of the Kongo Kingdom.* Scriv Service, Uppsala, Sweden.
Ember, Carol R.
1974 An Evaluation of Alternative Theories of Matrilocal Versus Patrilocal Residence. *Behavior Science Research* 9:135-149.
Ember, Carol R., Melvin Ember and Burton Pasternak
1974 On the Development of Unilineal Descent. *Journal of Anthropological Research* 30:69-94.
Ember, Melvin
1973 An Archaeological Indicator of Matrilocal Versus Patrilocal Residence. *American Antiquity* 38: 177-182.
Flannery, Kent V.
1972 The Origins of the Village as a Settlement Type in Mesoamerica and the Near East: A Comparative Study. In *Man, Settlement and Urbansim,* edited by P. Ucko, R. Tringham, and G. Dimbleby, pp. 23-53. Duckworth, London.
Frankenstein, Susan and Michael Rowlands
1978 The Internal Structure and Regional Context of Early Iron Age Society in South-Western Germany. *Bulletin of the Institute of Archaeology of London* 15:73-112.
Friedman, Johnathan
1982 Catastrophe and Continuity in Social Evolution. In *Theory and Explanation in Archaeology,* edited by C. Renfrew, M. Rowlands and B. Segraves, pp. 175-96. Academic Press, New York.
Friedman, Johnathan and Michael Rowlands
1977 Notes Towards an Epigenetic Model of the Evolution of "Civilisation." In *The Evolution of Social Systems,* edited by Johnathan Friedman and Michael Rowlands, pp. 201-75. Duckworth, London.
Gibbon, Guy and Clark Dobbs
1991 The Mississippian Presence in the Red Wing Area, Minnesota. In *New Perspectives on Cahokia,* edited by J. Stoltman, pp. 281-306. Prehistory Press, Madison.
Griffin, James B.
1978 The Midlands and Northeastern United States. In *Ancient Native Americans,* editied by Jesse Jennings, pp. 221-280. W.H. Freeman, San Francisco.
1993 Cahokia Interaction with Contemporary Southeastern and Eastern Societies. *Midcontinental Journal of Archaeology* 18:3-17.
Helms, Mary
1970 Matrilocality, Social Solidarity, and Culture Contact: Three Case Histories. *Southwestern Journal of Anthropology* 26:197-212.
1979 *Ancient Panama: Chiefs in Search of Power.* University of Texas Press, Austin.
1988 *Ulysses' Sail.* Cambridge University Press, New York.
Kapches, Mima
1980 Wall Trenches on Iroquoian Sites. *Archaeology of Eastern North America* 8:98-105.
Kelly, John
1980 *Formative Developments at Cahokia and the Adjacent American Bottom: A Merrell Tract Perspective.* Ph.D. dissertation, University of Wisconsin. Madision.
Kowalewski, Stephen and Suzanne Fish
1990 *The Archaeology of Regions.* Smithsonian, Washington, D.C.
Lehmer, Donald J.
1971 *Introduction to Middle Missouri Archaeology.* National Park Service, Washington, D.C.
Meillassoux, Claude
1978 "The Economy" in Agricultural Self-Sustaining Societies: A Preliminary Analysis. In *Relations of Production,* editied by D. Seddon, pp. 127-157. Frank Cass, London.
Milner, George R.
1990 The Late Prehistoric Cahokia Cultural System of the Mississippi River Valley: Foundations, Florescence, and Fragmenation. *Journal of World Prehistory* 4:1-43.

Murdock, George P. and Douglas White
1969 The Standard Cross-Cultural Sample. *Ethnology* 8:329-369.
O'Brien, Patricia
1978 Steed-Kisker: A Western Mississippian Settlement System. In *Mississippian Settlement Patterns*, edited by B. Smith, pp. 1-20. Academic Press, New York.
Pauketat, Timothy
1992 The Reign and Ruin of the Lords of Cahokia: A Dialectic of Dominance. In *Lords of the Southeast*, edited by A.W. Barker and T.R. Pauketat, pp. 31-52. Archaeological Papers of the American Anthropological Association, Number 3, Washington, D.C.
Peebles, Christopher S.
1987 The Rise and Fall of the Mississippian in Western Alabama: The Moundville and Summerville Phases, A.D. 1000 to 1600. *Mississippi Archaeology* 22:1-31.
Peregrine, Peter
1991a Prehistoric Chiefdoms on the American Midcontinent: A World-System Based on Prestige-Goods. In *Core/Periphery Relations in Precapitalist Worlds*, edited by C. Chase-Dunn and T. Hall, pp. 193-211. Westview Press, Boulder, CO.
1991b A Graph-Theoretic Approach to the Evolution of Cahokia. *American Antiquity* 56(1):66-75.
1991c Some Political Aspects of Craft Specialization. *World Archaeology* 23(1):1-11.
1992a *Mississippian Evolution: A World-System Perspective.* Prehistory Press, Madision, Wisconsin.
1992b Social Change During the Woodland-Mississippian Transition: A Study of Household and Community Patterns in the American Bottom. *North American Archaeologist* 13(2):131-47.
1993 An Archaeological Correlate of War. *North American Archaeologist* 14:139-151.
1994a Raoul Naroll's Contribution to Archaeology. *Cross-Cultural Research* 28:351-363.
1994b Trade and Matrilineality: A Hypothesis Based on World-Systems Theory. *Cross-Cultural Research* 28:99-110.
1995a *Archaeology of the Mississippian Culture.* Garland Research Guides to Ancient Civilizations, Volume 6. Garland Publishing, New York.
1995b Networks of Power: The Mississippian World-System. In *Native American Interactions*, edited by M. Nassaney and K. Sassaman, pp.247-265. University of Tennessee Press, Knoxville.
Peregrine, Peter, Peter Cunningham, and James Stuby
n.d. *An Analysis of Late Archaic and Middle Woodland Burial Objects in Midcontinental North America.* Manuscript on file, Anthropology Laboratory, Lawrence University.
Renfrew, Colin
1982 Polity and Power: Interaction, Intensification and Exploitation. In *An Island Polity: The Archaeology of Exploitation in Melos*, edited by C. Renfrew and M. Wagstaff, pp. 264-290. Cambridge University Press, New York.
Renfrew, Colin and Paul Bahn
1991 *Archaeology: Theory and Method*. Thames and Hudson, London, UK.
Schortman, Edward and Patricia Urban
1992 The Place of Interaction Studies in Archaeological Thought. In*: Resources, Power, and Interregional Interaction*, edited by E. Schortman and P. Urban, pp. 3-15. Plenum, New York.
Shannon, Thomas R.
1989 *An Introduction to the World-System Perspective.* Westview Press, Boulder.
Snow, Dean
1980 *The Archaeology of New England*. Academic Press, New York.n
1995 Migration in Prehistory: The Northern Iroquoian Case. *American Antiquity* 60:59-79.

Steponaitis, Vincas P.
1986 Prehistoric Archaeology in the Southeastern United States, 1970-1985. *Annual Review of Anthropology* 15:363-404.
1991 Contrasting Patterns of Mississippian Development. In *Chiefdoms: Power, Economy, and Ideology*, edited by T. Earle, pp. 193-228. Cambridge University Press, Cambridge.
Styles, Bonnie
1981 *Faunal Exploitation and Resource Selection.* Northwestern University Archaeological Program, Evanston.
Tainter, Joseph
1975 *The Archaeological Study of Social Change: Woodland Systems in West-Central Illinois.* Ph.D. dissertation, Department of Anthropology, Northwestern University. University Microfilms, Ann Arbor.
1977a Woodland Social Change in West-Central Illinois. *Midcontinental Journal of Archaeology* 2:67-98.
1977b Modeling Change in Prehistoric Social Systems. In *For Theory Building in Archaeology*, edited by Lewis Binford, pp. 327-51. Academic Press, New York.
1983 Woodland Social Change in the Central Midwest: A Review and Evaluation of Interpretive Trends. *North American Archaeologist* 4:141-61.
Tiffany, Joseph
1991a Models of Mississippian Culture History in the Western Prairie Peninsula: A Perspective from Iowa. In *Cahokia and the Hinterlands*, edited by T.E. Emerson and R.B. Lewis, pp. 183-192. University of Illinois Press, Urbana.
1991b Modeling Mill Creek-Mississippian Interaction. In *New Perspectives on Cahokia*, edited by J. Stoltman, pp. 319-347. Prehistory Press, Madison.
Trigger, Bruce G.
1978 Iroquoian Matriliny. *The Pennsylvania Archaeologist* 48:55-65.
Wallerstein, Immanuel
1974 *The Modern World-System I.* Academic Press, New York.
Welch, Paul
1991 *Moundville's Economy.* University of Alabama Press, Tuscaloosa.

Chapter 5

The Limits of World-Systems Theory for the Study of Prehistory

Randall H. McGuire
SUNY - Binghamton

In the 1980s many archaeologists grew weary of a cultural ecology that directed analysis to local, environmentally circumscribed regions. Cultural ecology had (and continues to be) a very productive source of information about prehistoric diet and adaptation, but after 20 years of such research some scholars argued that we needed to take a broader view to understand prehistory. Instead of limited studies of individual river valleys many archaeologists adopted some type of world-systems approach for their research on prehistory. Whether they embraced a specific world-systems theory, such as Immanuel Wallerstein's, or merely espoused a more generalized world-systems perspective these archaeologists were drawn to a vision of a prehistory driven by economic interconnections (Blanton et al. 1981; Baugh 1982, 1984; Plog et al. 1982; Plog 1983; Upham 1982; Di Peso 1983; Blanton and Feinman 1984; Whitecotten and Pailes 1986; Kohl 1987).

An expansive view of an interconnected prehistory is valuable for archaeology, and indeed predates the use of world-systems theory in archaeology. However, prehistoric developments often do not fit the expectations of a world-systems theory or the assumptions of a world systems perspective. This is clearly the case in the prehistory of the Hohokam of southern Arizona. In this case the region was never as economically or politically integrated as the world-systems model would assume. A world-systems approach with its emphasis on functionally integrated interregional systems fails to capture the dynamic and often contradictory interplay of social relations at various scales that shaped this prehistory. The antithetical peer polity perspective, that retreats to the myopia of processes in a single region, also fails to capture this dynamic and contradictory interplay. In place of these oppositional positions archaeologists should ask about processes of uneven development in social relations at various scales in specific historical sequences to arrive at understandings of how long range interactions and local developments interrelated in prehistory.

World-Systems: Theories and Perspectives

The core notions of the world-systems approach, including the broad inter-regional perspective and the notion of uneven development in prehistory, were not new to archaeology. Archaeologists have long talked about key and dependent areas (Palerm and Wolf 1957), cores and buffers (Rathje 1971), and heartlands and hinterlands (R.M. Adams 1965). Even in cultural ecology some archaeologists advanced models of regions linked through relations of symbiosis (Sanders and Price 1968). A world-systems approach differed from these earlier notions because it directed archaeologists to ponder how the growth of cores stems from the creation of peripheries and nudged the focus of analysis from diffusion and adaptation to exploitation and dependency.

World-systems theory originated in the work of Immanuel Wallerstein (1974, 1978, 1980, 1989), but has grown considerably beyond his formulations. At the most general level Wallerstein's ideas incorporate a world-systems perspective that can be found in the work of many other researchers including some who preceded him. In the 1990s some archaeologists have moved away from Wallerstein's model to consider other world-systems theories, especially that of Hall and Chase-Dunn (this volume). Other archaeologists have reacted to the popularity of a world-systems approach by advocating a peer polity interaction as an alternative to world-systems models.

Wallerstein's Theory of World-Systems

In the first volume of his monumental work *The Modern World System I*, Immanuel Wallerstein (1974:3) identifies two great watersheds in the history of the world, the neolithic revolution and the creation of the modern world. The goal of Wallerstein's theory of world-systems is to account for the rise of capitalism and the modern world that it created. This is a European tale. He gives some consideration to the world empire of Rome that preceded the creation of Europe, and to the great world empires Europe encountered such as the Ottoman and the Chinese. In Wallerstein's story, Europe gobbles up the non-capitalist economies that occupied most of the globe and transforms them into functionally related components of the modern world-system. Their prior form is less important to Wallerstein than the role they come to play in the European-centered world-system. Wallerstein's (1974, 1980, 1989) great work is thus both historical and Euro-focused (Wolf 1982).

Wallerstein (1978) has made some generalizations about world systems other than the modern. These generalizations derive from Polanyi's (1957) substantive economics. Wallerstein (1978) identifies four possible modes of production in world history: reciprocal mini-systems, redistributive empires, a capitalist world economy, and a hoped for socialist world government. In reciprocal mini-systems all able-bodied individuals engage in production, and processes of reciprocal exchange create inequalities favoring senior males. World empires contain a stratum of non-producers who pre-empt the surplus of others through a tribute network controlled by a centralized political system. Wallerstein sees world empires as stable long lived entities lasting hundreds of years. World economies derive from a functional and geographic division of labor but differ from world empires in their lack of an over-arching centralized government. According to Wallerstein, before the advent of the modern world-system, world economies had always been fragile and short lived. Either they developed into world empires or they were enveloped by a world empire. What makes the modern capitalist world economy unique is that it has lasted for 500 years.

In this formulation Wallerstein overgeneralizes from the European experience. Archaeologists, historians, and anthropologists have found that the variation in non-capitalist economic systems is far greater than Wallerstein allows and that many of his generalizations about types of world-systems are incorrect.

Philip Kohl (1989) evaluated the applicability of Wallerstein's theory for the Bronze Age of west Asia and found many problems with applying it to this case. He found much evidence for world economies and little evidence that there was an innate tendency for them to collapse quickly or change into world empires. He suggests that the stability that Wallerstein sees in world empires is a consequence of him generalizing from a limited number of cases, the Roman, Ottoman, Persian, and Chinese, and not an inherent characteristic of such societal types. Finally, Kohl concludes that in Bronze Age West Asia peripheries had considerable power visa vis cores because the technological gap between cores and peripheries was minimal or non-existent, and because peripheries could shift relations between multiple, competing, cores.

A more important problem with Wallerstein's theory for prehistory is its premise that core-periphery relations will be based on economics and that all groups and relations in a world economy can be ranked. These are questionable assumptions. A great number of contrasts can be made between social groups based on linguistics, culture, adaptation, religion, etc. and these distinctions may be ranked or not (Marquardt and Crumley 1987:11). Furthermore, in prehistoric societies the notion of a distinct economic sphere has little meaning, and long range interaction networks may depend as much on social, political, or religious relations as economics (Renfrew 1986; Kohl 1989; C.E. Adams 1991; Hosler 1994).

A World-Systems Perspective

Numerous archaeologists have rejected a direct application of Wallerstein's theory of world-systems to prehistory because it does not fit the kinds of economies that they study. But, these same individuals argue that a world-systems perspective remains useful for archaeology (Kohl 1987; Shortman and Urban 1987; Peregrine's introduction to this volume). There can then exist many theories within a world-systems perspective.

In the introduction to this volume, Peregrine defines a world-systems perspective as a way of viewing the world that "allows one to perceive the world as a set of autonomous political units linked into a larger functioning unit through economic interdependence." This larger unit is the "world" and it is seen as a dynamic entity constantly remaking itself. Furthermore, this world will always be made up of two geographical units, a core and a periphery, and these units will be in competition with each other.

Peregrine argues that such a perspective is valuable in the study of prehistory for three reasons: (1) it is inherently spatial with a focus on geographically defined units (cores and peripheries) and the spatial relationships between them; (2) it is multi-leveled with layers within layers; and, (3) it is evolutionary, proposing a topology of societal forms that a given culture will move through under specified conditions.

Thus, a world-systems perspective is a highly generalized construct that can be applied to a great variety of cases. At its most basic level it assumes that social entities are systems. Such systems are made up of interconnected parts that form a whole so that change in one part, or subsystem, will alter the other parts or subsystems. The perspective seems to presume that such systems exist to do something, e.g. exploit a periphery, advance an elite, etc. and they are therefore functionally integrated.

This systems logic has several implications for how scholars study, interpret, and account for cultural change. One rarely stated implication of this logic is that units in comparable position within the system, e.g. peripheral areas, will become more similar over time as they respond and restructure themselves in response to the demands made upon them by the system (Wallerstein personnel communication). This process suggests that such systems should become more stable over time as their components remake themselves to fit their roles in the system. The world-systems perspective however, suggests that such stability will never occur because as Wallerstein (1974:347) said the life of the system "is made up of the conflicting forces which hold it together by tension, and tear it apart as each group seeks eternally to remold it to its advantage". Finally, the perspective is atomistic, because it accepts that social systems are themselves bounded and made up of bounded units. As Chase-Dunn and Hall (1991:858) argue: "Setting bounds for empirically existing intersocietal interactions is the methodological core of world-systems analysis."

World-Systems Theories

Sociologists, anthropologists, historians, and archaeologists using a world-systems perspective have advanced numerous world-systems Theories to account for the human history before the modern era (for example, Ekholm and Friedman 1982, 1985; Abu-Lughod 1990; Frank 1990; Frank and Gills 1990; Chase-Dunn and Hall 1991, 1993; Santley and Alexander 1992). Some of these theories argue that a single mode of production has characterized world history for the last 5,000 years or more, and reject the idea of qualitative changes in this period (Ekholm and Friedman 1982, 1985; Frank 1990; Frank and Gills 1990; Santley and Alexander 1992). Others, argue that transitions have occurred over this period with qualitatively different modes of production coming into existence while older forms disappeared (Chase-Dunn 1989; Chase-Dunn and Hall 1991, 1993).

Of these theorists, the substantivist world-systems formulations of Thomas Hall and Christopher Chase-Dunn have attracted the most attention among U.S. archaeologists (this volume, also Chase-Dunn 1989; Chase-Dunn and Hall 1991; Hall 1989). Both these sociologists begin with Wallerstein's theory but substantially improve on it as a general theory of human history. They both have read extensively in the archaeological and anthropological literature, and their understanding of non-capitalist economics is considerably richer than Wallerstein's superficial reading of Polanyi.

Hall and Chase-Dunn (this volume) define a world system as an intersocietal network in which interaction is an important condition for the reproduction of the internal structures of the composite units and significantly affects the changes that occur in these local structures. They do not assume that all intersocietal systems will have core/periphery hierarchies. They argue instead that we have to prove the existence of exploitation, domination and unequal exchange.

They retain from Wallerstein, however, the key notion of these intersocietal networks as systems. If these networks are systems then they must consist of regular interacting or interdependent societies that form a unified whole. The functioning of the system is not reducible to any of the individual societies that make it up, but the system can be broken down into unique entities and subsystems. Given this perspective Hall and Chase-Dunn focus on three issues as key to understanding world systems: (1) how do we define the boundaries of the system; (2) how do we define the subunits that make up the system; and (3) how do we typologize world-systems. This systems logic works best when economics are being discussed.

The systems logic of the world-systems perspective asserts itself in all of the alternative world-systems theories that have been offered. In fact few if any of the alternative theories capture the ambiguity and tension between stability and change that Wallerstein so carefully tries to build into his ideas. They are generally even more systemic than the work that inspired them. Hall and Chase-Dunn's three issues clearly reflect the atomistic bases of the systems logic. All three are concerned with defining the boundedness of units, subsystems, and the overall system.

Systems logic also structures the two revisionist foci in alternative world-systems theory that Peregrine identifies in the introduction to this volume. The first of these foci concerns how we define the nature of geographic differentiation within world-systems. This is in part the topological question of how to define core, periphery, and semi-periphery, as well as arguments as to their universality. The second foci concerns how important were different aspects or sub-systems to characterizing world-systems and to the dynamics of such systems. Here scholars debate if world-systems must be based on subsistence goods or if they can arise from prestige goods exchange. Embedded in this debate is the more fundamental issue of whether relations of production should be given priority over relations of reproduction.

Archaeologists have, and can use either strong or weak readings of a world-systems approach. In a strong reading the archaeologist advocates a particular world-systems theory to interpret prehistory. In a weak reading the archaeologist invokes a world-systems perspective, or, even more weakly, that long range interactions are important to understanding local developments.

World-systems theories are, at their core, economic models that emphasize how economic interactions lead to relations of dependency and exploitation between bounded units that are themselves altered by these relations. Despite assertions of researchers such as Hall and Chase-Dunn (this volume) that world-systems may be based on other than economic relations few if any scholars have attempted to theorize on the form or dynamics of such systems. Equally under-theorized is Hall and Chase-Dunn's assertion that world-systems can exist in the absence of hierarchical social relations.

The contention that world-systems may-be based on a variety of relations (economics, intermarriage, religion etc), and that hierarchical social relations may or may not be present, could lead to a very weak reading of the world-systems perspective. Such a perspective comes down to one idea: that social units must be studied as parts of interconnected systems and not in isolation. On the face of it this would appear to be a truism, except for the fact that a large body of archaeological theory rejects, or downplays this idea.

Cultural Ecology and Peer Polity Interactions

The cultural ecology of the 1960s and 1970s stressed the study of adaptation within environmentally defined areas, such as valleys, basins, and plateaus that were thought to define natural and cultural ecosystems (Sanders and Price 1968; cf. Kowalewski, this volume). Cultural ecologists sought to explain cultural change in terms of adaptation to this ecosystem. Exchange from outside the ecosystem might establish symbiotic relations between regions but the major emphasis remained on the adaptation to a localized area. This research program was very successful in reconstructing aspects of prehistoric diet and adaptation. We learned much about these things from it and many aspects of an ecological archaeology remain basic to archaeological research. Increasingly in the 1990s, however, archaeologists have moved towards more social and political considerations of the past.

A number of archaeologists working in Europe have proposed the notion of peer polity interaction as an alternative to a world-systems approach (Renfrew 1986). This alternative has been applied to regions outside of Europe including the Southwest (Minnis 1989). The model of peer polity interaction puts the emphasis on an intermediate scale of analysis between the local and the inter-regional. The stress is on interactions within a region and it is assumed that the interactions within the region are of more importance to cultural change than external links to other region.

> Peer polity interaction designates the full range of interchanges taking place (including imitation and emulation, competition, warfare, and the exchange of material goods and information) between autonomous (i.e. self governing and in that sense politically independent) sociopolitical units which are situated beside or close to each other within a single geographical region, or in some cases more widely (Renfrew 1986:1).

Renfrew (1986:7-8) proposes four hypotheses that archaeologists can use to test for peer polity interaction: (1) if one polity exists, then other polities of comparable size and complexity will also exist in the same region; (2) social transformations will occur in multiple polities at the same time; (3) features shared by the polities will not have a single origin or locus of invention; and (4) a range of different types of interactions including warfare, emulation, and the flow of objects will bring about changes.

Despite the clear and fundamental disagreement on the proper scale and unit of analysis, peer polity interaction and world-systems approaches share a number of fundamental assumptions. Both programs begin with the notion of bounded social units that are systemic in character. They differ on how broadly they define the system to be studied and in the degree of boundedness between units. Both of these approaches are fundamentally evolutionary. Peer polity interaction does not really address or reject the use of a world-systems approach for the modern world. It instead argues that the world-systems approach does not apply to pre-state systems, where peer polity interaction is the more appropriate model.

The world-systems perspective and peer polity interaction are not so much opposing social theories as they arguments for the importance of analysis at different scales. Thus, there are dangers in framing an either/or choice between a peer polity and world-systems model. Renfrew's (1986) idea of peer polity interaction is an argument against *a priori* assumptions of economically and politically defined cores and peripheries. It is, however, every bit as problematic to assume that the polities we are dealing with in a given case are peers, as it is to *a priori* assume cores and peripheries. Our analyses need to look for both possibilities in the study of real historical sequences such as the Hohokam of southern Arizona.

The Hohokam

Archaeologists usually divide the Formative Southwest into four major cultural units; the Anasazi, the Mogollon, the Patayan, and the Hohokam (Cordell 1984). Hohokam remains occur in the Sonoran desert of southern Arizona and along the northern frontiers of Sonora (Crown 1990; Gumerman 1991). Archaeologists frequently speak of the Hohokam region in terms of a core, the Phoenix basin, and a periphery extending from Flagstaff, Arizona on the north, south to the international border and from the San Pedro river on the east to the Gila Bend on the west (Figure 5.1) (McGuire 1991).

The Hohokam range encompasses all of the Lower Sonoran desert in southern Arizona. The Lower Sonoran desert is part of the Basin and Range physiographic province, consisting of a series of drop-faulted mountain ranges divided by extensive block-faulted basins. Low precipitation (3 to 12 inches a year across the region) and summer temperatures in excess of 100°F make the availability of water the main determinate of agricultural production and reliability in the desert. Two perennial rivers, the Gila and the Salt, pass through the core area. The seasonal flow of these streams varies greatly, but they provide well watered floodplains for agriculture and people could extract water from either using minimal technology.

Prehistory

Archaeologists divide Hohokam prehistory into four periods; Pioneer, Colonial, Sedentary, and Classic.

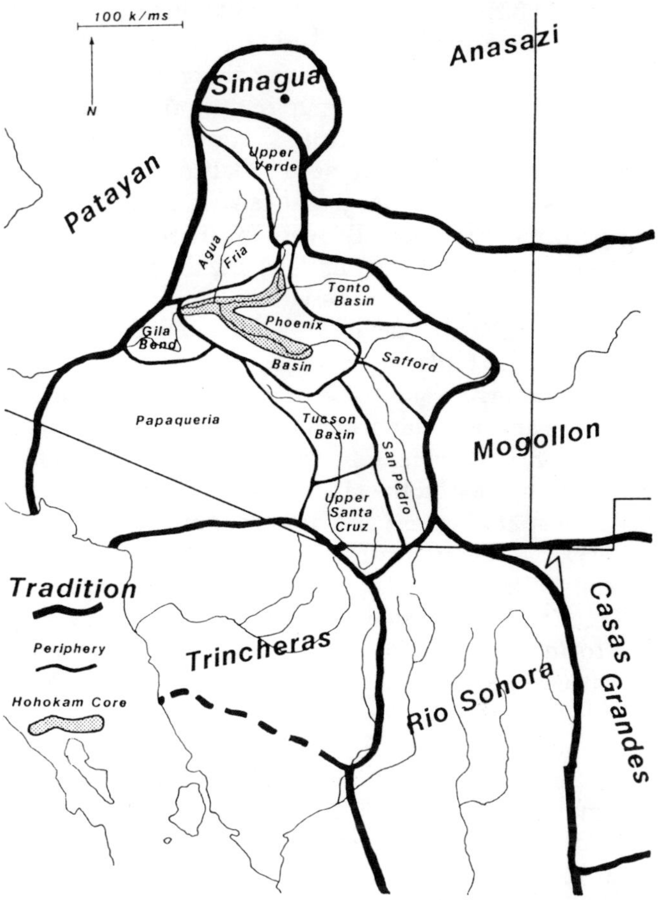

Figure 5.1. The Hohokam World at the Beginning of the Sedentary Period (from McGuire 1991:figure 8.1).

Considerable debate exists concerning the dating of the sequence and I have used Eighmy and McGuire's (1988) interpretation of the chronology (but see also Dean 1991).

Pioneer period (AD 150-725) settlements appear principally in the core area with some late Pioneer villages in the periphery. Core villages consisted of a handful of shallow pithouses, usually along the flood plains of the Gila and Salt Rivers. During the Pioneer period the Hohokam began using irrigation agriculture, but wild plants and game continued to make up most of the diet (Gasser and Kwiatkowski 1991). Hohokam potters produced a red-on-grey pottery in the earliest phases of the period but by the end of the period they had developed this ware into the typically Hohokam red-on-buff style. The first evidence of marine shell obtained from the Gulf of California appear in this period as does the typically Hohokam ritual assemblage of censors, palettes, and long serrated projectile points. At the beginning of the period burial was by inhumation but the Hohokam practiced cremation by the end of the period.

The aptly named Colonial period is usually divided into two phases, Gila Butte (AD 725-825) and the Santa

Cruz (AD 825-1000). During the Gila Butte phase the Hohokam tradition spread over most of southern Arizona. Core area villages exist along major canals. They continued to be made up of pithouses but these now tended to cluster in groups around shared courtyards with an adjacent cemetery. Ballcourts appear in this phase and at the largest sites such as Snaketown capped platform mounds were built around central plazas. Cremation burial has become the norm in this phase. This basic culture assemblage continues in the Santa Cruz phase as canals are extended and more and larger villages built.

The patterns established in the Colonial period continue and are elaborated in the Sedentary period which contains a single phase, the Sacaton (AD 1000-1100). In this period the Hohokam tradition reaches its greatest spatial extent and artistic expression (Haury 1976:356). A hierarchy of settlements exist with villages lacking ballcourts, villages with a single ballcourt, and villages with multiple ballcourts, central plazas, and platform mounds. Despite the expansion of public architecture, domestic structures continue to be relatively ephemeral shallow pithouses little changed from the Gila Butte phase.

Dramatic changes in the Hohokam material culture assemblage and spatial distribution usher in the Classic period, which is divided into two phases, the Soho (AD 1100-1300) and the Civano (AD 1300-1450). In the Soho the Hohokam regional system that extended all across southern Arizona appears to collapse and the term Hohokam is best only applied to the core area. Despite this seeming regional retraction, during the Classic period the Hohokam expand the canal systems in the Gila and Salt basins to their greatest extent. Settlements become more compact with compounds replacing the courtyards of earlier periods and above ground adobe rooms replacing pithouses. The Hohokam continued to build pithouse villages in marginal areas of the core and perhaps on the edges of larger settlements. During the Soho ballcourts cease to be used and platform mounds become residential spaces with domestic structures on them. In the Civano some Hohokam settlements cover areas of greater than a square mile and include specialized administrative centers such as Casa Grande. Cremation continues throughout the Classic with cemeteries near compounds but starting in the Soho individuals are also buried within compounds and in special mortuary structures such as Clan House 1 at Casa Grande.

The overall distribution of Hohokam traits also changes dramatically in the Classic Period. During the Colonial and Sedentary Periods the Phoenix Basin is clearly the center of the Hohokam world, both in the geographic sense and because the traits used to identify Hohokam appear earliest and are most elaborated in this area (Figure 5.2). In the Classic Period the Phoenix basin continues to be the most heavily populated region in southern Arizona with the largest and most elaborate towns, but it has lost its centrality in terms of traits. Of the various traits that define the Classic Period, such as Salado Polychrome pottery, platform mounds, Sonoran Brownware pottery (particularly the type Tanque Verde Red-on-brown), and *cerros de trincheras* sites, only the distribution of platform mounds appears centered on the Phoenix basin (Figure 5.3). In terms of ceramic distributions the Phoenix basin is at the western edge of the Salado polychrome distribution and the Tucson Basin and Papagueria are in a separate Sonoran Brownware distribution.

The large settlements of the Classic period seem to be abandoned by the late 15th century. A subsequent El Polvoron phase (AD 1450-?) appears to be the product of a remnant population, sometimes living in the ruins of the large centers. When the Spanish first entered the area in the late 17th century they found the Salt river valley

Figure 5.2. Distribution of Hohokam Material Culture in the Sedentary Period (from McGuire 1991:figure 8.2).

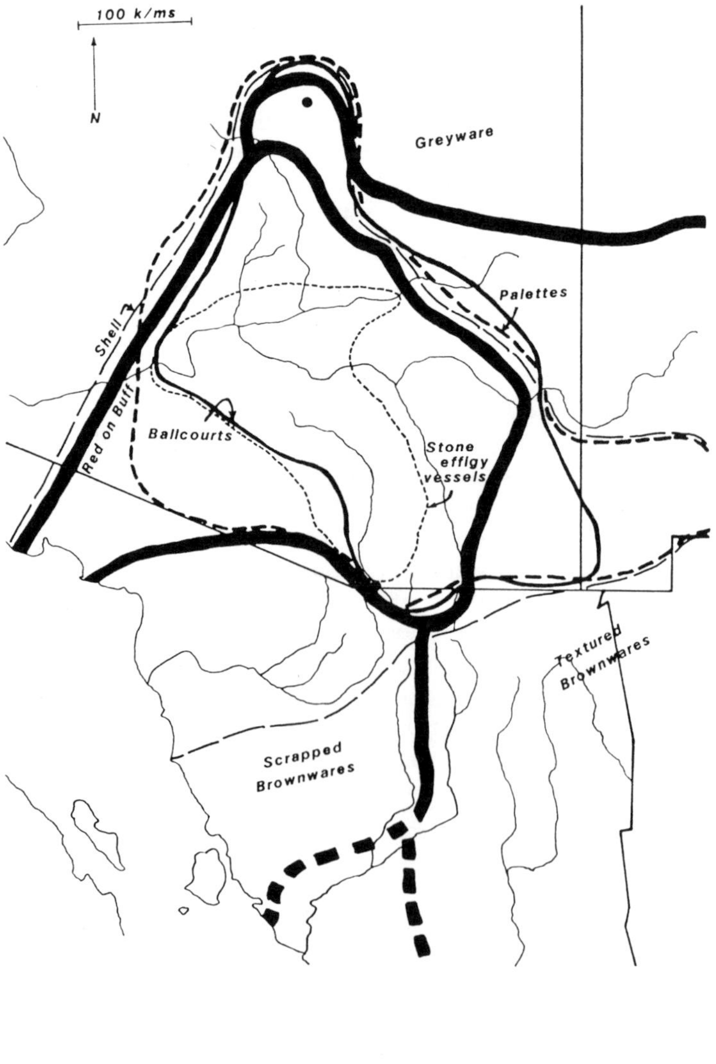

abandoned by settled agriculturalists and only a few villages of O'odham (Pima) on the Gila River.

Hohokam Core and Periphery

Traditionally archaeologists thought that the Hohokam were a bounded linguistic and cultural group, that migrated into the Phoenix basin, expanded outward, and then contracted (Haury 1976). Today, most archaeologists in southern Arizona speak of the Hohokam as having been a regional system that incorporated multiple ethnic, linguistic, and cultural groups (Crown 1990; Gumerman 1991). They work with an explicit concept of a Hohokam core surrounded by areas that are in some sense peripheral to that core. Hohokam archaeologists tend to see developments in these peripheral areas as originating in and dependent upon what happens in the core. The movement of styles, products, and items are often assumed to be one way from the core out. These peripheries are somehow viewed as being incapable of existence, at least as Hohokam, apart from the core. Archaeologists may discuss the core without reference to the peripheries but they seldom discuss peripheries without reference to the core. At first glance the Hohokam regional system would appear to be a prime example of a Pre-Columbian world-system.

Figure 5.3. Distribution of Hohokam Material Culture in the Civano Phase (From McGuire 1991:figure 8.3).

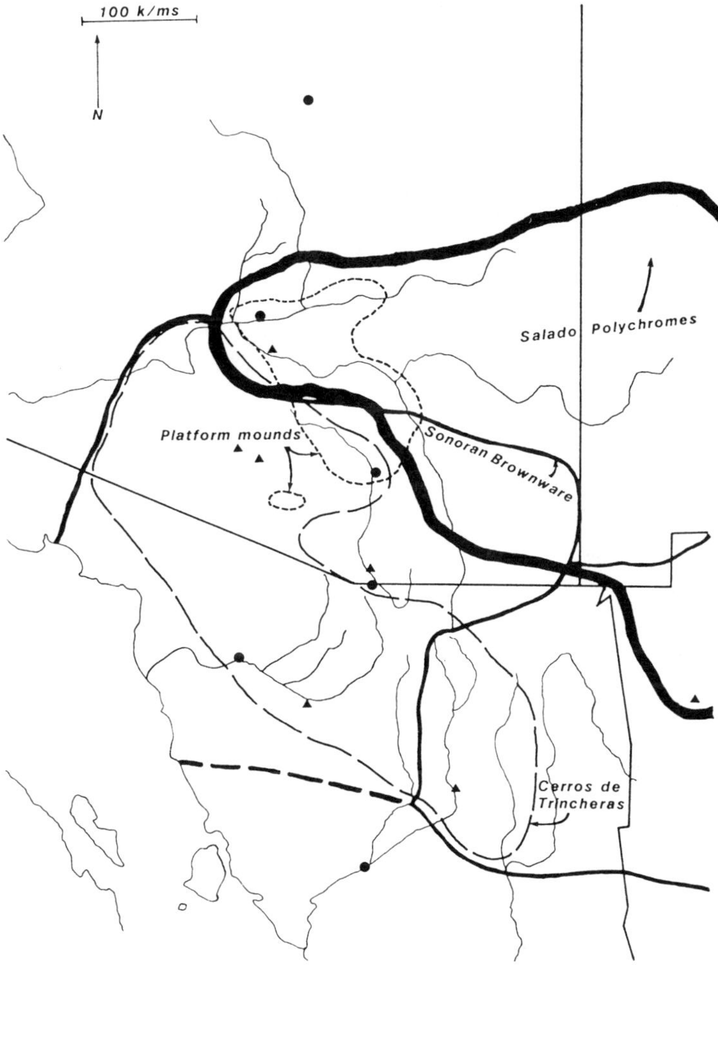

In both the traditional and the regional systems view scholars regard the Hohokam as a bounded unit, with internal subdivisions that change through time. Further, they assume that the nature of that unit (be it a culture or a regional system) remains the same throughout the sequence. That is they do not entertain the idea that formally similar distributions of artifacts may represent qualitatively different social formations. Thus, in almost all current interpretations of Hohokam prehistory a distribution of ceramic styles and artifact traits is either seen as representing a culture or a regional system. Few archaeologists consider that at one time a distribution may reflect a culture, in another a regional system, and in another still something else.

Archaeologists generally regarded the Phoenix basin as the core of the system and the rest of the Hohokam range as peripheral. The most elaborate expressions of the Hohokam tradition occur in the Phoenix basin including the largest sites, the biggest ballcourts and platform mounds, the most extensive irrigation networks, the most lavish ritual objects, and the highest percentage of red-on-buff pottery. Most of these things occur in the peripheral areas but they are less elaborated and appear later in time than in the core. Prehistorians have variously classified and described the peripheries of the Hohokam with only a few systematic attempts to consider the entire regional system (Gladwin et al. 1936; Di Peso 1956, 1979; Schroeder 1960, 1979; Haury 1976; Gumerman and Haury 1979; Wilcox and Sternberg 1983; Neitzel 1984; Teague 1984). They recognize a set of sub-areas which correspond to major basins and river valleys. These areas include the Tucson Basin, the Gila Bend, the Papaguería, the San Pedro river, the Safford area, the Agua Fria river, the Upper Verde river, the Upper Santa Cruz river, and the Phoenix Basin. Like the Hohokam in general, archaeologists regard these peripheries as bounded units, reflecting a social unit that changes over time.

When researchers start in the Phoenix basin and look out at the "peripheries" they cannot help but be struck by the similarities between the Phoenix Basin and the other sub-areas. Upon examining these similarities they easily conclude that the Phoenix Basin was a hot area of cultural development and the source of a common cultural pattern and/or economy over the larger region. If researchers start with "peripheral" areas and look in they encounter more diversity than shared similarities to the core. The prehistory of three peripheries, the Upper Verde, the Papaguería and the Trincheras region illustrate the variability that existed within the system (McGuire 1991).

Hohokam archaeologists often interpret these three peripheries as having different cultural and economic relationships to a Phoenix basin core. The Papaguería is generally regarded as a peripheral area in the Hohokam tradition for all of its Formative period prehistory. Many archaeologists see the Upper Verde region as first a periphery of the Hohokam and then later as the southern edge of a Sinagua culture. The relationship of the Trincheras culture of northern Sonora to the Hohokam is highly controversial, with some scholars claiming this area is part of the Hohokam tradition and others maintaining it was a separate tradition. As these debates suggest, the three areas are quite distinctive from each other in spite of their shared status as Hohokam peripheries.

Throughout the history of Hohokam archaeology all three of these regions have been regarded as peripheral to a core Phoenix basin Hohokam and their prehistories largely interpreted in relation to this core area. Despite this shared status the patterns of material culture, sequence of development, and relationship to the core differ greatly between each area.

Hohokam-style material culture appears in each of these areas at some point in their prehistory but beyond this similarity the development of each area is quite different. In the Upper Verde, Hohokam traits appear early in the sequence but never make up a majority of the material culture. In the late prehistoric most prehistorians would consider the area to be Sinagua, not Hohokam. In the Papaguería the earliest Formative ceramics and architecture were virtually identical to core area assemblages. Through time the artifact assemblage of the region increasingly looks more like that of the Tucson Basin than the core area. The Trincheras materials are initially distinctive from the core but then in the late prehistoric the archaeology of the Altar Valley in this area greatly resembles that of the Papaguería and the Tucson Basin, while the rest of the region continues as a distinctive region. At no time does the archaeology of the Trincheras area mirror that of the core.

Hohokam World-Systems and Peer Polities

The use of either a world-systems approach or peer polity interaction in the Hohokam case could be seriously misleading. The changes in the Hohokam regional system over time do not fit very well with the expectations of either approach. At a given time certain aspects of the case appear congruent with one or the other of the models but at other times this congruence is lost. At no time does either model seem to capture the variation that exists in Hohokam prehistory. Furthermore, the sequence of change in the Hohokam archaeological record does not conform to the expectations of the evolutionary perspective that underlies both approaches.

World-systems theory holds that diverse peripheries will become more alike and less different, economically, politically, and culturally, due to their shared economic relationship to a core. The concept of periphery has analytical value because of this convergence. Once a world-system incorporates a region, the relationship of that periphery to the core will shape its development and therefore the core-periphery relationship becomes the key to understanding changes in the periphery.

Hohokam prehistory offers little evidence of such functional convergence. The pattern of change in fact contradicts the predictions of world-systems theory. Peripheral areas have very similar looking archaic manifestations and look most like each other and the core at the beginning of the Colonial period. Over time these areas diverge from each other and the core rather than converge. The Papaguería and the Upper Verde both start the Colonial period with red-on-buff pottery, Hohokam style pithouses, and other Hohokam material manifestations. By the Classic period the material culture of both regions was greatly different from each other and from the Phoenix basin.

Hohokam prehistory lacks functional convergence because southern Arizona was never as economically or politically integrated as the world-systems model assumes. Few archaeologists would argue that large scale, long distance trade in basic commodities existed among the prehistoric Hohokam. Even the models of food trade into the Papaguería do not require that the amount be more than a fraction of total subsistence to buffer irregular supplies in the local environment. Furthermore, in this case the Papaguerian peoples may have traveled to the food in times of stress rather than the other way around. The technology available to move foodstuffs would have allowed the regular redistribution of foodstuffs over distances 50 to 60 kilometers (Lightfoot 1979; Hassig 1988:64). Food redistribution networks could have covered areas of 7,800 to 11,232 square kilometers. All of the Hohokam peripheries are approximately this size except the Papaguería and the Trincheras which are considerably larger.

The Hohokam peripheries such as the upper Verde, Tonto Basin, Tucson Basin, Agua Fria and the others had to have been primarily self-provisioning. The Hohokam must have forged the connections in their regional system primarily through the exchange of preciosities. Trade in preciosities will link areas producing cultural convergence and dependencies that form the locus of cultural change.

Such trade will not, however, lead to large scale functional convergence and uniform peripheries because the local economic/ecological relations remain primary. We cannot arrive at an adequate understanding of cultural change in large regions without integrating trade in preciosities with local economic relations. To do this we must once again emphasize the difference between peripheries without denying the interconnections.

The boundaries that separate the peripheries from each other and from the core are at best fuzzy. At the scale of the regional system the distinction between the Upper Verde and the Agua Fria appears distinct but as the scale is lowered the line drawn on the smaller scale map blurs and disappears. The same can be said for the Phoenix Basin and the Papagueria. It is not at all clear that the Hohokam regional system was made up of inter-connected societies or polities. Or, more importantly that it was made up of bounded units at all.

The shift from the Sedentary Period to the Classic Period is often seen as a dramatic and sudden transformation in Hohokam history. Such a comparison is, however, misleading because the transformation was not sudden but rather a matter of small quantitative changes building up to a major qualitative shift at the end of the Sedentary followed by a hundred years or more of reorganization. Peripheral areas such as the upper Verde and the Papaguería began to diverge from the core area cultural pattern from the Colonial period onwards.

We can see these small shifts in the prehistory of the Tucson basin, the Papaguería, and the Trincheras. Red-on-buff ceramics remain the dominant type in the Tucson basin until the Rillito phase when the local brownware style begins to dominate in the southern half of the basin (Doelle and Wallace 1991). In the eastern Papaguería red-on-brown frequencies exceed red-on-buffs in the Sedentary period. In both the western Papagueria and the Trincheras area Sonoran brownwares become the dominant ceramic types only in the Classic period.

By the Classic Period the Phoenix Basin is no longer at the center of a Hohokam regional system but on the western edge of a Salado regional system. Meanwhile the Papaguerian and Trincheras regions appear to have been incorporated into a O'otam regional system (McGuire 1991). The development of Saladoan and O'otam regional systems in the late prehistoric might be taken to indicate a declining role for the Phoenix basin. The basin appears to have lost its hot status as a center of innovation and become a cultural periphery receiving innovation. This perception is not consistent, however, with economic and political developments in the basin that suggest increased production, and greater social differentiation. In the Classic period the irrigation system reaches its greatest extent, villages include elite residences on mounds, and at least one specialized administrative center, Casa Grande, exists.

The Hohokam network was never as economically, politically or in any other way integrated as the approach assumes. As a result, over time the peripheries become more distinct rather than more alike as they should if they were integrated into a international division of labor. The network was not made up of bounded units or polities. The divisions between regions were always very fuzzy and thus these regions only exist when the prehistory is examined at a certain scale. Finally, even as the Phoenix Basin looses its position as a cultural and stylistic core in the Classic Period it becomes more economically and politically more developed.

Hohokam history in the Pioneer to Sedentary periods also does not fit the first three of Renfrew's (1986:7-8) expectations for peer polity interaction. Renfrew's fourth condition, that a variety of interactions bring about change, does seem to apply. My evaluation here keys on the question of what should be the region that Renfrew's four conditions applies to. If we define the region narrowly, such as the Phoenix Basin then each of the conditions can be seen, but clearly this smaller region is embedded in larger processes that the peer polity model does not stress.

Few, if any, Hohokam archaeologists hold that the Phoenix Basin was ever under the sway of a single polity. Multiple social and political groups clearly existed in the basin at all points in time. Although some towns were bigger than others no one town stands out at any period as the preeminent center of the basin. In this sense Renfrew's first condition of neighboring polities of comparable scale is met. However, if we look out side of the basin to the other parts of the Hohokam world it is clear that the largest and most important towns were in the Phoenix basin.

Renfrew's second condition that polities will undergo the same transformations at about the same time again works in the restricted context of the basin but not in the greater Hohokam world. As the previous review of Hohokam peripheries demonstrates, the rate and nature of change varies across the Hohokam world.

Finally, for most of the Hohokam sequence (Pioneer to Sedentary Periods) there is a clear center or core, the Phoenix Basin, from which innovation and change seems to originate. This is contrary to Renfrew's expectation that no single locus of innovation and change will be identified.

The peer polity model does seem to have more applicability in the Classic Period. At this time no clear core exists in the Hohokam world and indeed some of us have argued that no Hohokam world exists at all. Within the Salado Regional System there are many towns of comparable size and no clear center. Crown (1994) has suggested that a religious cult united this world.

Underlying all of the debate on world-systems and peer polity interactions is an evolutionary premise. All of the participants in the debate accept the idea that the modern world may be so greatly integrated that the

World is the proper unit of analysis. The essential issue is did a sufficient degree and kind of integration exist in evolutionary more "simple" times for similar processes to operate in the prehistoric past? The advocates of peer polity interaction have been the clearest on this point suggesting that peer polity interaction characterizes pre-state societies and world-systems follow with the evolution of states.

Yet in the Hohokam sequence this evolutionary trajectatory seems reversed. In the earliest time periods (Pioneer to Sedentary) a Hohokam world exists with a core in the Phoenix basin and peripheries filling about half the modern state of Arizona. Over time this world gradually transforms itself as the peripheries become more different and the Phoenix Basin less like a core. Despite this fact developmental change occurred as populations grew, energy capture intensified, technology became more elaborate, inter-regional exchange and economic specialization increased, and settlement patterns more complex. In one sense these societies seem to be evolving, yet in another they appear to be digressing.

Beyond World-Systems and Peer Polities

The limitations with the use of either a world-systems perspective or peer polity interaction in Hohokam prehistory spring from the attempt to account for the totality of social reality with a single totalizing theory (Thomas 1991). These attempts reduce the rich variation of history to a handful of categories, a few processes, and a high order scale.

The Trouble With Systems

A world-systems perspective takes a systemic view, that stresses the units (cores, peripheries, and semi-peripheries) that are linked in such a system rather than the relations that create the units. Classificatory terms such as core and periphery unite areas in terms of a specified set of similarities but in doing so, they mask or hide important variation between regions placed in the same category. The theory identifies inequalities in the processes of economic exchange and development as the driving forces for change in history. In world-systems theory a social group becomes core because of its functional position in the international division of labor. A social group may, however, be central because of its position in a web of religious, social, economic, or political relations. One group may be the center for one set of relations, e.g. religion, while a different group in the center for another set of relations, e.g. economic.

A world-systems perspective maintains that processes occur in multiple functionally interrelated layers. Yet in all the world-system theories that have been advanced the emphasis is on how the highest order processes drive change on lower levels. People, however, live and act in a world of varying scales and their relations with others change as their scale of reference changes. The processes that occur at different scales are linked, but they are not reducible, one to another (Marquardt and Crumley 1987:2).

I would agree that the scale of analysis defined by the peer polity model is an important one for looking at cultural change. The processes that occur in local river valleys or basins are often too restricted and those operating at the level of the whole of the Southwest are too grand to account for most of the changes in prehistory. We also doubt that the Southwest was ever a single network of peer polity interaction so at any given time multiple networks could have existed. This model, however, gives us little or no guidance on how external relations articulate networks or affect process of change. The peer polity model runs the risk of being a new isolationism that frames research questions in a way that blinds us to any significant impacts long range interactions may have had on the prehistory of the Southwest. It only gives us the idea of emulation, a new term for the old notion of influence, to account for far ranging similarities in cultural change.

The notion of bounded units that change over time underlies both the peer polity and the world-system approach. We live in a world of bounded entities, cities, counties, states, and nation states. A border, a line on a map, defines each of these units. At least in theory, the stuff that makes up these units, the culture of the nation, the authority of the government, or the relations of the economy, should extend evenly and completely from border to border. Again, at least in theory there is a hierarchy to these units. They should fit neatly one inside the other like a set of Russian dolls. We all know this model does not often work. We find this neat ordering only in political units, yet the model structures how we view the world so that we try and fit any social phenomena with a spatial aspect into it. This modern notion of bounded units is a creation of modern history and the invention of nation states (Anderson 1983; Smith 1991). Such bounded, nested, spatial, units are modern creations (Wolf 1982). In prehistoric cases, like the Hohokam, the boundaries between social groups are ill defined and very fuzzy; yet we draw hard lines around them to define neat units.

Uneven Development and Scale

A world-systems perspective points to an important aspect of social relations, unevenness in development, and to the contradictions that occur from this unevenness. Archaeologists can take this notion of unevenness and examine it as a much more multidimensional phenomena than the world-systems theory allows. To do so, we need to avoid a totalizing theory that uses *a priori* functionally related categories such a core and periphery and that assumes that processes of social change are best understood at a single scale. Instead we need to examine the unevenness of cultural development in terms multiple dimensions and at multiple scales.

Marquardt and Crumley (1987:2) speak of the "effective scale" of research, that being "any scale at which pattern may be recognized or meaning inferred." As we change the effective scale of our analysis we frame a different web of relations. The unevenness in these relations will disappear at a different scale as a new pattern of unevenness appears. Social groups also live and act in a world of varying scale and their position *viz-a-viz* others changes as their scale of reference changes. Our choice of an effective scale, therefore, brackets an area for study allowing us to view a particular set of social relations while denying us access to sets visible at other scales. Also, we will find that some theoretical models are more informative at one scale and others at a different scale, so that our choice of models in part also depends on the scale of our analysis. The prehistoric world we wish to understand was a complex product of the intersection of all these scales. Thus our studies of prehistory need to be multi-scaler. As we change scales the boundaries that seemed sharp at one level become fuzzy and disappear.

All of this assumes that the goal of our analyses is to understand history as a material social process and not to build sterile generalizations about world-systems in all times and places. To study this kind of history we ask about the commonalities and differences between social groups and the larger historical, environmental context in which these commonalities and differences emerged. We also need to look for unevenness in historical developments. Uneven development begets social groups that have different interests within a social order, and as they act to meet these interests, they create conflicts that drive social change. Such a history should be multi-scaler. As we change our scale of analysis, we frame a different set of relations; the unevenness in these relations will disappear at a new scale as a fresh pattern of unevenness appears.

References Cited

Abu-Lughod, Janet
1990 *Before European Hegemony: The World System A.D. 1250-1350.* Oxford University Press, Oxford.
Adams, E. Charles
1991 *The Origin and Development of the Pueblo Katsina Cult.* Univeristy of Arizona Press, Tucson.
Adams, Robert McC.
1965 *The Land Behind Baghdad.* University of Chicago Press, Chicago.
Anderson, Benedict
1983 *Imagined Communities.* Verso, London.
Baugh, Timothy G.
1982 *Edwards I (34BK2): Southern Plains Adaptations in the Protohistoric Period.* Oklahoma Archaeological Survey, Norman.
1984 Southern Plains Societies and Eastern Frontier Pueblo Exchange During the Protohistoric Period. *Papers of the Archaeological Society of New Mexico* 9:154-167.
Blanton, Richard E., and Gary Feinman
1984 The Mesoamerican World System. *American Anthropologist* 86:673-682.
Blanton, Richard E., Stephen A. Kowalewski, Gary Feinman, and Jill Appel
1981 *Ancient Mesoamerica.* Cambridge University Press, Cambridge.
Chase-Dunn, Christopher
1989 *Global Formation: Structures of the World-Economy.* Basil Blackwell, Cambridge.
Chase-Dunn, Christopher and Thomas D. Hall
1991 *Core/Periphery Relations in Precapitalist Worlds.* Westview Press, Boulder.

1993 Comparing World-Systems: Concepts and Working Hypotheses. *Social Forces* 71:851-886.

Cordell, Linda S.
1984 *Prehistory of the Southwest.* Academic Press, Orlando.

Crown, Patricia
1990 The Hohokam of the American Southwest. *Journal of World Prehistory* 4(2):223-255.
1994 *Ceramics and Ideology: Salado Polychrome Pottery.* University of New Mexico Press, Albuquerque.

Dean, Jeffrey S.
1991 Thoughts on Hohokam Chronology. In *Exploring the Hohokam: Prehistoric Desert Dwellers of the American Southwest*, edited by G.J. Gumerman, pp. 417-459. University of New Mexico Press, Albuquerque.

Di Peso, Charles C.
1956 The Upper Pima of San Cayetano del Tumacacori. *Amerind Foundation Publications* 7. Dragoon.
1979 Prehistory: Southern Periphery. In *Southwest*, edited by Alfonso Ortiz, pp. 152-161. *Handbook of North American Indians*, Vol. 9. Smithsonian Institution, Washington D.C.
1983 The Northern Sector of the Mesoamerican World System. In *Forgotten Places and Things*, edited by A. E. Ward, pp. 11-22. Center for Archaeological Studies, Albuquerque.

Doelle , William H. and Henry D. Wallace
1991 The Changing Role of the Tucson Basin in the Hohokam Regional System. In *Exploring the Hohokam*, edited by G.J. Gummerman, pp. 279-346. University of New Mexico Press, Albuquerque.

Eighmy, Jeffery and Randall H. McGuire
1988 Archaeomagnetic Dates and the Hohokam Phase Sequence. *Colorado State University Archaeomagnetic Lab Technical Series* 3, Ft. Collins.

Ekholm, Kasja and Jonathan Friedman
1982 Capitalism, Imperialism, and the Exploitation in the Ancient World System. *Review* 6:87-110.
1985 Towards a Global Anthropology. *Critique of Anthropology* 5:97-119.

Frank, Andre Gunder
1990 A Theoretical Introduction to 5,000 Years of World System History. *Review* 13:155-248.

Frank, Andre Gunder and Barry K. Gills
1990 The Culmination of Accumulation: Theses and Research Agenda for 5,000 of World-System History. *Dialectical Anthropology* 15:19-42.

Gladwin, Harold S., E.W. Haury, E.B. Sayles, and Nora Gladwin
1936 Excavations at Snaketown I: Material Culture. *Medallion Papers* 25, Globe.

Gasser, Robert E. and Scott M. Kwiatkowski
1991 Food For Thought: Recognizing Patterns in Hohokam Subsistence. In *Exploring the Hohokam*, edited by G.J. Gumerman, pp. 417-459. University of New Mexico Press, Albuquerque.

Gumerman, George
1991 *Exploring the Hohokam: Prehistoric Desert Dwellers of the American Southwest.* University of New Mexico Press, Albuquerque.

Gummerman, George C. and Emil W. Haury
1979 Prehistory: Hohokam. In *Southwest*, edited by Alfonso Ortiz, pp.75-90. *Handbook of North American Indians*, Vol. 9. Smithsonian Institution, Washington D.C.

Hall, Thomas D.
1989 *Social Change in the Southwest, 1350-1880.* University of Kansas, Lawrence.

Hassig, Ross
1988 Structure and Growth of the Aztec Empire. Paper presented at the annual meetings of the Society for American Archaeology, Phoenix.

Haury, Emil
1976 *The Hohokam:Desert Farmers and Craftsmen.* University of Arizona Press, Tucson.

Hosler, Dorthy
1994 *The Sounds and Colors of Power*. The MIT Press, Cambridge.
Kohl, Philip
1987 The Use and Abuse of World-Systems Theory. *Advances in Archaeological Method and Theory*, Vol. 11, edited by M.B. Schiffer, pp. 1-35. Academic Press, San Diego.
1989 The Use and Abuse of World-Systems Theory: The Case of the "Pristine" West Asian State. In *Archaeological Thought in America*, ed. by CC. Lamberg-Karlovsky, pp. 241-267. Cambridge University Press, Cambridge.
Lightfoot, Kent G.
1979 Food Redistribution Among Prehistoric Pueblo Groups. *The Kiva* 44(4):319-340.
Marquardt, William and Carole L. Crumley
1987 Theoretical Issues in the Analysis of Spatial Patterning. In *Regional Dynamics: Burgundian Landscapes in Historical Perspective.* edited by C.L. Crumley and W.H. Marquardt, pp.1-18. Academic Press, Orlando.
McGuire, Randall H.
1991 On the Outside Looking In: The Concept of Periphery in Hohokam Archaeology. In *Exploring the Hohokam*, edited by G.J. Gumerman, pp. 347-383. University of New Mexico Press, Albuquerque.
Minnis, Paul E.
1989 The Casas Grandes Polity in the International Four Corners. In *The Sociopolitical Structure of Prehistoric Southwestern Societies*, edited by Steadman Upham, K.G. Lightfoot, and R. A. Jewitt, pp. 269-305. Westview Press, Boulder.
Neitzel, Jill E.
1984 The Organization of the Hohokam Regional System. *American Archaeology* 4(3):207-216.
Palerm, Angel and Eric R. Wolf
1957 Ecological Potential and Cultural Development in Mesoamerica. In *Studies in Human Ecology*, pp. 1-37. Anthropological Society of Washington D.C.
Plog, Fred
1983 Political and Economic Alliances on the Colorado Plateaus, AD 400 - 1400. *Advances in World Archaeology* 2:289-330.
Plog, Fred, Sted Upham and Phillip C. Weigand
1982 A Perspective on Mogollon-Mesoamerican Interaction. In *Mogollon Archaeology: Proceedings of the 1980 Conference*, edited by P.H. Beckett, pp. 227-238. Acoma Books, Ramona.
Polanyi, Karl
1957 *The Great Transformation: The Political and Economic Origins of Our Time.* Beacon Press, Boston.
Rathje, William
1971 The Origin and Development of Lowland Classic Maya Civilization. *American Antiquity* 36:275-285.
Renfrew, Colin
1986 Introduction: Peer Polity Interaction and Socio-Political Change. In *Peer Polity Interaction and Socio-Political Change*, ed. by Colin Renfrew and J.F. Cherry, pp. 1-18. Cambridge University Press, Cambridge.
Sanders, William T. and Barbara Price
1968 *Mesoamerica: The Evolution of a Civilization.* Random House, New York.
Santley, Robert and Rani Alexander
1992 The Political Economy of Core-Periphery Systems. In *Resources, Power, and Interregional Interaction*, edited by E. Schortman and P. Urban, pp. 17-21. Plenum, New York.
Schortman, Edward and Patricia Urban
1987 Modeling Interregional Interaction in Prehistory. In *Advances in Archaeological Method and Theory*, Vol. 11, edited by M.B. Schiffer, pp. 37-95. Academic Press, San Diego.

Schroeder, Albert H.
1960 The Hohokam, Sinagua, and Hakataya. *Society for American Archaeology Archives of Archaeology*, Vol. 5.
1979 Prehistory: Hakataya. In *Southwest*, edited by Alfonso Ortiz, pp. 100-107. *Handbook of North American Indians*, Vol. 9. Smithsonian Institution, Washington D.C.
Smith, Anthony D.
1991 *National Identity.* University of Nevada Press, Reno.
Teague, Lynn S.
1984 The Organization of Hohokam Economy. In *Hohokam Archaeology Along the Salt Gila Aqueduct* (Central Arizona Project, Vol 9), ed. by L.S. Teague and P.L.Crown, pp. 187-250. Arizona State Museum, Tucson.
Thomas, Julian
1991 *Rethinking the Neolithic.* Cambridge University Press, Cambridge.
Upham, Stedman
1982 *Politics and Power*. Academic Press, New York.
Wallerstein, Immanuel
1974 *The Modern World-System I.* Academic Press, New York.
1978 Civilization and Modes of Production. *Theory and Society* 5:1-10.
1980 *The Modern World-System II.* Academic Press, New York.
1989 *The Modern World-System III.* Academic Press, Orlando.
Whitecotten, Joseph W. and Richard A. Pailes
1986 New World Pre-Columbian World-Systems. In *Ripples in the Chichimec Sea: New Considerations of Southwestern-Mesoamerican Interactions*, edited by F.J. Mathian and R.H. McGuire, pp. 183-204. Southern Illinois University Press, Carbondale.
Wilcox, David R. and Charles Sternberg
1983 *Hohokam Ballcourts and Their Interpretation.* Arizona State Museum, Tucson.
Wolf, Eric
1982 *Europe and the People Without History.* University of California Press, Berkeley.

Chapter 6

A Macroregional Comparison of the American Southwest and Highland Mesoamerica in Pre-Columbian Times: Preliminary Thoughts and Implications

Gary M. Feinman
Linda M. Nicholas
University of Wisconsin-Madison

Steadman Upham
University of Oregon

In a special issue of *Review* (Upham, Feinman, and Nicholas 1992), we began a comparative effort to consider macroregional similarities and differences in the political economies of the pre-Columbian American Southwest and highland Mesoamerica during the late pre-contact period. The discussion here expands on key points made in the *Review* article, while at the same time, it discusses several related issues and new directions for future macroregional research that go beyond the concerns raised previously. In this introductory section of the paper, we address a number of theoretical debates and considerations concerning the application of macroregional approaches in archaeology. A preliminary discussion and focused comparison of highland Mesoamerica and the American Southwest follows. In the concluding section, several implications are drawn from these comparisons, and suggestions are made concerning macroregional approaches and the contemporary debates stimulated by their application to precapitalist contexts. A central thesis of this analysis is that, while a macroregional perspective is essential for understanding long-term histories and processes, archaeologists must approach this scale without facilely accepting the flawed assumptions of an earlier archaeological paradigm (traditional culture history) that also seriously considered broad spatial phenomena (see Kowalewski's and Peregrine's contributions to this volume for related perspectives).

Although we strongly advocate the examination of human phenomena at the macroregional scale, we do not see this analytical perspective as the sole (or even the principal) unit of analysis. Rather, in our view, human socioeconomic systems are best investigated at several analytical scales simultaneously. One of the advantages that we see for archaeology in the frameworks that have their tap roots in the writings of Braudel (1972), Wallerstein (1974), and Wolf (1982) is that they do provide a structure for articulating material, energy, and information exchanges at the broad, macroregional scale with more local and regional processes.

Nevertheless, a macro-scale perspective is clearly necessary to address the kinds of issues that were discussed recently in *American Antiquity* by Gordon Willey (1991), who contrasts episodes (to use his terminology) of "horizon-style unifications" with "marked regional stylistic diversity" in Mesoamerica and Peru. Likewise, archaeologists in both Mesoamerica and the Southwest have defined complex and massive episodes of transition that crosscut regional boundaries, affecting much larger spatial domains. Here, for example, we might include the period between A.D. 650-900, when many of Mesoamerica's extant centers declined greatly in size and importance (see Diehl and Berlo 1989), or the series of "hinge points" in Southwestern prehistory (e.g., A.D. 1000-1150) during which major cultural transitions appear to have affected many different regions simultaneously (Cordell and Gumerman 1989). In each of these cases, local factors alone appear inadequate to account for these widespread transitions.

In this discussion, we refer to 'macroregions' rather than 'world-systems' for several reasons. First, we explicitly endeavor to avoid criticisms generated by the misguided view that 'world-systems' necessarily operate only at the entire world or global scale. As Peregrine discusses in the introduction to this volume, such an intent clearly was never meant in reference to multi-societal systems (Wallerstein 1974:15), but certain archaeologists unfamiliar with Wallerstein's original work persist in thinking otherwise. Second, in comparing these two ancient American macroregions, we prefer to make the question of 'systemness' an empirical issue rather than an assumed point of departure. While use of the term, 'macroregion,' implies a degree of interaction and interconnection between the component regional populations, it does not presuppose that such interrelations always constitute a defined or boundable system.

In the consideration of political and economic relations at the macroregional perspective, we follow Janet Abu-Lughod (1989; also see Hall and Chase-Dunn, this volume) in recognizing that a given macroregion (or world system) need not be defined or dominated by a single, predominant core. Likewise, significant macro-scale interactions that have important local consequences are not viewed as exclusive to class-based societies (Chase-Dunn and Hall 1991; Chase-Dunn 1992; Collins 1992). Only through the contrast and comparison of highly stratified and stateless macroregions can we begin to understand the different kinds of interconnections (or 'system logics') that interdigitated these ancient worlds at the macro-scale (Chase-Dunn 1992). Finally, we explicitly reject the ever-present supposition that core-periphery relationships are either static over time or defined exclusively by environmental or geographic parameters (cf. Kowalewski, this volume). In both the indigenous Southwest and prehispanic Mesoamerica, relatively large alluvial basins (like the Phoenix Basin of southern Arizona or the Valley of Mexico) were not core regions of political or demographic power throughout the entire sequence.

By comparing the North American Southwest and Mesoamerica, we face another difficult issue, since some researchers combine the two areas into a single "world" or world-system. Although we certainly recognize important prehispanic interaction between these two macroregions (such as the movement of turquoise, copper bells, and macaws), we suggest that these two prehispanic worlds are profitably compared and contrasted nonetheless. In a sense, this question lies within the critical domain of boundaries and boundedness that is faced by those of us who wish to investigate macroregions. As reviewed by Chase-Dunn and Hall (1991) in the introductory section of their volume, *Core/Periphery Relations in Precapitalist Worlds* (see also their chapter in this volume), the challenges are both to discriminate the components of macroregions, as well as to define the temporally specific parameters of macroregional systems.

Geographers use both formal and nodal (or interactive) properties to identify complex regions (e.g., Haggett 1966:241-253), and these same basic criteria seem applicable to macroregional investigation (but see Upham 1992). In contrast, archaeologists have tended to rely on qualitative or formal properties in identifying geographic units. These would include descriptive environmental variables or general impressions of material cultural distributions. Although such considerations may be important for the examination of transportation technologies or certain other issues, the investigation of macroregional articulations requires increased focus on nodal or interactive properties, that is, the nature (and potentially the quantification) of the flows within and between regions (for a more contemporary example, see Johnson 1980:Fig. 5).

Whether formal or nodal criteria are applied, it is our (rather impressionistic) view that Mesoamerica and the American Southwest are best considered as separate (yet inter-connected) macroregions, although the diachronic comparison of the volume of internal versus external flows (and what that conveys about boundaries) is a research problem for future investigation. Here it is worth remembering that Jane Schneider (1977) and Janet Abu-Lughod (1989) have noted significant flows between the separate pre-capitalist macroregions of the Old World, although (as with Mesoamerica and the Southwest) the internal linkages were presumably far more intense than those that cross macroregions. In brief, we advocate and employ a flexible, nested, multi-scale approach to study past human behaviors, rather than one that identifies a single unit of analysis or selects a static set of analytical categories.

Comparision of Mesoamerica and the American Southwest

A full or even synthetic comparison of the pre-Columbian American Southwest with pre-Columbian Mesoamerica is beyond the scope of this paper. Instead, we have confined our analysis to issues and hypotheses raised by Philip Kohl (1989), Christopher Chase-Dunn and Thomas Hall (Chase-Dunn and Hall 1991; Chase-Dunn 1992) and others (e.g., Schortman and Urban 1987; Edens 1992) in prior comparative discussions of ancient macroregions.

Neither Mesoamerica nor the Southwest was ever politically consolidated by a single core state or empire. No polity in either area ever solidified a multi-nodal, macroregional structure to form an all-encompassing world empire as happened in Egypt, China, and for relatively brief episodes, in Mesopotamia. Throughout the pre-Columbian era, both of these New World macroregions were multicentric, with specific cores as defined by demographic nucleation, architectural elaboration, and the apparent concentration of political and military power, which varied in importance over time (albeit to different degrees). Having said this, however, we emphasize that during some periods of the pre-Columbian era in both areas, polities emerged that exercised degrees of influence and control over substantial regions.

In a recent paper, also prepared for *Review*, Blanton, Kowalewski, and Feinman (in 1992; see also Blanton and Feinman 1984) discuss cycling in the Mesoamerican political economy. During certain eras, such as the Middle Horizon (ca. A.D. 300-700), large core polities (like Teotihuacan) exerted considerable influence (both direct and indirect) over interregional exchange and boundaries in sections of the Mesoamerican "world." These core-dominated episodes were marked by a dichotomization between core and peripheral areas, and by powerful political/urban institutions, agricultural intensification in the immediate vicinity of the cores, and the relative codification of religious iconography. Alternatively, other eras were marked by less obvious distinctions between core and peripheral areas. At these times, strategies of agricultural intensification and the use of labor in construction were less differentiated over space. Furthermore, dynamic transitions in core/periphery status occurred, and there was greater emphasis on the long-distance movement of portable wealth.

Waxing and waning in the nature and directionality of macroregional connections also was highly characteristic of the pre-Columbian Southwest. The spread of the Chacoan system in the northern Southwest following A.D. 900 (Judge and Schelberg 1984; Neitzel 1989; Crown and Judge 1991) or the emergence of large population centers circa A.D. 1285 across the Colorado Plateaus and Mogollon Rim country (Upham 1982; Upham and Reed 1989; Adams 1991) represent large-scale developments for the Southwest. The extent of the demographic, economic, or power differentials between core and peripheral areas, however, never approached that seen during the core-dominated eras in Mesoamerica. While this is neither a new or surprising observation, it does constitute a key distinction between these macroregions.

From our perspective, prestige goods or preciosities had an important role in the articulation of both the Southwest and Mesoamerica. As we (Upham 1982, 1986; Feinman and Nicholas 1991) and others (Friedman and Rowlands 1977; Schneider 1977; Blanton and Feinman 1984; McGuire 1986; Brumfiel 1987) have discussed elsewhere, these goods are not epiphenomenal, but rather they are linked to social reproduction and energy flows through various mechanisms, most basically (although not solely) through the establishment and maintenance of leader-follower, patron-client relations (cf. Kowalewski, this volume). Thus, the recognition that inter-polity relations may have significant ramifications for local distributions of power and produce does not imply a restricted focus on basic or utilitarian commodities (cf. Edens 1992).

Peter Peregrine (1991) has drawn a useful distinction between exotics and other preciosities that acquire relatively little added labor (such as an unmodified shell, an animal tooth, or an exotic cobble) and other items that do require massive and skilled craftwork to finish (such as woven cloth or a finished stone bowl). Whereas exchange of the former goods presents little necessity or potential for marked labor differentiation over space, the latter "labor-value-added" goods could enhance such divisions (and so interdependency), if exchanged in sufficient volume. Although systematic comparative research has not been undertaken, it is our perception that value-added preciosities (such as formed stone and shell beads, stone bowls, or metalwork) had a comparatively greater role in Mesoamerica (at least during certain times) than in the Southwest. Yet, this difference is certainly of degree rather than kind, with such labor intensive preciosities more prevalent later (rather than earlier) in the pre-Columbian Southwest.

This discussion of macroregional similarities already has touched on several key differences. Mesoamerica, relative to the Southwest, was the focus of more concentrated cores, more hierarchical and stratified social systems, greater interdependencies, and more apparent spatial divisions of labor. In support of a hypothesis advanced by Hall and Chase-Dunn (this volume), these differences seem to be related to the greater continuity and longevity of Mesoamerican cores as opposed to those of the Southwest (both at the scale of single core settlements and core regions) (Hantman 1983). While more elaborate social stratification, greater regional interdependency, and more marked labor divisions over space may engender core stability, the relative longevity of highland Mesoamerican cores suggests reconsideration of Friedman and Rowlands' (1977) assertion that the economic importance of prestige goods and preciosities necessarily entails core instability. Modification of their argument would seem to require both an examination of the nature of the specific articulations between the circulation of preciosities, labor recruitment and production strategies, and an evaluation, on the lines of Peregrine (1991), as to the specific preciosities involved and how their manufacture affects interdependency and labor divisions over space. Here, it also would be important to dissect the specific and diverse roles that portable wealth or precious goods may have in different political economies (D'Altroy and Earle 1985; Blanton et al. in press).

Based on ethnohistoric and archaeological grounds, there seems to be little doubt that pre-Columbian-Mesoamerican political units tended to be larger in spatial and demographic size than those in the Southwest. Despite obvious difficulties concerning the scale of pre-Columbian polities, there is little solid evidence for political consolidations in the Southwest at the scale of the Aztec tributary domain or the areas under the hegemony of much earlier highland Mesoamerican polities centered at Teotihuacan or Monte Albán. At the same time, archaeological data indicate widespread adoption of ceramic design styles after A.D. 700 and striking similarities in other categories of material culture for specific groups throughout the Southwest and beyond (Upham 1994). Such data suggest that intergroup contact and interaction was structured and intense, yet little agreement exists about the exact nature of the political ties that bound Southwestern groups together. During the historic period, following massive population shifts and depopulation in the desert west region, widespread connectivity persisted between groups, but these interactive ties never led to more than relatively small-scale, traditional political alliances (Jorgensen 1980).

Despite the generally larger size of political units in Mesoamerica, most historical linguistic analyses have recognized two to three times as many language families in Mesoamerica as compared to the Greater Southwest (Figures 6.1 and 6.2; see illustrations in Coe, Snow, and Benson 1986:44-45, 86-87). In addition, published distributions of material cultural complexes (for want of a better term) traditionally identify at least twice the number of such divisions for pre-contact Mesoamerica (e.g., Willey, Ekholm, and Millon 1964:461) as for the Southwest (Cordell 1984:15) (Figures 6.3 and 6.4). Yet the spatial extent of these two macroregions was roughly comparable (Figure 6.5). Each measures slightly more than one million square kilometers. In fact, according to the boundaries drawn in the sources cited above, the Southwest macroregion may have been slightly larger.

As is evident from a comparison of the accompanying figures, there is somewhat less consensus on the limits of the greater Southwest than Mesoamerica (see Upham 1994; Kowalewski, this volume). We recognize that the borders of each macroregion were not stable nor closed through time (this may account for some of the variability in presentation). However, no matter which specific macroregional boundaries are accepted, the basic comparative findings would stand. Of course, more precise measurement would require much greater attention to the boundary issues raised in the first section of this paper.

Given the rough comparability in overall macroregional extent and the differences in polity size, culture historians may find it perplexing that spatially defined material cultural and linguistic variability was considerably greater in Mesoamerica than the Southwest. Many culture historians presume the isomorphism of political boundaries with ethnic units that are defined by relative homogeneity in language and material culture. Therefore, according to this perspective, smaller polity size and weaker macroregional interactions in the ancient Southwest should translate into greater cultural and linguistic diversity (as compared to more consolidated political landscape in Mesoamerica).

Certainly, the aforementioned counter-intuitive findings concerning the relative degrees of cultural variation and diversity in the ancient Southwest and Mesoamerica give little support to the now-fading notion of the small isolated Southwestern pueblo or the concept of the autonomous tribe in general. In addition, where analyses have been undertaken, the material attributes associated with specific Southwestern traditions and complexes have been shown to have distributions that are not neatly coterminous (Adams 1991; Crown 1991, 1994; Judge 1991). As Steve Plog (1980a, 1980b, 1989) and others (e.g., Hantman 1983; LeBlanc 1986; McGuire, this volume) previously have suggested, these results imply that Southwestern networks (through at least most of the prehistoric period) tended to be rather open, far-ranging, fluid, and overlapping. Relative to Mesoamerica, community and regional boundaries must have been weak and porous compared to the linkages that interconnected those social segments. Such findings do not preclude the foundation of political hierarchies and confederations in the Southwest (e.g. Spielmann 1994). But, they suggest that these complex, vertically organized entities were shorter-lived and less able to establish, manipulate, and limit flows across boundaries than was the case for hierarchical formations in Mesoamerica. Here it is worth noting that an episode (A.D. 1000-1150) marked by expanding political formations in the ancient American Southwest actually coincided with increasing ceramic heterogeneity across this macroregion (Cordell and Gumerman 1989:10).

To paraphrase Eric Wolf (1982:6-7), many theorists (even some with macroregional concerns) implicitly

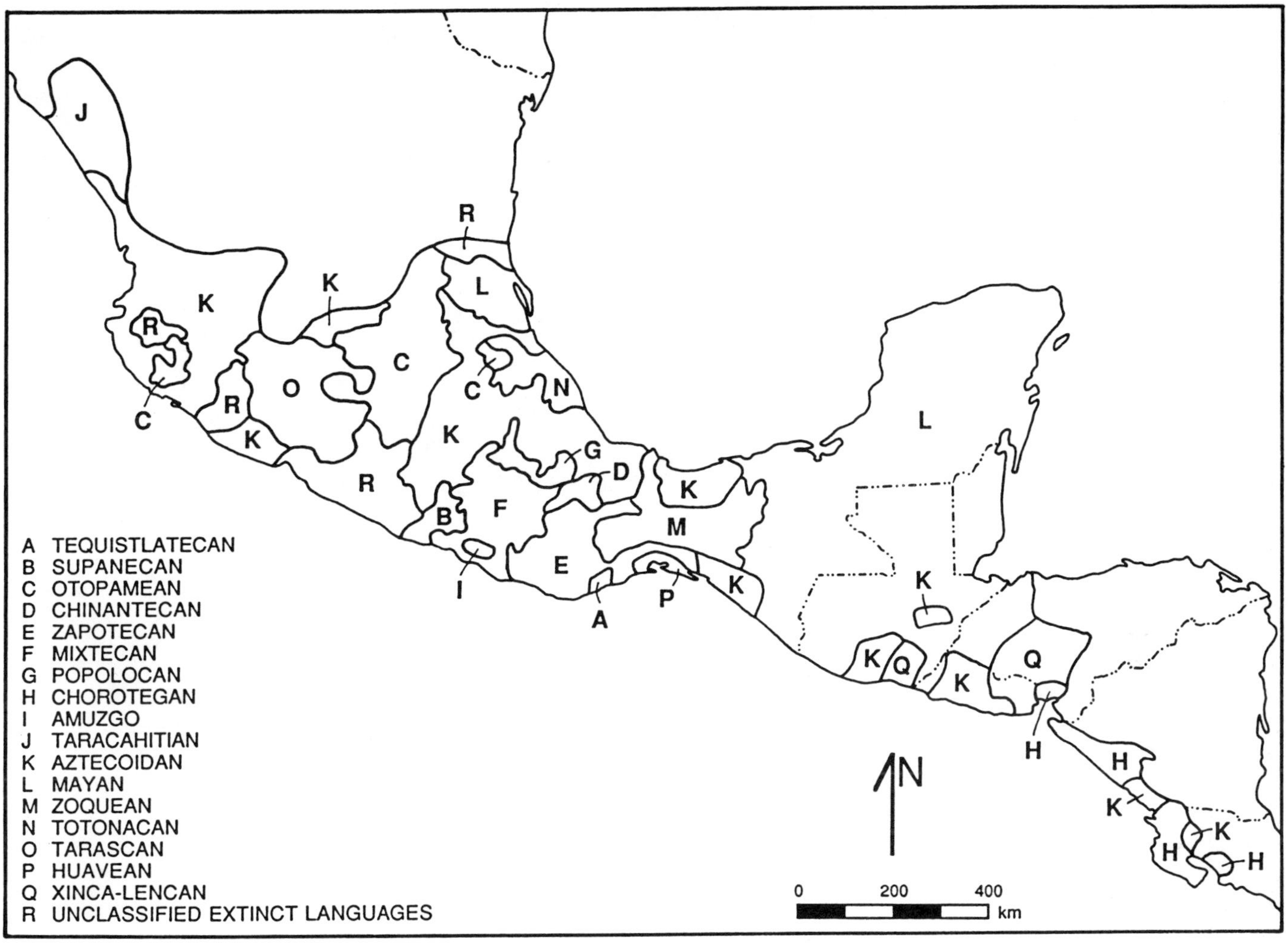

Figure 6.1. Mesoamerican language families (adapted and simplified from Snow, Coe, and Benson 1986:86-87).

envision small non-state societies as bounded "billiard balls" that are politically, socially, and economically discrete and autonomous (also see McGuire, this volume). According to these theorists, these geographically bounded "balls" are then "cued up" in the formation of more hierarchical entities, such as states. But, is it reasonable to consider these less stratified, less hierarchical formations as discrete and bounded? In other words, are complex formations, like states, made by breaking down barriers and binding together what were small, independent polities, or are state formation and expansion actually processes that may make and solidify boundaries on landscapes where social divisions previously were broadly spaced, fluid, or weakly defined due to a diverse array of overlapping interconnections?

For Mesoamerica, we suggest (see Kowalewski et al. 1983) that states, particularly centralized, primate states with large political capitals, actually helped to make and solidify social and cultural barriers. Linguistically and material culturally, the Maya region (Figures 6.1 and 6.3), which tended to be a less centralized and politically consolidated segment of Mesoamerica, is more homogeneous in terms of material culture and language than highland Mesoamerica. Alternatively, the highlands, where the macroregion's largest, most centralized, and economically specialized polities were located, are marked by greater artifactual and linguistic diversity. Since the Southwest is more similar environmentally to the semi-arid Mesoamerican highlands than to the eastern Maya lowlands, this relationship would not seem to be geographically or environmentally determined in some simple fashion. The aforementioned comparative homogeneity of the Maya lowlands, a region now recognized to have been densely inhabited at least during some phases of its pre-contact history (Culbert and Rice 1990), also implies that demography alone cannot account for the frequency or specific distribution of social boundaries, although it is a factor that requires further consideration (Blau 1970, 1977:134).

We suspect that, during the politically unifying reign of highland Mesoamerican polities, the crystallization of social and cultural boundaries and barriers actually

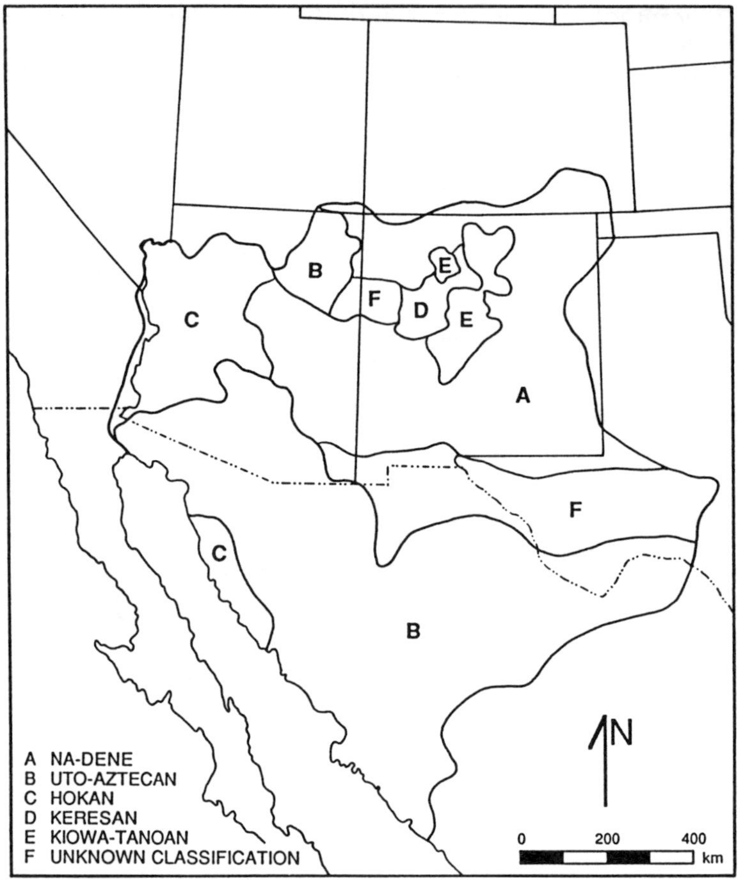

Figure 6.2. Southwestern language families (adapted from Snow, Coe, and Benson 1986:44-45).

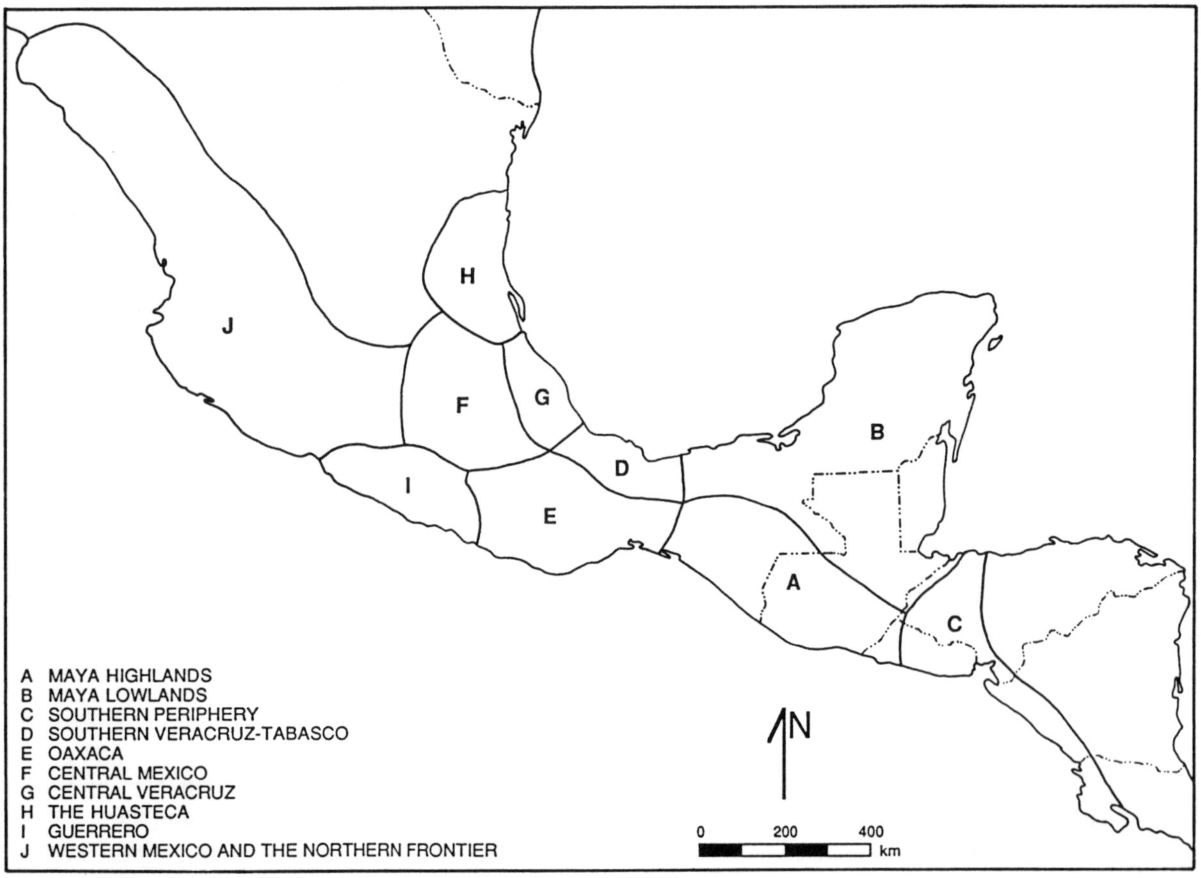

Figure 6.3. Mesoamerican cultural complexes (adapted from Willey, Ekholm, and Millon 1964:461).

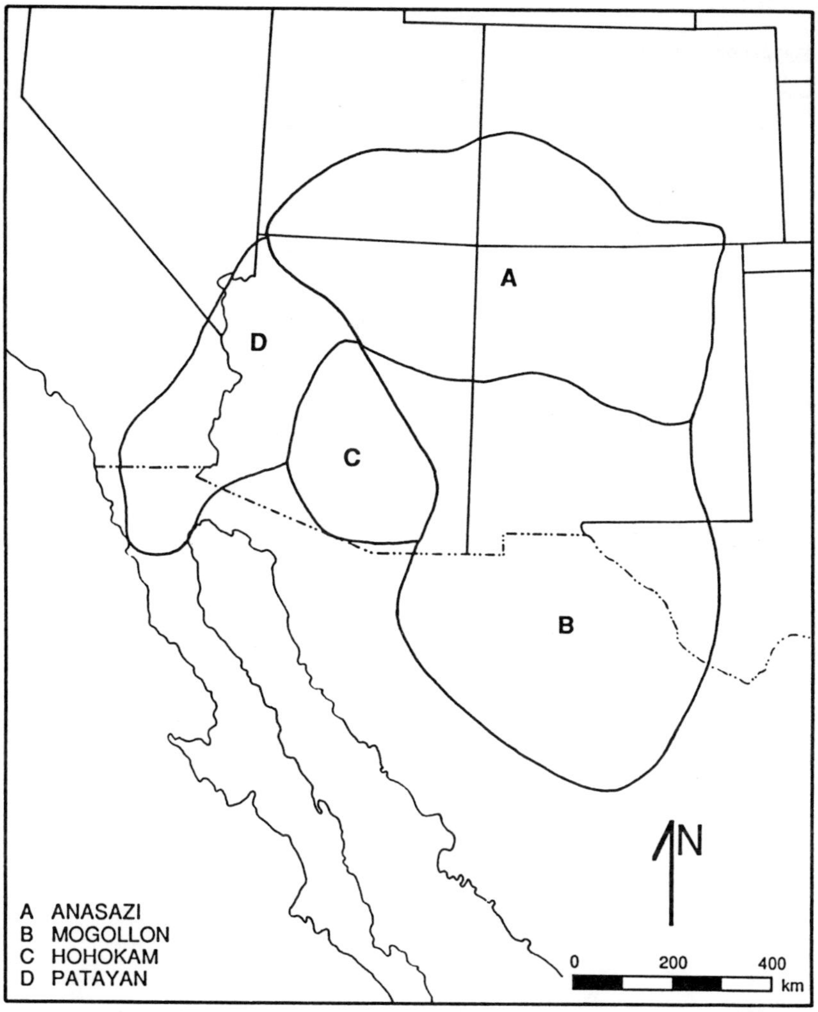

Figure 6.4. Southwestern cultural complexes (adapted from Cordell 1984:15).

was fostered in several ways. These might have included the control and channeling of interregional flows toward the center (at the expense of horizontal linkages) (e.g. Brumfiel 1980), the manipulation of important boundary relations and exchanges in proportionally fewer hands (limiting cross-regional household-to-household flows) (Feinman 1991), the establishment of economic interdependencies and so spatial divisions of labor (and so the creation of other differences that such economic distinctions entail—-a process that Chase-Dunn and Hall (1991) refer to as "backwash"), and the formation and demarcation of interest groups and culturally defined entities under the broad political umbrella formed by hierarchical polities (e.g., Hall 1983).

In comparable fashion, Yoffee (1988:64) has suggested that, through several episodes of early Mesopotamian empire formation, ethnic and linguistic diversity became more heterogeneous, not less so. He further argues that "the development of a political ideology of Mesopotamian unity was in contradiction to the growing ethnic heterogeneity in the land." Among other things, these arguments imply that it would behoove us to go beyond Willey's (1991) distinction between "horizons" and "regional stylistic diversity," and do a better job at distinguishing between artifactual patterning that signifies broad household-to-household relations from that marking elite communication or political consolidation.

Conclusion

In sum, this comparative effort has led us to a number of suggestions concerning macroregional approaches and contemporary debates. We strongly advocate investigation of macroregional relations and processes, but such broad-scale analyses must be undertaken with investigations at the regional and various local scales. In other words, debates over 'the' appropriate unit of analysis or arguments over the 'proper' unit of selection seem somewhat misguided (as Lewontin [1970] argued several decades ago for biological evolution).

We question whether social systems characterized by broad-scale, relatively open networks are even properly

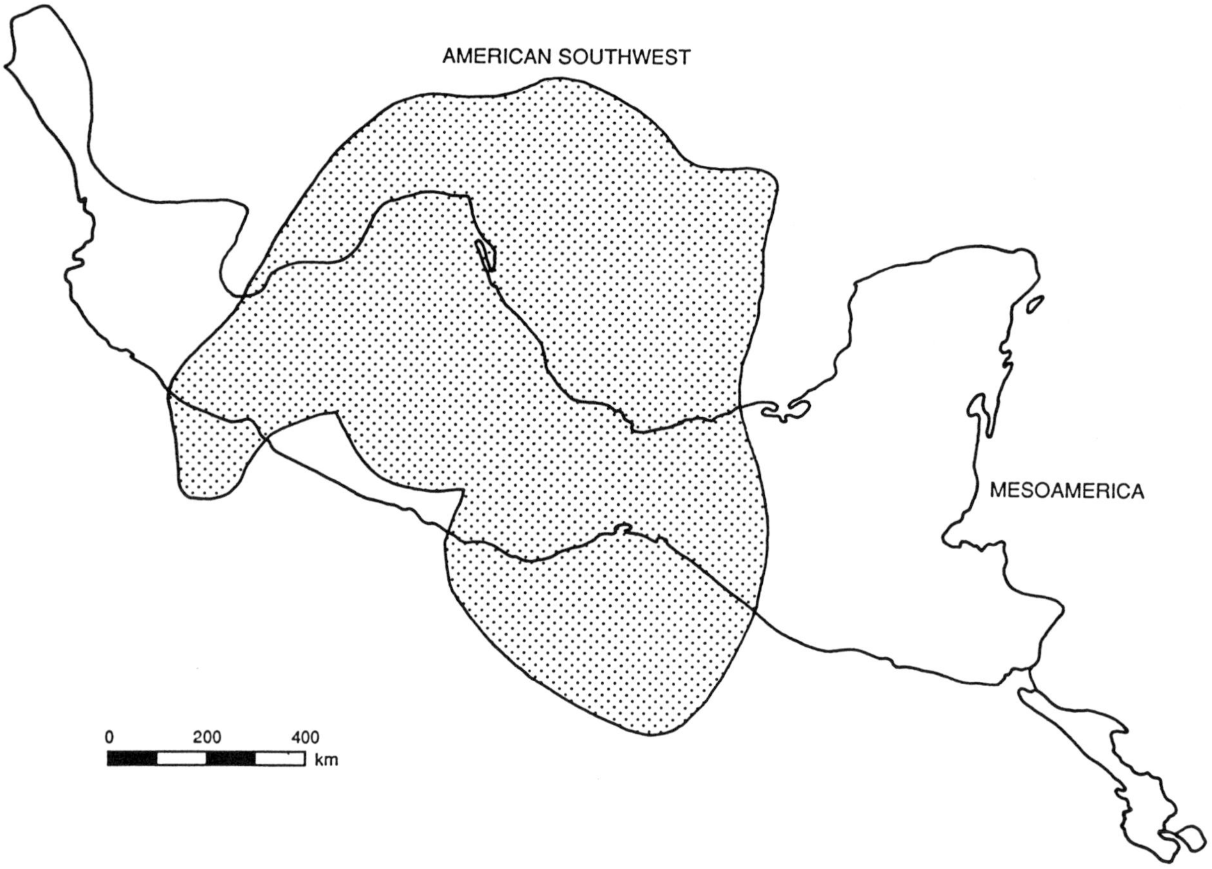

Figure 6.5. Comparison of the areal extent of Mesoamerica and the American Southwest.

conceptualized as a multitude of bounded, discrete societies, cultures (Shennan 1978), or "tribes" (Upham, Crown, and Plog 1994). Might not these characterizations be a less than useful residue from the type casting of the early contact period or the ethnographic present (as several geographers [e.g., Murphy 1991], as well as Timothy Taylor [1992] in his *Scientific American* article on the Gundestrup cauldron, have proposed)?

Although we concur with many recent studies that impart significant economic and ideological implications to the transfer of preciosities, we have proposed parameters for the examination of significant diversity in these systems that are sometimes simply lumped under a single monicker, such as "prestige-good economies." For example, in the later (Puebloan) Southwest, precious exotics (like textiles) may have been associated with more corporate forms of ritual power rather than the accumulation of great personal wealth (e.g. Saitta 1994; Spielmann 1994). While wealth exchanges, individual accumulation, and elaborate personal ornamentation were typical for Classic Maya lords and the rulers of the Mesoamerican epiclasssic period (A.D. 800-1100), it seems to be less typical of Classic period Teotihuacan (Blanton, Kowalewski, Feinman 1992; Blanton et al. in press). Yet, long distance exchange in obsidian and other goods certainly was important in the Teotihuacan world. On-going research to establish the nature and diversity of the links between such exchanges and various systems of production, reproduction, and power should continue.

Finally, if greater concern with broad-scale phenomena is truly to pay off theoretically for archaeology (and the historical human sciences, in general), then we should keep tuned to the broad historical and cross-cultural questions laid out in the works of Wallerstein (1974), Wolf (1982), Schneider (1977), and others. That is, archaeologists must continue to build frameworks for the comparative study of long-term histories, while consciously avoiding a knee-jerk return either to the "shreds and patches" trait listing or the "milk-toast" diffusionism associated with past archaeological frameworks. A modified macroregional approach that reopens questions about the nature and causes of social boundaries, while holistically examining the different economic, political, and ideological strategies and behaviors that bridged them would seem to offer a potentially promising approach.

References

Abu-Lughod, Janet L.
1989 *Before European Hegemony: The World System A.D. 1250-1350.* Oxford University Press, New York.
Adams, E. Charles
1991 *The Origin and Development of the Pueblo Katsina Cult.* University of Arizona Press, Tucson.
Blanton, Richard E., and Gary M. Feinman
1984 The Mesoamerican World-System. *American Anthropologist* 86:673-682.
Blanton, Richard E., Gary M. Feinman, Stephen A. Kowalewski, and Peter N. Peregrine
in press A Dual-Processual Theory for the Evolution of Mesoamerican Civilization. *Current Anthropology* 37(1).
Blanton, Richard E., Stephen A. Kowalewski, and Gary M. Feinman
1992 The Mesoamerican World-System. *Review* 15 (3):419-426.
Blau, Peter M.
1970 A Formal Theory of Differentiation in Organizations. *American Sociological Review* 35:201-218.
1977 *Inequality and Heterogeneity: A Primitive Theory of Social Structure.* The Free Press, New York.
Braudel, Fernand
1972 *The Mediterranean and the Mediterranean World in the Age of Phillip II,* 2 vols. Harper and Row, New York.
Brumfiel, Elizabeth M.
1980 Specialization, Market Exchange, and the Aztec State. *Current Anthropology* 21:459-478.
1987 Elite and Utilitarian Crafts in the Aztec State. In *Specialization, Exchange, and Complex Societies,* edited by E. M. Brumfiel and T. K. Earle, pp. 102-118. Cambridge University Press, Cambridge.
Chase-Dunn, Christopher
1992 The Comparative Study of World-Systems. *Review* 15 (3):313-333.
Chase-Dunn, Christopher, and Thomas D. Hall
1991 Conceptualizing Core-Periphery Hierarchies for Comparative Study. In *Core/Periphery Relations in Precapitalist Worlds,* edited by C. Chase-Dunn and T. D. Hall, pp. 5-44. Westview Press, Boulder, CO.
Coe, Michael, Dean Snow, and Elizabeth Benson
1986 *Atlas of Ancient America.* Facts on File, New York.
Collins, Randall
1992 The Geo-Political and Economic World-Systems of Kinship-Based and Agrarian-Coercive Societies. *Review* 15 (3):373-388.
Cordell, Linda S.
1984 *Prehistory of the Southwest.* Academic Press, New York.
Cordell, Linda S., and George J. Gumerman
1989 Cultural Interaction in the Prehistoric Southwest. In *Dynamics of Southwestern Prehistory,* edited by L. S. Cordell and G. J. Gumerman, pp. 1-17. Smithsonian Institution Press, Washington, DC.
Crown, Patricia L.
1991 The Role of Exchange and Interaction in Salt-Gila Basin Hohokam Prehistory. In *Exploring the Hohokam: Prehistoric Desert Peoples of the American Southwest,* edited by G. J. Gumerman, pp. 383-415. University of New Mexico Press, Albuquerque.
1994 *Ceramics and Ideology: Salado Polychrome Pottery.* University of New Mexico Press, Albuquerque.
Crown, Patricia L., and W. James Judge
1991 *Chaco and Hohokam: Prehistoric Regional Systems in the American Southwest.* School of American Research Press, Santa Fe.

Culbert, T. Patrick, and Don S. Rice
1990 *Pre-Columbian Population History in the Maya Lowlands.* University of New Mexico Press, Albuquerque.
D'Altroy, Terrance N., and Timothy K. Earle
1985 Staple Finance, Wealth Finance, and Storage in the Inka Political Economy. *Current Anthropology* 26:187-207.
Diehl, Richard A., and Janet Catherine Berlo
1989 *Mesoamerica after the Decline of Teotihuacan A.D. 700-900.* Dumbarton Oaks Research Library and Collection, Washington, DC.
Edens, Christopher
1992 Dynamics of Trade in the Ancient Mesopotamian "World System." *American Anthropologist* 94:118-139.
Feinman, Gary
1991 Demography, Surplus, and Inequality in Highland Mesoamerica. In *Chiefdoms: Power, Economy, and Ideology*, edited by T. K. Earle, pp. 229-262. Cambridge University Press, Cambridge.
Feinman, Gary M., and Linda M. Nicholas
1991 New Perspectives on Prehispanic Highland Mesoamerica: A Macroregional Approach. *Comparative Civilizations Review* 24:13-33.
Friedman, Jonathan, and Michael Rowlands
1977 Notes Towards an Epigenetic Model of the Evolution of 'Civilization.' In *The Evolution of Social Systems*, edited by J. Friedman and M. J. Rowlands, pp. 201-278. Duckworth, London.
Haggett, Peter
1966 *Locational Analysis in Human Geography.* St. Martin's Press, New York.
Hall, Thomas D.
1983 Peripheries, Regions of Refuge, and Non-State Societies: Toward a Theory of Reactive Social Change. *Social Science Quarterly* 64:582-597.
Hantman, Jeffrey L.
1983 *Social Networks and Stylistic Distributions in the Prehistoric Plateau Southwest.* Ph.D. dissertation, Arizona State University, Tempe.
Johnson, Gregory A.
1980 Rank-Size Convexity and System Integration: A View from Archaeology. *Economic Geography* 56:234-247.
Jorgensen, Joseph G.
1980 *Western Indians.* W.H. Freeman and Company, San Franscisco.
Judge, W. James
1991 Chaco: Current Views of Prehistory and the Regional System. In *Chaco and Hohokam: Prehistoric Regional Systems in the American Southwest*, edited by P. L. Crown and W. J. Judge, pp. 11-30. School of American Research Press, Santa Fe.
Judge, W. James, and John D. Schelberg
1984 *Recent Research on Chaco Prehistory.* Reports of the Chaco Center, Number 8. Division of Cultural Research, National Parks Service, Albuquerque.
Kohl, Philip L.
1989 The Use and Abuse of World-Systems Theory: The Case of the "Pristine" West Asian State. In *Archaeological Thought in America*, edited by C. C. Lamberg-Karlovsky, pp. 218-240. Cambridge University Press, Cambridge.
Kowalewski, Stephen, Richard Blanton, Gary Feinman, and Laura Finsten
1983 Boundaries, Scale, and Internal Organization. *Journal of Anthropological Archaeology* 2:32-56.
LeBlanc, Steven A.
1986 Aspects of Southwestern Prehistory: A.D. 900-1400. In *Ripples in the Chichimec Sea*, edited by F. J. Mathien and R. H. McGuire, pp. 105-134. Southern Illinois University Press, Carbondale.

Lewontin, R. C.
1970 The Units of Selection. *Annual Review of Ecology and Systematics* 1:1-18.
McGuire, Randall H.
1986 Economies and Modes of Production in the Prehistoric Southwestern Periphery. In *Ripples in the Chichimec Sea*, edited by F. J. Mathien and R. H. McGuire, pp. 243-269. Southern Illinois University Press, Carbondale.
Murphy, Alexander B.
1991 Regions as Social Sonstructs: The Gap between Theory and Practice. *Progress in Human Geography* 15:22-35.
Neitzel, Jill
1989 The Chacoan Regional System: Interpreting the Evidence for Sociopolitical Complexity. In *The Sociopolitical Structure of Prehistoric Southwestern Societies*, edited by S. Upham, K. G. Lightfoot, and R. A. Jewett, pp. 509-556. Westview Press, Boulder, CO.
Peregrine, Peter
1991 Some Political Aspects of Craft Specialization. *World Archaeology* 23:1-11.
Plog, Stephen
1980a *Stylistic Variation in Prehistoric Ceramics: Design Analysis in the American Southwest.* Cambridge University Press, Cambridge.
1980b Village Autonomy in the American Southwest: An Evaluation of the Evidence. In *Models and Methods in Regional Exchange*, edited by R. E. Fry, pp. 135-146. SAA Papers No. 1, Society for American Archaeology, Washington, DC.
1989 Ritual, Exchange, and the Development of Regional Systems. In *The Architecture of Social Integration in Prehistoric Pueblos*, edited by W. D. Lipe and M. Hegmon, pp. 143-154. Occasional Papers No. 1. Crow Canyon Archaeological Center, Cortez, CO.
Saitta, Dean J.
1994 Class and Community in the Prehistoric Southwest. In *The Ancient Southwestern Community: Models and Methods for the Study of Prehistoric Social Organization*, edited by W. H. Wills and R. D. Leonard, pp. 25-43. University of New Mexico Press, Albuquerque.
Schneider, Jane
1977 Was There a Pre-Capitalist World-System? *Peasant Studies* 6:20-29.
Schortman, Edward M., and Patricia A. Urban
1987 Modeling Interregional Interaction in Prehistory. *Advances in Archaeological Method and Theory*, Vol. 11, edited by M.B. Schiffer, pp. 37-95. Academic Press, San Diego.
Shennan, Stephen J.
1978 Archaeological Cultures: An Empirical Investigation. In *The Spatial Organization of Culture*, edited by I. Hodder, pp. 113-139. University of Pittsburgh Press, Pittsburgh.
Spielmann, Katherine A.
1994 Clustered Confederacies: Socio-Political Organization in the Protohistoric Rio Grande. In *The Ancient Southwestern Community: Models and Methods for the Study of Prehistoric Social Organization*, edited by W. H. Wills and R. D. Leonard, pp. 45-54. University of New Mexico Press, Albuquerque.
Taylor, Timothy
1992 The Gundestrup Cauldron. *Scientific American* March:84-89.
Upham, Steadman
1982 *Polities and Power: An Economic and Political History of the Western Pueblo.* Academic Press, New York.
1986 Imperialists, Isolationists, World-Systems, and Political Realities: Perspectives on Mesoamerican-Southwestern Interaction. In *Ripples in the Chichimec Sea*, edited by F. J. Mathien and R. H. McGuire, pp. 205-219. Southern Illinois University Press, Carbondale.
1992 Interaction and Isolation: The Empty Spaces in Pan-Regional Political and Economic Systems. In *Resources, Power, and Interregional Interaction*, edited by E. M. Schortman and P. A. Urban, pp. 139-156. Plenum Press, New York.

1994 Nomads of the Desert West: A Shifting Continuum in Prehistory. *Journal of World Prehistory* 8 (2):113-168.

Upham, Steadman, Patricia Crown, and Stephen Plog
1994 Alliance Formation and Cultural Identity in the American Southwest. In *Themes in Southwestern Prehistory: Grand Patterns and Local Variations in Culture Change*, edited by G. J. Gumerman and L. S. Cordell, pp. 183-210. School of American Research Press, Santa Fe.

Upham, Steadman, Gary M. Feinman, and Linda M. Nicholas
1992 New Perspectives on the Southwest and Highland Mesoamerica: A Macroregional Approach. *Review* 15 (3):427-451.

Upham, Steadman, and Lori Stephens Reed
1989 Regional Systems in the Central and Northern Southwest: Demography, Economy, and Sociopolitics Preceding Contact. In *Columbian Consequences: Archaeological and Historical Perspectives on the Spanish Borderlands West*, edited by D. H. Thomas, pp. 57-76. Smithsonian Institution Press, Washington, DC.

Wallerstein, Immanuel
1974 *The Modern World-System I.* Academic Press, New York.

Willey, Gordon R.
1991 Horizontal Integration and Regional Diversity: An Alternating Process in the Rise of Civilizations. *American Antiquity* 56:197-215.

Willey, Gordon R., Gordon F. Ekholm, and Ren_ F. Millon
1964 The Patterns of Farming Life and Civilization. In *Natural Environment and Early Cultures*, edited by R. C. West, pp. 446-498. *Handbook of Middle American Indians*, Vol. 1. University of Texas Press, Austin.

Wolf, Eric R.
1982 *Europe and the People Without History.* University of California Press, Berkeley.

Yoffe, Norman
1988 The Collapse of Ancient Mesopotamian States and Civilization. In *The Collapse of Ancient States and Civilizations*, edited by N. Yoffee and G. L. Cowgill, pp. 44-68. University of Arizona Press, Tucson.

Chapter 7

Periphery and Frontier in Southern Mexico: The Mixtec Sierra in Highland Oaxaca

Laura Finsten
McMaster University

Archaeological and other studies of ancient complex social systems have tended to focus on their seemingly "more complex" central parts, particularly large urban centers and their immediate hinterlands or sustaining areas, although there are some notable exceptions (e.g. Feinman and Nicholas 1990, 1992). This is no less true of many analyses adopting a world-system perspective where, despite the explicit emphasis given multisocietal units of analysis, little effort has been made to collect and analyze primary data from the less flamboyant of the societies making up the macroregional mix, or to the full range of the socioeconomic spectrum within the constituent societies. Truly multiregional approaches, i.e. those that employ regional scale data from different societies constituent parts of macroregions, are even more rare although the need for such studies has long been noted (Wright 1986). As a result, our ability to distinguish exogenous from endogenous processes, to isolate and study the emergent properties of macroregions and, hence, to develop general theory about world-systems is hampered.

Hall and Chase-Dunn (this volume, also Chase-Dunn and Hall 1993:863) identify two aspects of core/periphery relations as key to the development of world-systems theory: core/periphery differentiation and core/periphery hierarchy. How variable are multisocietal systems in the degrees of differentiation among their constituent societies in complexity and population density? Is domination (economic, political, and/or ideological) among the societies of world-systems a universal characteristic and played out in the same way in all multisocietal systems? World-system theorists generally have assumed that cores are more complex and populous than peripheries, and that domination necessarily flows from core to periphery, using the modern world-system as their model (Wallerstein 1974). A number of recent studies (summarized in Chase-Dunn and Hall 1993) have suggested that core/periphery relations are more variable than Wallerstein's classic formulation assumed. Variation in the nature of and linkages between intersocietal differentiation and core/periphery domination require further investigation (Chase-Dunn and Hall 1993:864).

In the specific arena of understanding the long-term development of ancient complex societies, the roles peripheries have played in change in cores, and vice-versa, have long been neglected. Were peripheries largely passive and dependent, while cores alone were the active centers of change? Is structural change in one dependent upon structural change in the other, and how do the structures of peripheries and cores differ?

Are demographic processes in cores and peripheries fundamentally different, and are they interconnected in a systematic way? How dynamic are the boundaries between core and peripheral societies within world-systems?

This paper represents a modest effort to begin answering some of these questions. Its broad goal is to examine core/periphery relations diachronically, over several millennia, in adjacent regions of pre-Columbian Mesoamerica. As is described in greater detail below, the Mixtec Sierra, the region forming the principle focus of this paper, is a marginal mountainous periphery between two of Mesoamerica's "nuclear zones": the Valley of Oaxaca and the Mixteca Alta. One specific objective is to examine the long-term, internal dynamic of a marginal area which was, at least during some periods, the periphery of a small-scale macroregional or world-system. How did this marginal region's structure change over the course of its settlement history, and how much of this change is the result of linkages with either or both adjacent regions? Are changes in regional complexity related to ties with a macroregional core such as the Valley of Oaxaca? Were the relationships between the Mixtec Sierra and the adjacent nuclear zones typically characterized by dominance emanating from core to periphery? A second objective is specifically to explore change in the nature of the Mixtec Sierra's role as a frontier and boundary zone. How was interregional interaction between the Mixtec Sierra and its neighbors related to various boundary processes within this mountainous marginal zone?

The Peñoles Project Area

The Peñoles Project Area consists of 1,000 square kilometers of rugged mountains in the Mixtec Sierra of the southern Mexican highlands, between the Valley of Oaxaca and the smaller valleys of the Mixteca Alta, including the Nochixtlán Valley (Figure 7.1).[1] It is bounded to the north by the continental divide and the Pan-American Highway and to the south by the modern road to San Antonio Huitepec from Zaachila. Its eastern boundary adjoins the Valley of Oaxaca Settlement Pattern Project survey area, an area of 2,150 square kilometers (Kowalewski et al. 1989). To the northwest, the study area abuts against the Nochixtlán Valley survey area (Spores 1972); south of this, parts of the Mixtec Sierra survey area boundary approach to within about one kilometer Byland and Pohl's Jaltepec study area (Byland and Pohl 1987; Pohl and Byland 1994). The modern *municipio* of Santa María Peñoles lies near the geographic center of the project area.

The project area was chosen in part because it was a frontier and boundary zone during much of the pre-Columbian era. Within this part of the Mixtec Sierra are major communication routes, past and present, linking the Valley of Oaxaca to the Mixteca Alta and beyond to the central plateau. It contains the contact zone where the Zapotec and Mixtec languages and cultures met during most pre-Columbian periods, as did the two valleys' distinctive ceramic styles. The frontiers and boundaries of large regional states based in the Valley of Oaxaca and the Mixteca Alta were established in the Mixtec Sierra.

The second salient characteristic of the study area is its ecological marginality compared to the broad, more populous highland valleys that border it. Virtually the entire Peñoles Project Area consists of steep-sided mountains and sharply incised, very narrow river valleys. The highest elevations approach 3,000 meters above sea level, and most of the survey area lies between 2,300-2,800 meters above sea level. Compared to the much richer adjacent Nochixtlán and Oaxaca valleys, the Peñoles area clearly is agriculturally marginal today and would have been in the pre-Columbian era as well. Agricultural productivity is limited by steep slopes and erosion, prolonged frost due to high elevations and/or temperature inversions, very limited water sources suitable for irrigation, and marked seasonality in rainfall (Garvin 1994). The viability of terracing systems is limited by the availability of labor for their construction and, most important, the labor-intensive maintenance required in an area of great vertical relief. Resources that would have been plentiful in the Peñoles region but much more scarce in the adjacent valleys include game such as deer, fruit trees, and especially wood products, the most important of which probably were oak for making charcoal and tall pines for construction beams (Drennan 1989; Garvin 1994). The Peñoles region may have been a net exporter of labor during some pre-Columbian periods, as it is today (Brito de Marti 1982).

Data Recovery Methods

The survey methods used were those developed for systematic regional-scale survey in highland valleys (Sanders, Parsons, and Santley 1979; Blanton et al. 1982) but adapted to mountainous terrain. These methods are discussed in greater detail elsewhere (Finsten 1995; Finsten et al. n.d.). Survey crews combed all principle and secondary ridgelines as well as many lesser ones, mapping archaeological features wherever they were found. After examination of several river valleys in the Peñoles region, including a major one carved by the Peñoles River, failed to yield any evidence of pre-Columbian occupation or activity, we focused our efforts exclusively on ridgetops. We are confident that no major sites were missed. More

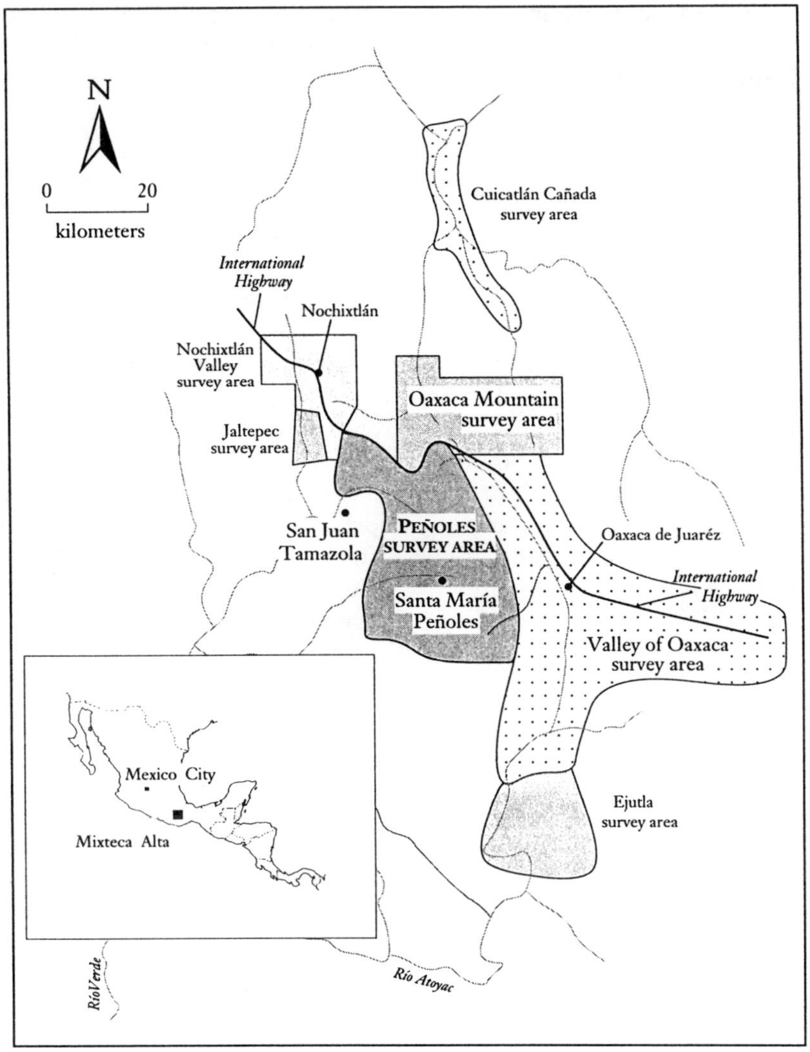

Figure 7.1 The state of Oaxaca, Mexico.

than 500 pre-Columbian settlements were located, mapped and described. At more than 100 sites, architecture was sufficiently preserved to be measured by pacing and drawn to scale. Architectural features included terraces, mounds, house foundations, plazas, patios, walls, gateway-like constructions and roadways. Surface collections of ceramic and other artifacts were made at many sites and notes about surface remains were taken at uncollected locations. Dates for sites and site segments were assigned on the basis of the distribution of pottery styles of known age in the Valley of Oaxaca and the Nochixtlán Valley.

Sites were found throughout the Peñoles Project Area, with the notable exception of the divide separating the drainages of the Upper Atoyac and the Rio Nochixtlán. This divide runs north-south, toward the western boundary of the Peñoles study area and is only extremely sparsely populated today. Reasons for the dearth of sites on the divide may include its very high elevation (generally 2800-3000 meters above sea level) and its often thin, granitic soils, both of which would have made successful agriculture unlikely. Furthermore, the absence of modern springs in the area today suggests that a lack of water for domestic uses in pre-Columbian times may have discouraged sustained settlement (Garvin 1994).

Long-Term Internal Dynamic

Although analyses of the Peñoles Project Area data are not yet complete, the distribution of settlements across the study area over time suggests two general conclusions about the long-term internal dynamic of the Peñoles region: long-term regional settlement continuity reflecting an enduring if small-scale polity, and relatively little hierarchical structure. Below I examine the settlement pattern and other evidence that supports these conclusions.

The presence of a long-standing, small-scale polity, perhaps from as early as Late Formative through Late Postclassic times (ca. 400 B.C. to A.D.1521), indicates persistence and continuity at the regional, if not the local, level that are surprising given the fragility of the mountain environment (Garvin 1994) and the considerable change in relationships between the Peñoles region and its valley neighbors. Most early sites date to the Late Formative (ca. 400 B.C. to A.D.200); only a few are Middle Formative (ca. 850-400 B.C.) in age. Nearly half of the Late Formative sites are concentrated in the south of the Peñoles region, around the modern town of San Miguel Peras, although at its northern limit this concentration extends to Santa María Peñoles (Figure 7.2). This is the only part of the study area to have any significant Middle Formative occupation, and many of the Late Formative sites in this relatively intensively occupied "Peras-Peñoles zone" became important centers in the succeeding Classic period.

Compared to Late Formative sites, Classic period settlements are far more numerous, more variable in size but generally larger, and seem to have been more densely occupied (Figure 7.3).[2] Twenty-three of the Classic period occupations occur in sites that are more than one kilometer long, and another measures more than two kilometers along its longest axis.[3] The Peras-Peñoles cluster contains many of the largest, most architecturally complex sites of the Classic period. However, sites of this time are widespread throughout the survey area and are not limited to this central zone.

Postclassic occupation is dense and continuous (Figure 7.4). Sites of this period are entirely absent only from the Valley of Oaxaca/Nochixtlán Valley divide, and are rare only in the far southeastern and northwestern sectors of the survey area, just above the Nochixtlán and other valleys of the Mixteca Alta. Fifteen sites are longer than two kilometers, and 25 measure between one and two kilometers along their longest axis. Two are greater than three kilometers long. Sites on the eastern slopes of the Peñoles region over-

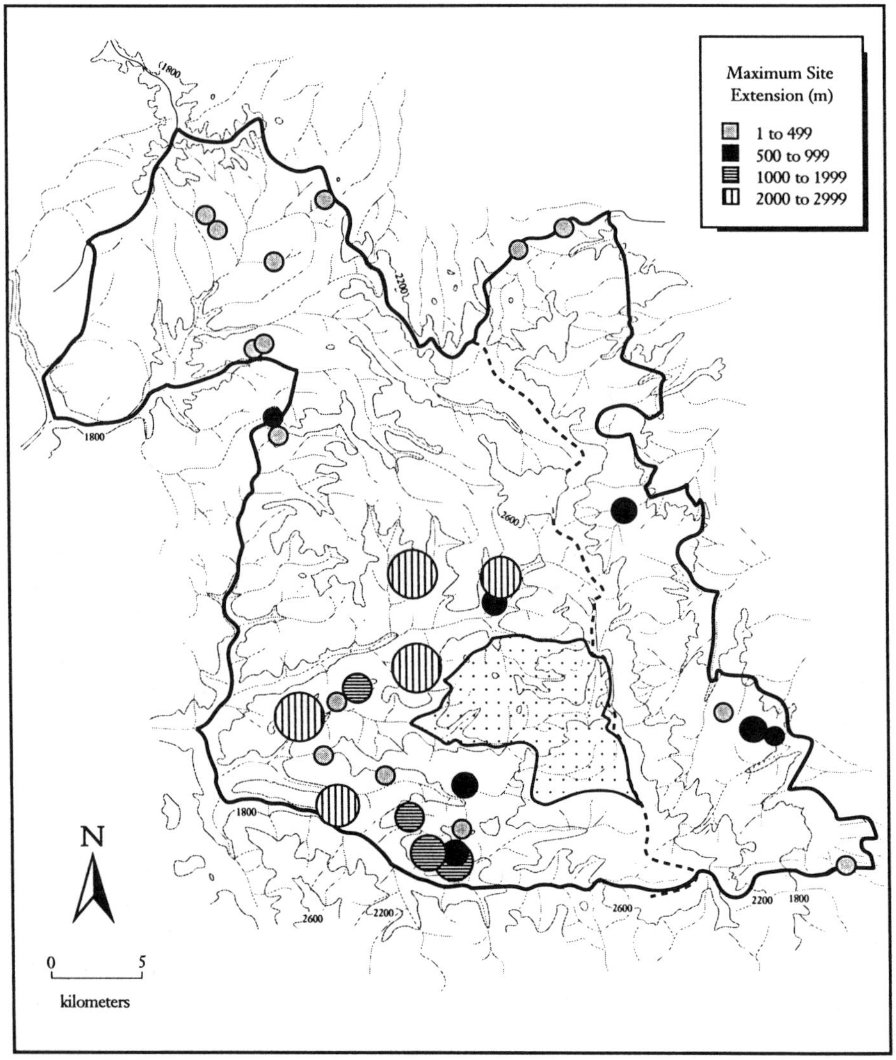

Figure 7.2 Formative period sites in the Peñoles Project area.

looking the Valley of Oaxaca, particularly where occupation is heavy, may be extensions of Late Postclassic Valley of Oaxaca-based petty kingdoms. Several fortified sites in this part of the Peñoles region are very similar to mountain redoubts located in the hills above the Valley of Oaxaca (see Elam 1989 for a description of these Valley of Oaxaca sites). The Postclassic demographic center of gravity was Ixquintepec, above the modern town of Santa María Peñoles, which probably was the seat of the Peñoles polity mentioned in sixteenth century sources (de Herrera y Tordesillas 1947; Gerhard 1993). A very rough estimate of population for the Peñoles region in the Postclassic period (5,000-15,000) suggests that the Classic period population had doubled. This size is broadly comparable to the average population of Late Postclassic petty kingdoms identified in the Valley of Oaxaca (Kowalewski et al. 1989:344-348). Using unoccupied shatter zones and population-weighted Thiessen polygons around large settlement aggregates, Kowalewski et al. (1989) tentatively identified ten to twenty territorial units in the Valley of Oaxaca that may correspond to the Late Postclassic petty kingdoms mentioned in sixteenth century documents, especially the *Relaciones Geográficas* (Acuña 1984). On average their estimated populations are about the same size as those of standard marketing areas (ca. 8,000) (Blanton 1985; Skinner 1963).

To summarize the Peñoles region's settlement history briefly, occupation was sparse and highly localized prior to the Classic period. The Peras-Peñoles zone in the central part of the survey area is the only part of the region with a significant concentration of Formative period occupation. This zone shows considerable occupational continuity from Late Formative through Classic to Postclassic times. The largest, most architecturally complex Classic period sites are found here. Despite this continuity, however, the greater intensity and more widespread distribution of settlement in the Postclassic period shift the demographic center of gravity northward to Peñoles proper.

Let us now turn to the second, more tentative conclusion about the internal dynamic of the Peñoles region

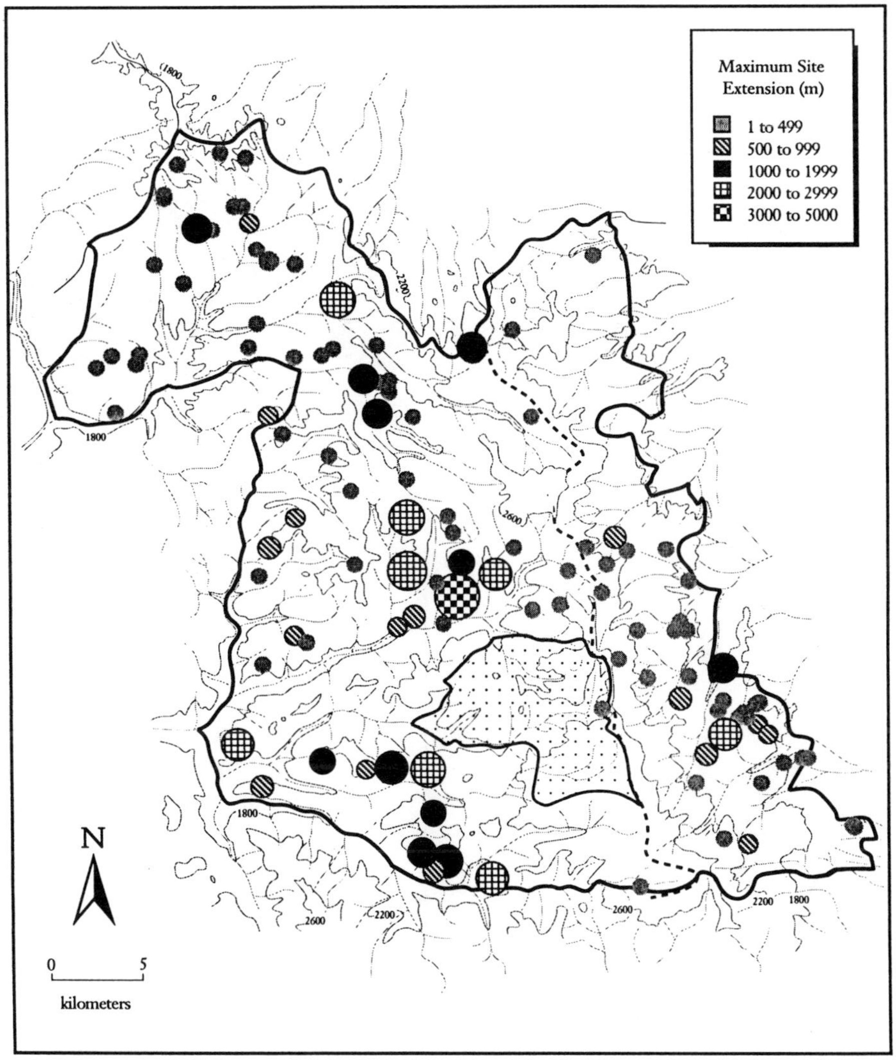

Figure 7.3 Classic period sites in the Peñoles Project area.

suggested by the present data. Hierarchical development appears to have been considerably less pronounced than was the case for comparable periods in the Valleys of Oaxaca and Nochixtlán, especially during the Formative and Classic periods. The Postclassic settlement system, however, is in many ways comparable in vertical complexity to the systems of neighboring Valleys. But it is not comparable in terms of settlement density. Even in the most intensively occupied period (the Postclassic), site density in the Peñoles region is less than half that found in the Valley of Oaxaca. The Valley of Oaxaca averages about 1.1 sites per square kilometer (Feinman and Nicholas 1992), while in the Peñoles region there are fewer than 0.5 sites per square kilometer.

Our measures of settlement size for Peñoles region sites are not directly comparable to those for valley sites because of the unusual configurations imposed on mountain settlements by the topography. Population estimation is also hampered by the often scant surface remains of earlier periods visible on the surface at multicomponent sites. Estimating population necessarily has had to rely on methods somewhat different from those used in southern highlands valleys where site area and density of occupational debris have been the primary variables used to determine the number of prehistoric inhabitants (see Blanton et al. 1982 and Kowalewski et al 1989 for a more detailed discussion of population estimation for Valley of Oaxaca settlements).

Despite these problems, however, it is clear that no Classic period settlements in the Peñoles region compare in overall size or population to contemporary secondary centers in the Valley of Oaxaca. Architectural analyses indicate that civic-ceremonial mounds are smaller, as well (Finsten 1995). The site-size and architectural patterns appear to reflect truncated rather than compressed hierarchical development. In other words, in both the Formative or Classic periods the Peñoles settlement system was less vertically complex than were the coeval systems in the adjacent Valley of Oaxaca. To some extent, the difficulty in detecting the presence of small sites lacking architecture in many

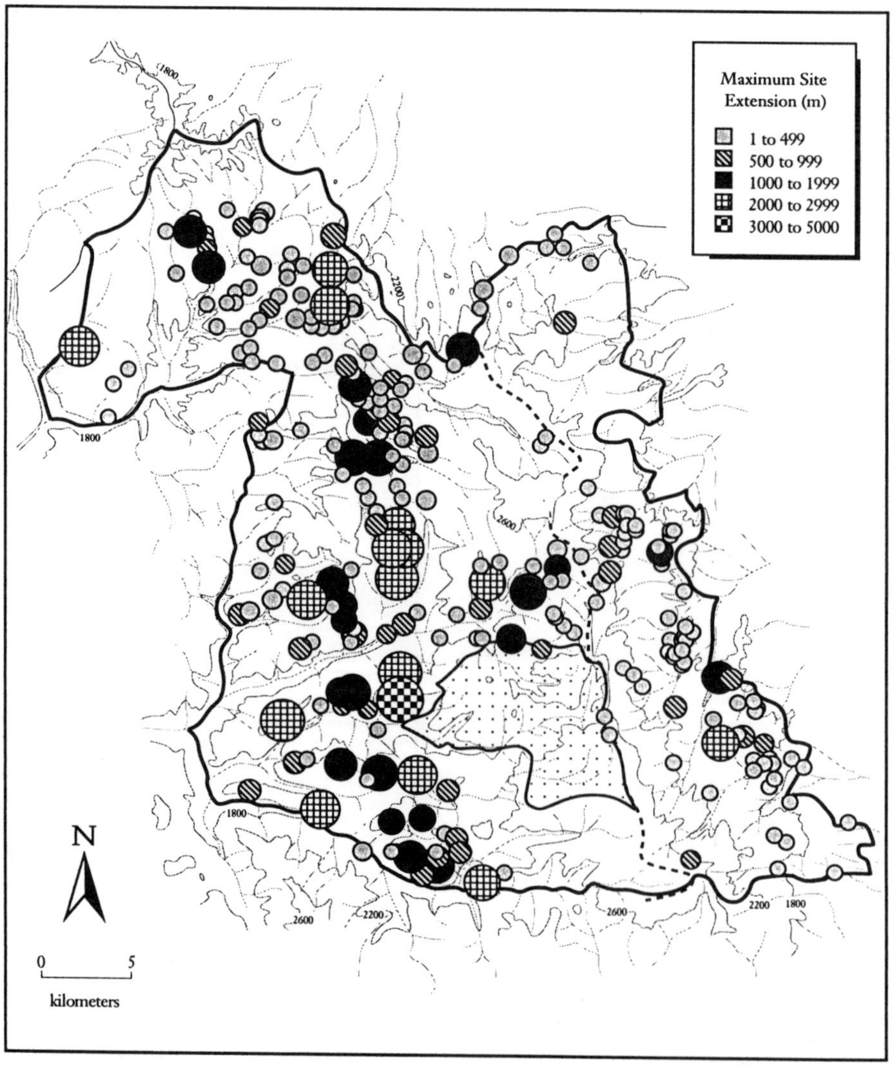

Figure 7.4 Postclassic period sites in the Peñoles Project area.

parts of the survey area may contribute to this picture. But visibility problems are not the whole explanation since many small Late Postclassic sites, often without apparent architecture, were found. In addition, sites lacking architecture tended to be toward the lower end of the site-size range; settlements missed here would not affect our perception of the number of hierarchical levels. The apparent standardization of large Classic period sites and the absence of Classic pottery from most mid-sized settlements are significant. Compared to the Valley of Oaxaca, in both the Formative and Classic periods, the Peñoles region had far less variation in site sizes, the largest settlements were considerably smaller and less populous than were secondary centers in the Valley of Oaxaca, and civic-ceremonial architecture was smaller in scale. All of these measures are consistent with less vertical complexity. The much lower site/population density in both the Formative and Classic periods as well as the simpler hierarchies in the Peñoles Project Area are consistent with the definition of a world-system periphery proffered by Hall and Chase-Dunn (this volume, also Chase-Dunn and Hall 1991). This analysis also supports the idea that core/periphery relations in world-systems typically are characterized by differential hierarchical development or vertical complexity, at least in early states.

In the Postclassic period, settlement patterns in the Peñoles Project Area were much more similar to those in the Valley of Oaxaca, although clearly the system differed in overall scale. At 1,000 square kilometers, the Peñoles region is nearly half the size of the Valley of Oaxaca survey area (2,140 square kilometers) (Kowalewski et al. 1989) but, as the figures discussed above indicate its density of Postclassic sites was much lower. Because the largest mountain sites are much smaller than first and second tier Valley of Oaxaca sites, population densities would have been even lower than the settlement density figures suggest.

The Peñoles region appears to have contained virtually all of a single petty kingdom (Ixquintepec/Santa María Peñoles) as well as smaller parts of several others, some based in the Valley of Oaxaca and at least one whose head town (Tamazola) was in the Mixteca Alta. This is a mere five to ten percent of the number present in the much richer Valley of Oaxaca and a fraction of those known from sixteenth century documents in the Nochixtlán and neighboring valleys of the Mixteca Alta. There is clear evidence, based on site differentiation in terms of size and internal (architectural) complexity, of more hierarchical development within the Peñoles Project Area than was apparent in earlier periods.

The Peñoles region had increased in scale and both vertical (hierarchical) and horizontal complexity in the Postclassic period, although its scale was still significantly smaller than that of the former core area (the Valley of Oaxaca) and its hierarchy continued to be less elaborate. But it was now more similar, structurally, to the adjacent valleys and to the rest of Mesoamerica, where virtually everywhere the fundamental constituent unit was the petty kingdom (cf. Hodge 1984).

The Peñoles region seems no longer have been a periphery of the Valley of Oaxaca in the Postclassic period. It continued to be marginal, because of its lesser agricultural productivity, dearth of some resources and, perhaps, because of the difficulties of transportation. But its status both within the Oaxacan multiregional system and *vis-á-vis* the Mesoamerican world-system was fundamentally altered as different mechanisms and institutions forged linkages among smaller, more comparably sized polities. In the evolutionary long-run, small-scale systems like those found in the Peñoles project area from Late Formative times on prevailed. The valley-based large, centralized states of Yucu–udahui and Monte Albán in the Classic period had given way to the ebb and flow of alliances among small, more comparably sized polities. The Peñoles region was transformed from an important margin on the frontier of a new, expanding state in the Late Formative to a heavily fortified periphery in the Classic period. By the Postclassic, it had become one of hundreds of petty kingdoms in Mesoamerica, and one of hundreds that were situated in disadvantaged, mountainous locations.

A Changing Frontier and Boundary Zone

To understand the nature of the Peñoles Project Area as a frontier and boundary zone it is necessary to examine the regional distributions of ceramic styles.[4] Architectural analysis, although the data are far less extensive, also provides important clues. Shared ceramic styles have long been employed as clues to regional interrelationships, although stylistic similarities alone do not provide straightforward answers to questions about the nature of those relationships and how they changed over time. We cannot readily distinguish actual movements of people, emulation of elite and/or other pot styles, elite level gift exchanges, and market exchange without considering other data. No clay source analyses have been conducted and so imports cannot be distinguished from local imitations with certainty. Architecture provides valuable information about administrative and other activities, and formal architectural styles may also provide clues about interregional relationships.

Late Formative settlement includes the relatively large aggregation of sites in the Peras-Peñoles zone discussed above, as well as a sparse string along the continental

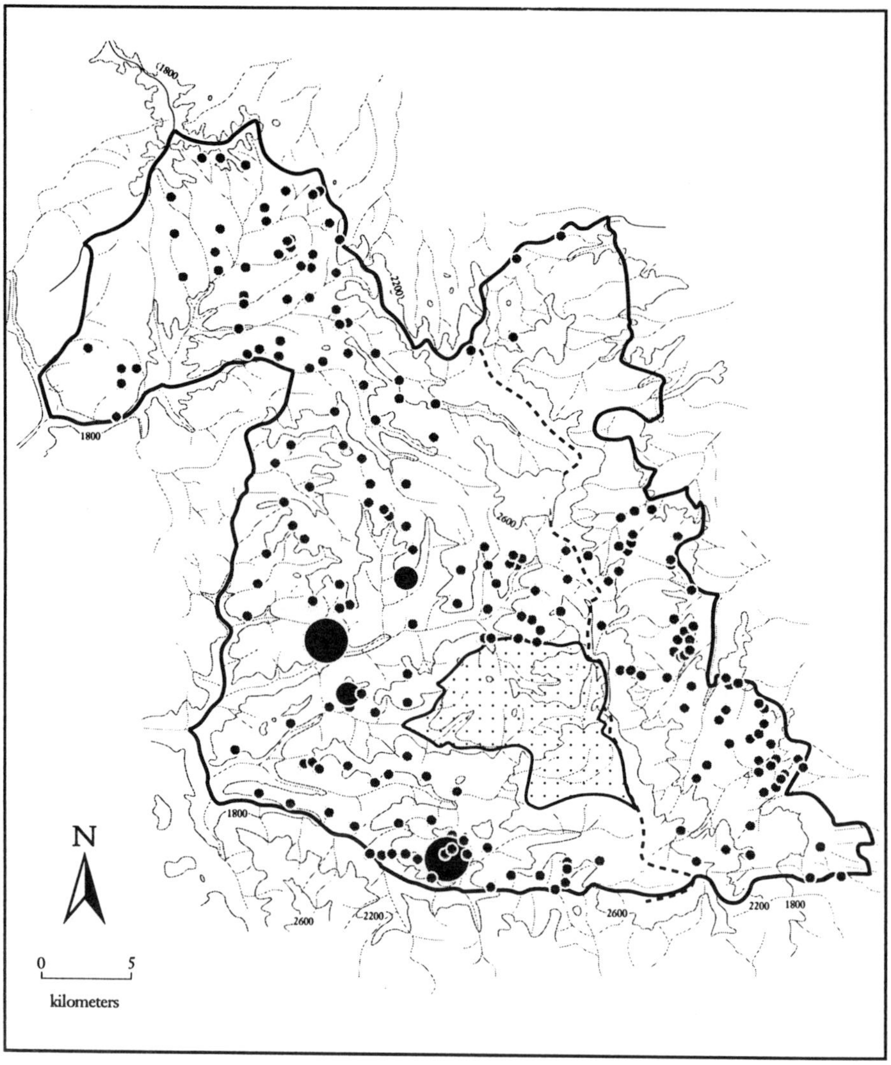

Figure 7.5 Brown sandy paste Peras bowls in the Peñoles Project area (darkened locations).

divide and several small sites to the northwest near the Nochixtlán Valley. Ceramics at all these sites include obvious Valley of Oaxaca diagnostics, while Late Formative styles specific to the Nochixtlán Valley are absent. Sites in the Peras-Peñoles zone have in addition a unique bowl form, unknown elsewhere in Oaxaca, made in local, Nochixtlán Valley-style but using typical Valley of Oaxaca grey and other pastes (Figure 7.5).

Both their pottery, which is visually indistinguishable from vessel fragments found at contemporary Valley of Oaxaca settlements, and their location suggest that Late Formative sites along the continental divide and in the northwest near the Nochixtlán Valley represent settlements along a communication corridor that must have been important to the Monte Albán state. The Late Formative is a well-documented time of expansion beyond the confines of the Valley of Oaxaca by the Monte Albán state (Marcus 1976, 1983; Redmond 1981; Spencer 1982). This corridor area lacks any indication of independent, local settlement in either the ceramic assemblages or site distributions. At sites in the Peras-Peñoles zone, too, there is evidence of clear ceramic ties to the Valley of Oaxaca in the presence of some pottery virtually identical to styles ubiquitous at contemporary Valley sites. However, these mountain settlements also have distinctive ceramics that are stylistically unlike any from the Valley of Oaxaca. Together with the relatively higher site density in this part of the Peñoles region, the ceramic evidence indicates the existence of a largely autonomous, local society in the Peras-Peñoles zone.

Everywhere Classic period ceramics were encountered, they are found in the style of Valley of Oaxaca greywares, although the subtle, macroscopic variations in paste color and temper suggest that most were made locally. The ceramic workhorse of the Valley of Oaxaca in the Classic , the G-35 bowl, is found at sites of this era throughout the entire study area, extending all the way over to the westernmost boundary (Figure 7.6) and probably beyond. Pottery in the style of the contemporaneous Las Flores phase of the Nochixtlán Valley is

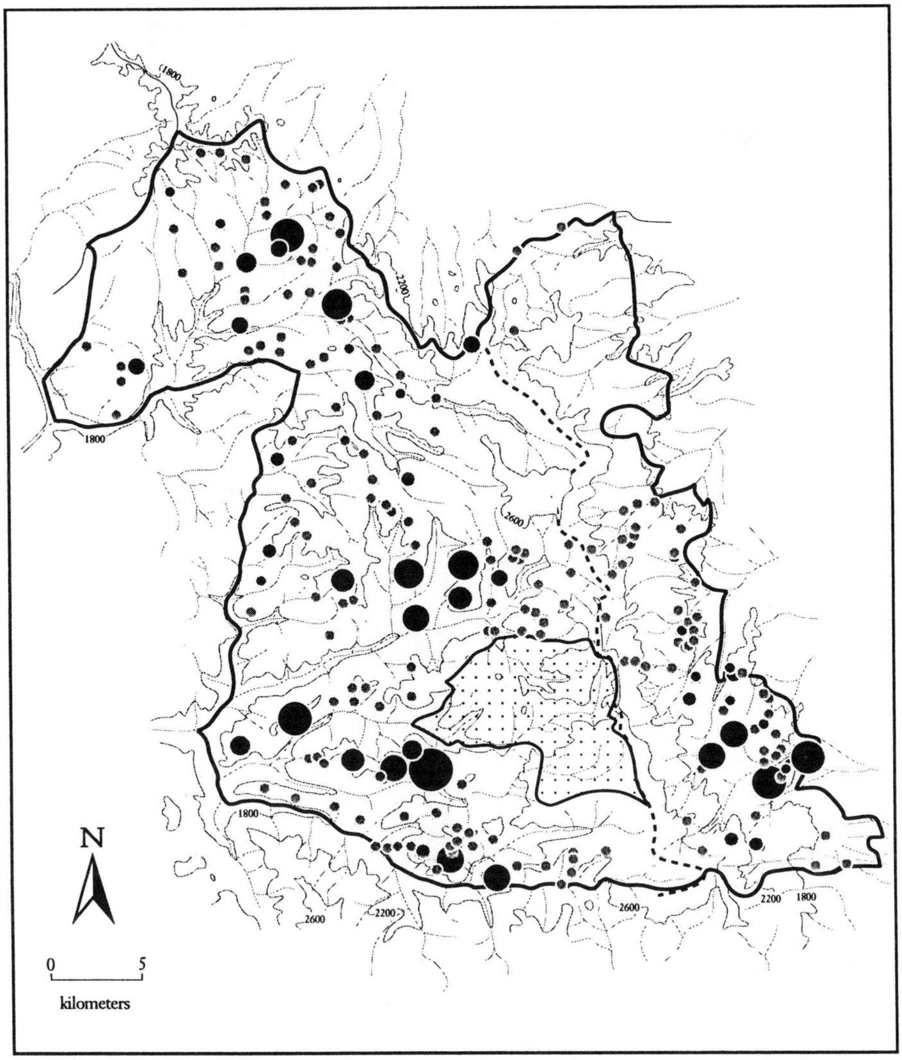

Figure 7.6 G-35 bowls in the Peñoles Project area (darkened locations).

rare. However, bowls with exactly the same form as the Valley of Oaxaca G-35 but made of the sandy cream paste commonly used for utilitarian wares in the Nochixtlán Valley also occur throughout the Peñoles Project Area (Figure 7.7). They are most frequent in the northwest, adjacent to the Nochixtlán Valley. The "ceramic boundary" with the Nochixtlán Valley lies at the western edge of the Peñoles Project Area, overlooking Nochixtlán. Further to the southwest, it may extend beyond the limits of our study area. The ceramic data suggest that in the Classic period, the Peñoles region's most significant interactions were with the Valley of Oaxaca, rather than to the west.

Many sites with Classic period occupations are large and have significant architecture, including mounds, patio groups, encircling walls and gateway features. The presence of walls and gateways at many sites with widespread Classic settlement is undoubtedly related to the Peñoles region's position on (and role in) the frontier of the Monte Albán state. Major Classic centers are found on every major ridgeline in the study area except the continental divide and the Valley of Oaxaca-Mixteca Alta divide (Figure 7.3). Since ridgecrests, rather than the narrow valley between them, were the important transportation corridors, these sites appear to have been situated to monitor and regulate movement within this mountainous frontier.

Postclassic ceramic distributions show a truly "fuzzy boundary" in which many Nochixtlán Valley and Valley of Oaxaca styles drop off across the Peñoles survey area, together forming east-west gradients, one apparently originating in the Valley of Oaxaca and the other in the Nochixtlán Valley. A few ceramic type distributions are sufficient to illustrate this.

Yanhuitlán Fine Creams dominate Natividad phase collections at Nochixtlán Valley sites, but are rare to absent in collections from contemporary Valley of Oaxaca sites (Spores 1972, 1974; Kowalewski et al.1989).[5] Their distribution in the Peñoles Project Area heavily emphasizes the west, adjacent to the Nochixtlán valley

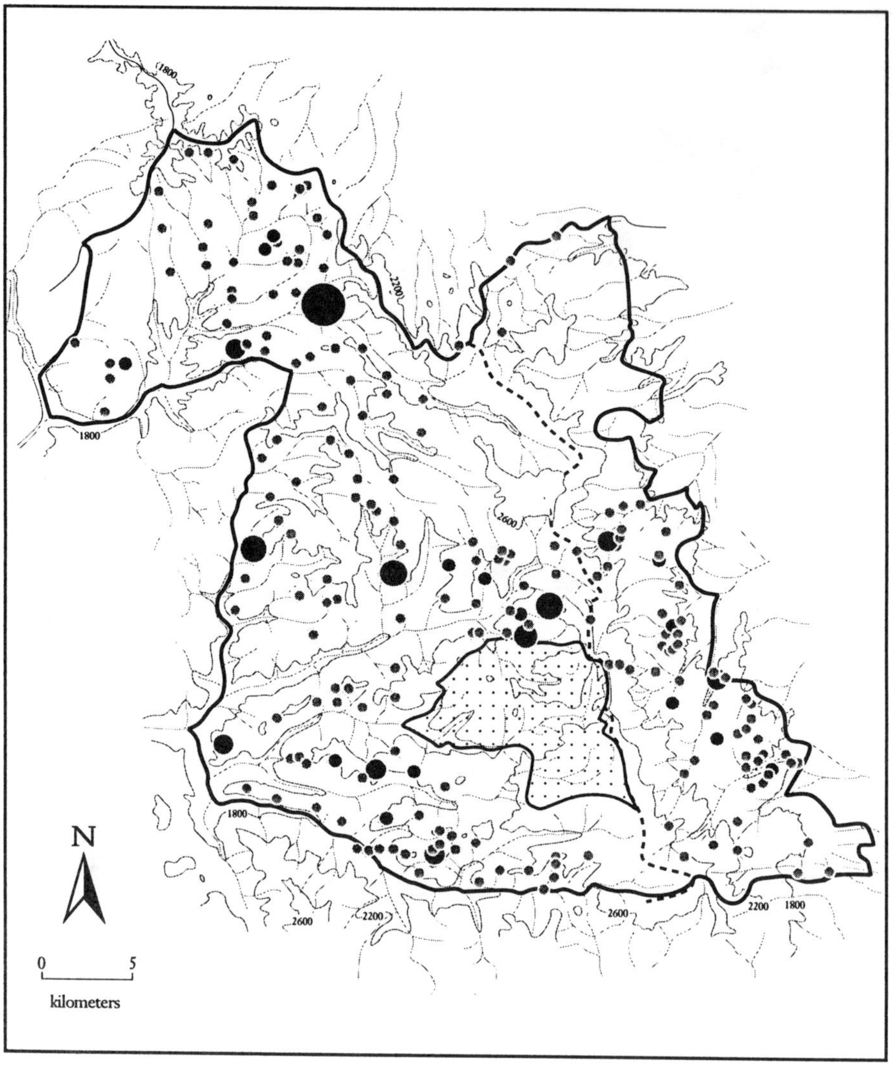

Figure 7.7 Sandy cream paste G-35 bowls in the Peñoles Project area (darkened locations).

(Figure 7.8). In the extreme east and, to a lesser extent, in the far south, Yanhuitlán Fine Creams are rare to absent, as they are in the Valley of Oaxaca.

Yanhuitlán Red-on-Cream, a decorated fine cream ware, is abundant in the Nochixtlán Valley and less frequently found at other Mixteca Alta and some Mixteca Baja Postclassic centers (Spores 1974). The distribution of this type in the Peñoles region is concentrated heavily in the south/central area, in and west of Ixquintepec (Figure 7.9). As was the case for fine creams, Yanhuitlán Red-on-Cream is absent to the east, near the divide with the Valley of Oaxaca.

G-3Ms are thin, hard-fired grey bowls that come in a variety of forms and dominate Late Postclassic ceramic assemblages in the Valley of Oaxaca. The simple, hemispherical variant is the most common in the Valley of Oaxaca as a whole. In the Valley's Tlacolula arm (the far east) where it is known to have been produced in at least two places, hemispherical bowls are the most frequent G-3M variant (Figure 7.10). In the Peñoles region, hemispherical bowls rank third among four shape modes in overall popularity. This form, like the outleaned wall G-3M, is relatively rare in the Peñoles region, occurring most often to the south (Figure 7.11), but is not abundant anywhere.

The least numerous variety of G-3M bowl in the Valley of Oaxaca is low and differentially fired to produce a white band under the lip. Despite its valley-wide scarcity, however, this is the most favored G-3M variant in the Etla arm of the Valley of Oaxaca (Figure 7.12), which borders much of the Peñoles Project Area. In the Peñoles region, it is also by far the most abundant, occurring more than twice as often in collections as the next most common form (the composite silhouette), and six times as often as the rarest form (outleaned wall bowl). Its distribution in the Peñoles region reflects a continuation of the Valley pattern into the Mixtec Sierra, focusing on the eastern part of the mountains adjacent to the Etla arm and the Central Area surrounding Monte Albán (Figure 7.13).

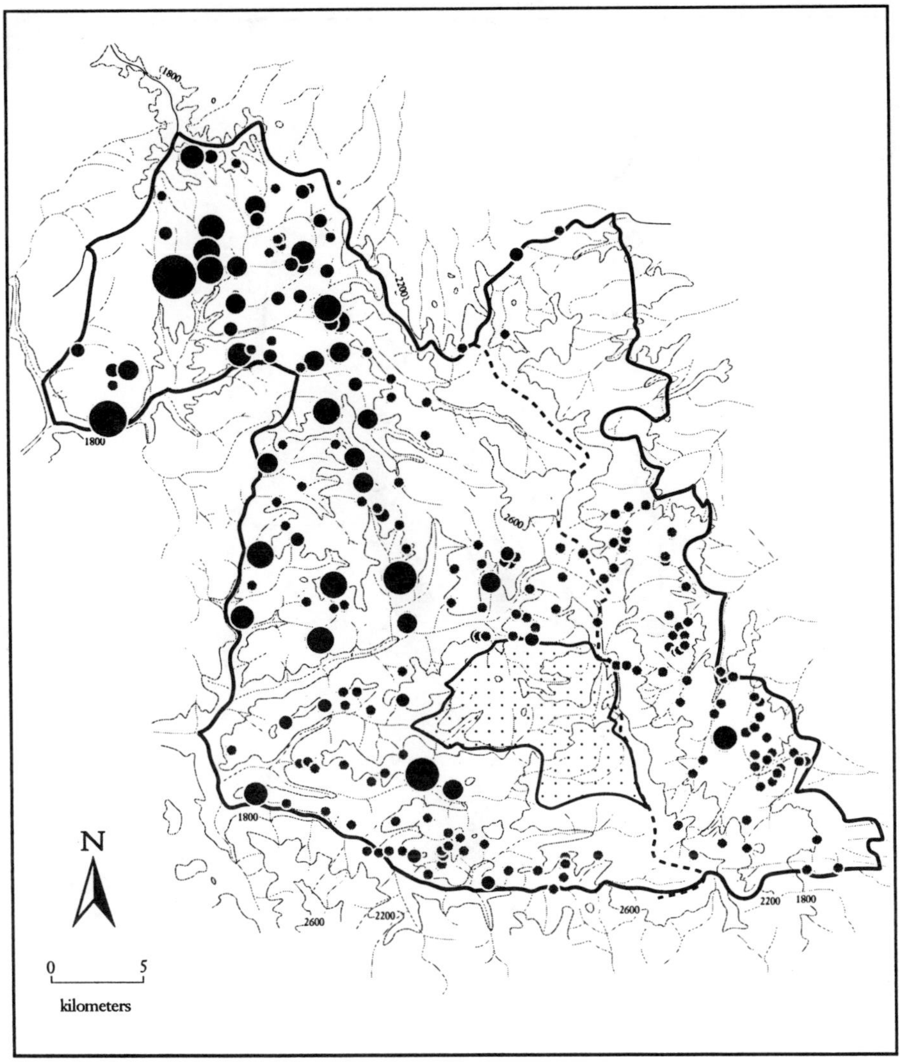

Figure 7.8 Yanhuitlán fine cream bowls in the Peñoles Project area (darkened locations).

Finally, Zaragosa bowls appear to be a Nochixtlán Valley variant of the low, differentially fired G-3M bowls found in parts of the Valley of Oaxaca and the Mixtec Sierra. Like the G-3Ms, Zaragosa bowls are low, differentially fired, and composite silhouette in form. Unlike the G-3Ms, they usually have an orange or tan rim and are tan or grey below the rim. Zaragosa bowls cluster in the extreme northwest of the Peñoles project area, in the area around the modern *municipio* of Santa Inez Zaragosa where the survey area begins to open up into the Nochixtlán Valley (Figure 7.14). Elsewhere in the mountains they are rare to absent, and this form is not known from the Valley of Oaxaca. Spores (1972) does not discuss it as a common ceramic type in the Nochixtlán Valley. As a local variant of the low, differentially fired, composite silhouette G-3M bowl, the Zaragosa bowl continues a pattern from Etla, through the Mixtec Sierra into the mountain frontier overlooking the Nochixtlán Valley.

As these few ceramic type distributions illustrate, there was no clear ceramic frontier dividing the Valley of Oaxaca and the Nochixtlán Valley in the Postclassic period. Nochixtlán Valley types (Yanhuitlán Fine Creams, Yanhuitlán Red-on-Cream) are found in decreasing frequency moving from west to east, approaching the Valley of Oaxaca. G-3M bowl variant distributions reflect a continuation of some Valley of Oaxaca distributional patterns into the Mixtec Sierra. Yet Postclassic site distributions, discussed above, suggest the presence of boundaries in the far southwest and in the far northwest, similar in many ways to those thought to delimit petty kingdoms in the Valley of Oaxaca.[6] Clearly, the spheres of market exchange through which ceramic vessels were distributed did not coincide with those of political dominance.

The analysis of ceramic style distributions supports a general conclusion that a system endured in the Peras-Peñoles zone despite considerable change in frontier

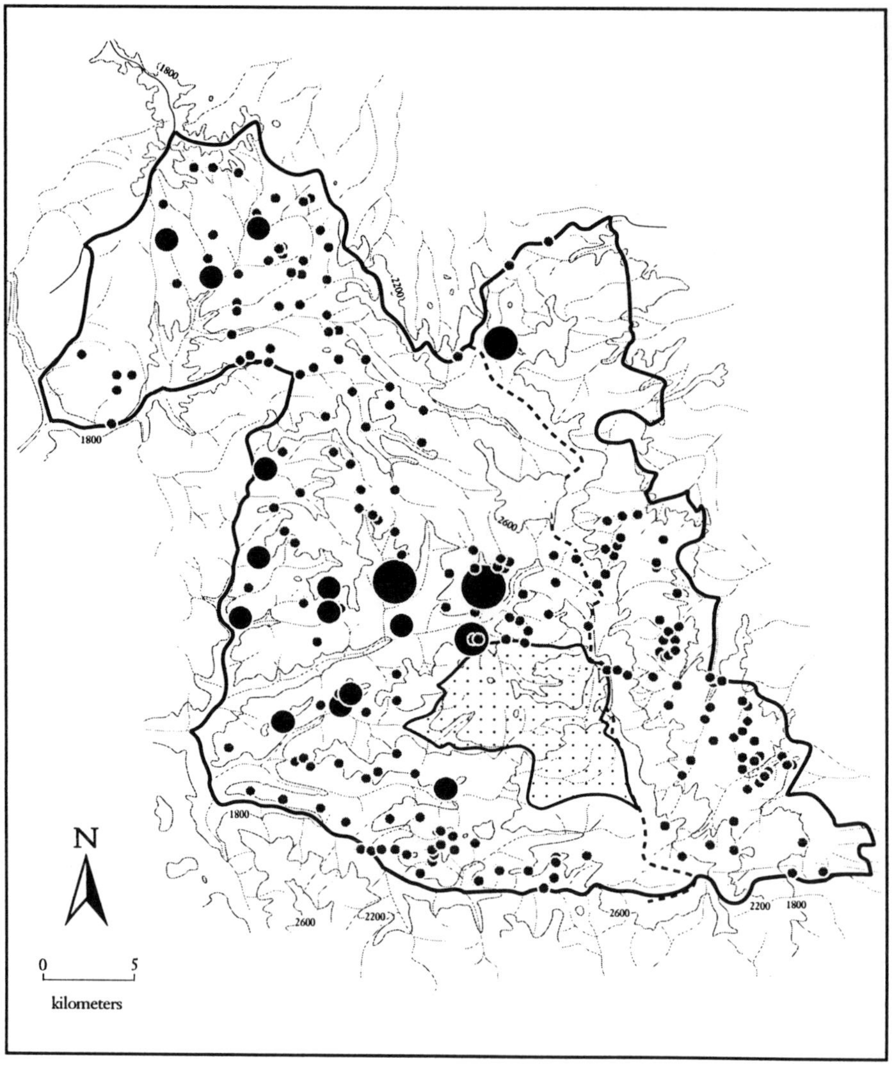

Figure 7.9 Yanhuitlán red-on-cream pottery in the Peñoles Project area (darkened locations).

relationships and loose but ever-present, if varying, ties to one or more adjacent valley systems.

Core-Periphery Relations and Long-term Change in the Peñoles Region

The Peñoles region, on the margins of one of Mesoamerica's pre-Columbian nuclear zones, was part of a larger, multiregional system that included the Valley of Oaxaca and/or valleys of the Mixteca Alta. This multiregional system was itself part of the Mesoamerican macroregion or world-system. In this paper, I have endeavored to analyze systematic regional-scale settlement pattern and other data from the Peñoles project area in order to examine changes in this marginal region's systemic structure over the long term (ca. 2,000 years). One objective of this analysis was to understand better the internal processes of marginal zones and frontier areas and their significance for change in neighboring states. As second goal was to evaluate world-system perspective concepts concerned with core/periphery relations. First, I focus on the significance of the results of the analyses for understanding the Peñoles region and its relationships to its nuclear zone neighbors in the Valley of Oaxaca and the Mixteca Alta.

In the Mixtec Sierra between the Valleys of Oaxaca and Nochixtlán, the major Mesoamerican ceramic periods are distinguishable and the pan-Mesoamerican gross secular trend toward growth is apparent. So is a Mesoamerica-wide Classic-Postclassic transition, which saw the fall of large-scale centralized states everywhere. But these marginal societies had an internal dynamic that cannot be explained entirely in terms of their relationships with their larger, at times more powerful neighbors.

In the Peñoles region, a small-scale polity emerged by at least Late Formative times and endured through the Late Postclassic period. Its fortunes were tied to those of one or other adjacent valley system to varying degrees and in different ways in the pre-Columbian era.

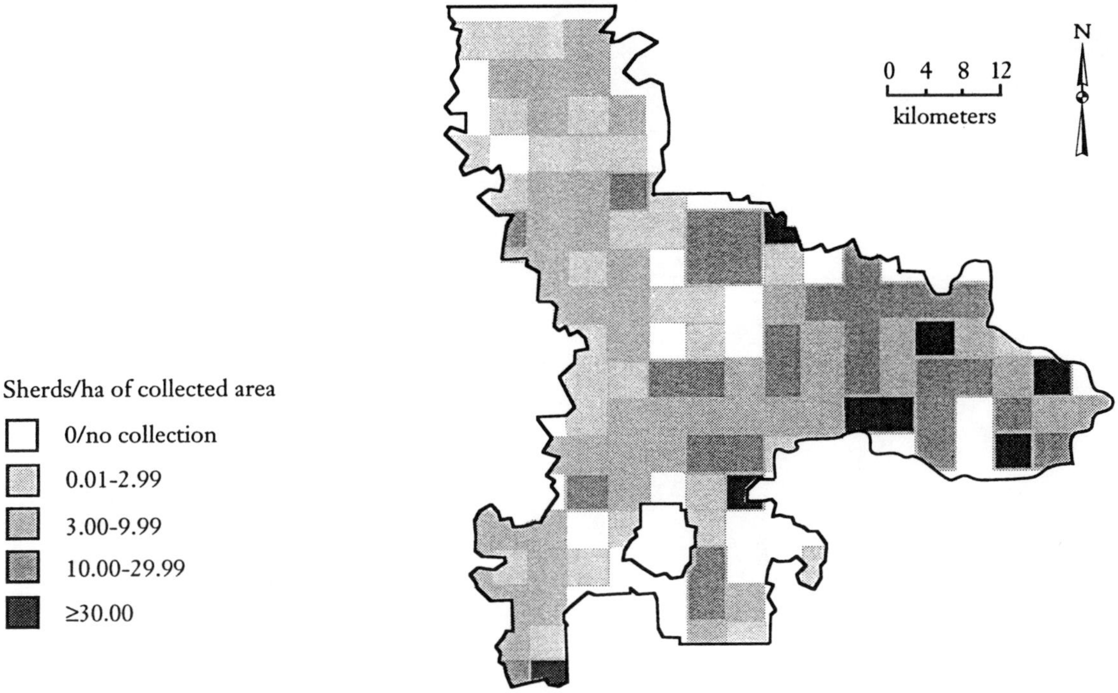

Figure 7.10 Valley of Oaxaca distribution of G-3M hemispherical bowls.

Sites whose very existence may have been related directly to Monte Albán expansionism in the Late/Terminal Formative are found only in the north, along the major corridor of the continental divide, and far northwest, overlooking the Nochixtlan Valley. The Peras-Peñoles zone, in the center of the study area, was considerably more autonomous. Some settlements in this zone may have been established as early as the Middle Formative period, before Monte Albán undertook expansion outside the Valley of Oaxaca. Monte Albán's imperial concerns may have improved access to fancier Valley of Oaxaca pottery in the Peras-Peñoles zone, but they were not the sole, or even primary, *raison d'être* for settlement and/or demographic growth.

Classic period settlement, ceramic and some architectural evidence suggests domination of the Peñoles region by the Valley of Oaxaca. The Late Formative continental divide corridor sites disappeared, but the Peras-Peñoles zone expanded spatially and sites grew in size and perhaps intensity of occupation, and increased in number. Many were heavily fortified. Some Classic sites may have fallen under the direct administration of Monte Albán or a secondary center such as Cerro San Cristobal, located on the eastern slope of the Mixtec Sierra overlooking the Valley of Oaxaca's Central Area. A local ceramic tradition was no longer distinguishable. Monte Albán's development of the Peñoles frontier was in part a response to boundary concerns, and may also have arisen in order to ensure a continuous supply of needed mountain resources. Although heavily fortified settlements fall within the Peñoles Project Area, it is apparent from ceramic distributions that Monte Albán's influence extended further west beyond the limit of the survey. Classic period concerns in this mountain frontier were broader than simple last-line of defense matters. For example, construction beams may have been a crucial part of the Monte Albán state's internal expansion, providing crucial materials for building the elaborate palaces and administrative complexes that both symbolized kingship and power and provided the space needed for decision-making. The Peñoles region may also have been an important source of immigrant labor necessary for the piedmont strategy that was central in supporting the Classic period Valley of Oaxaca state (see Kowalewski 1982).

In Postclassic period the Ixquintepec petty kingdom centered around the modern town of Santa María Peñoles emerged. The boundary distinguishing the distinctive ceramic traditions of the Valley of Oaxaca and the Nochixtlán Valley in earlier periods became extremely indistinct in the Postclassic period. Internal organization was more like that of the adjacent valleys than had been the case in earlier periods, as can be seen from the comparability in scale of the Peñoles polity and

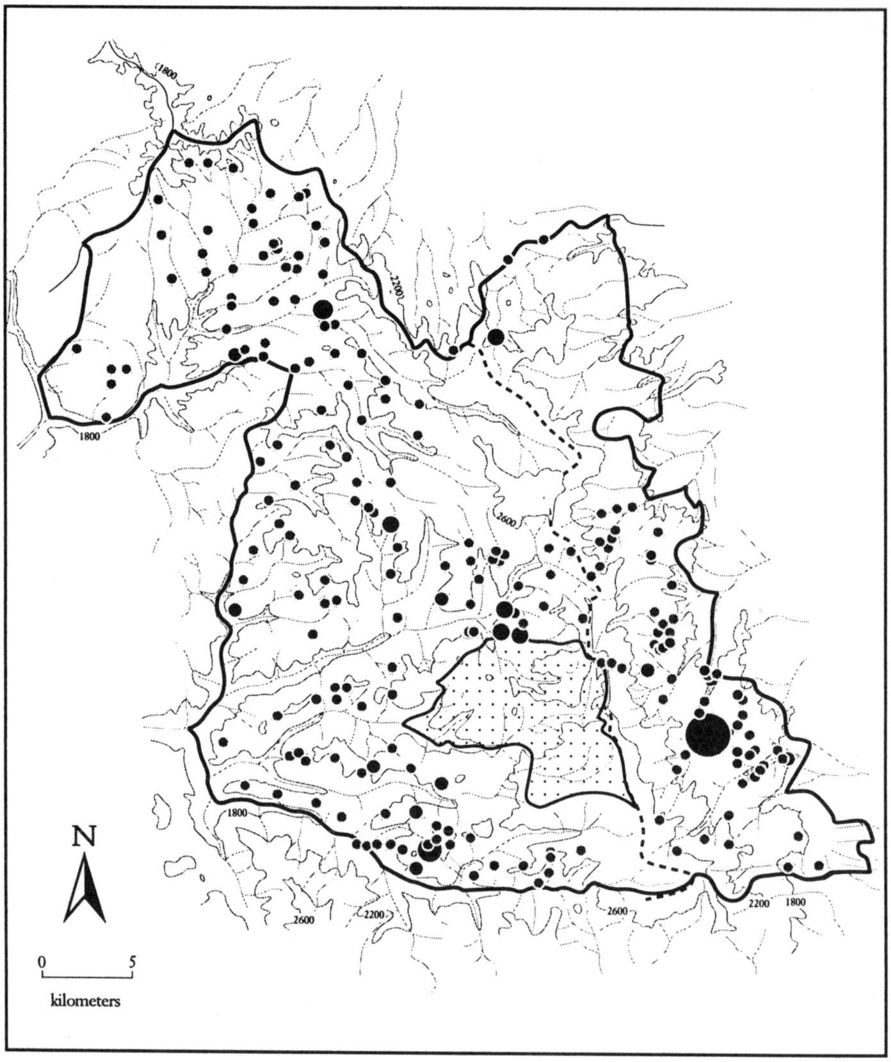

Figure 7.11 Peñoles Project area distribution of G-3M hemispherical bowls (darkened locations).

the basic Postclassic political units (petty kingdoms) found across Mesoamerica. Only in the Postclassic period was the Peñoles region on an equal footing with its neighboring polities, although this likely did not translate into political autonomy much of the time. Peñoles is listed as a dependency of the Valley of Oaxaca *cacicazgo* Etla in the sixteenth century (Gerhard 1993).

What do the Peñoles data suggest about core/periphery relations in early world-systems? As many earlier analyses have suggested, the Peñoles region was less complex in hierarchical system structure than the neighboring Valley of Oaxaca. And even in the Postclassic period, when its structure was much more like that of the Valley of Oaxaca regional system's, its population density was much lower. To some extent, though, these differences must be related to fundamentally different, and not well integrated, agroecosystems in the two regions.

Was domination characteristic of the relationships between the Peñoles region and the Valley of Oaxaca? Parts of the Mixtec Sierra were settled in the Late Formative period directly as a result of Monte Albán's expansionism, and these corridor sites were extensions of Valley of Oaxaca settlement. However, the Peras-Peñoles zone was much more independent. In the Classic period, large, heavily fortified and smaller settlements alike not only demonstrate close ties to the Valley of Oaxaca regional system but may be an extension of the Valley state into the mountainous western frontier. The study area seems clearly to have been dominated by the Valley of Oaxaca, and this domination was clearly political, probably economic, and perhaps ideological. By the Postclassic period, there is no evidence of domination although we know that Ixquintepec was a tributary of a Valley of Oaxaca petty kingdom by the Spanish conquest. Of course, late in the fifteenth century, all these Oaxacan kingdoms were in turn tributaries of the Aztec Triple Alliance. Tributary status likely did not mean domination in any real sense,

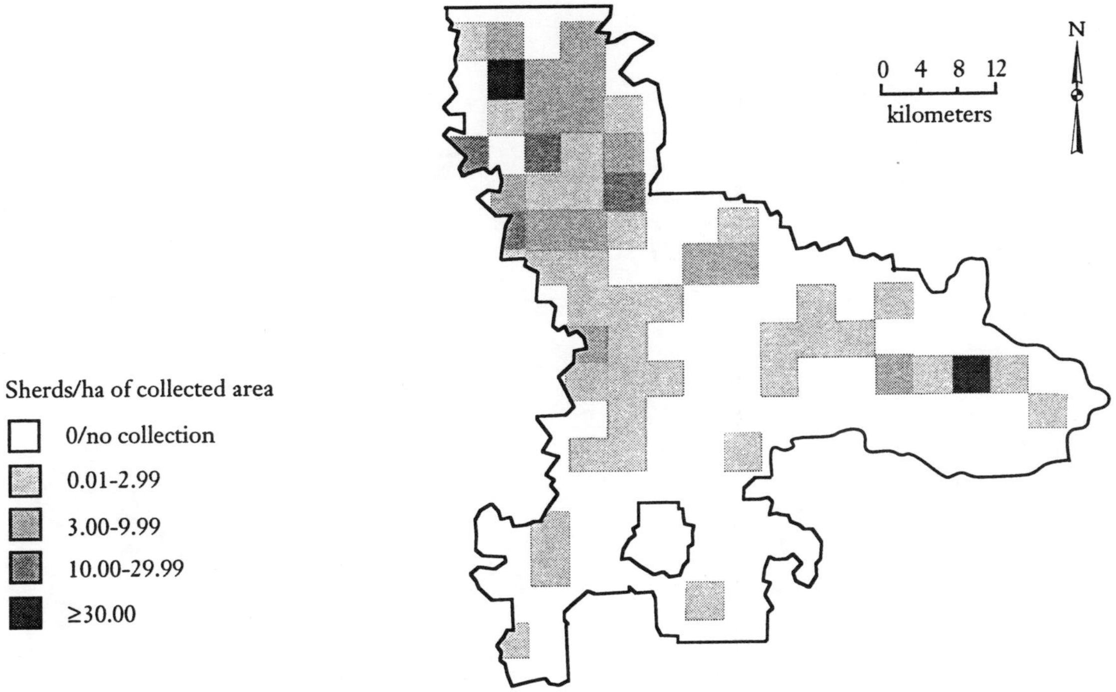

Figure 7.12 Valley of Oaxaca distribution of G-3M low, differentially-fired bowls.

although it likely did have an impact on the political economies of tributaries.

To what extent and how did its ties to neighboring valleys affect change in the Peñoles region? The Peras-Peñoles zone in the Late Formative was linked to Monte Albán, perhaps primarily through elite-level exchanges. It is not clear how these linkages affected development in either the Mixtec Sierra or the Valley of Oaxaca, however. There seems little doubt that greater internal hierarchical depth and increased scale in the Peñoles region in the Classic period were direct consequences of domination by Monte Albán, although internal factors may also have played a role. Yet the Mixtec Sierra remained less complex and populous than its dominating neighbor. Even in the Postclassic period, when it became structurally much more similar to the Valleys of Oaxaca and of the Mixteca Alta, the Peñoles region's population density was considerably lower. These qualities may have contributed to its relative stability over the long-term.

Notes

1. The Peñoles Project was co-directed by Laura Finsten and Stephen A. Kowalewski. Funding was provided by the Social Sciences and Humanities Research Council of Canada, the National Science Foundation, and the National Geographic Society. Permission to carry out the fieldwork was granted by El Instituto Nacional de Antropolog'a e Historia, México,D.F. I thank officials at El Centro Regional de Oaxaca-INAH for their assistance. I am grateful to the municipal and agrarian authorities and citizens of all the communities in the Peñoles Project Area who granted us permission to walk their land for both their cooperation and assistance. Members of the field crew whose unflagging efforts were key to the field project's success were Mark D. Borland, Oralia Cabrera C., Richard D. Garvin, Everardo Olivera D., Fausto Olivera M., Ian G. Robertson, Charlotte A. Smith and James A. Wilson. Charlotte A. Smith prepared Figure 1. Finally, I thank Mark Borland, Rick Garvin, Steve Kowalewski and Sammy Smith for their encouragement and comments.

2. Determining the extent of early occupations at multicomponent sites is a problem not yet completely resolved. Many sites in the Peñoles Project Area were undisturbed. Architectural preservation at such sites was excellent and consequently it was possible to make a detailed record of a range of features, including house foundations and fireboxes, that eventually will contribute greatly to our understanding of intracommunity organization. However, the same factors that contribute to superb architectural preservation act against producing abundant surface debris, including the pottery needed to date sites and site segments. At very few sites in the Peñoles Project Area was pottery

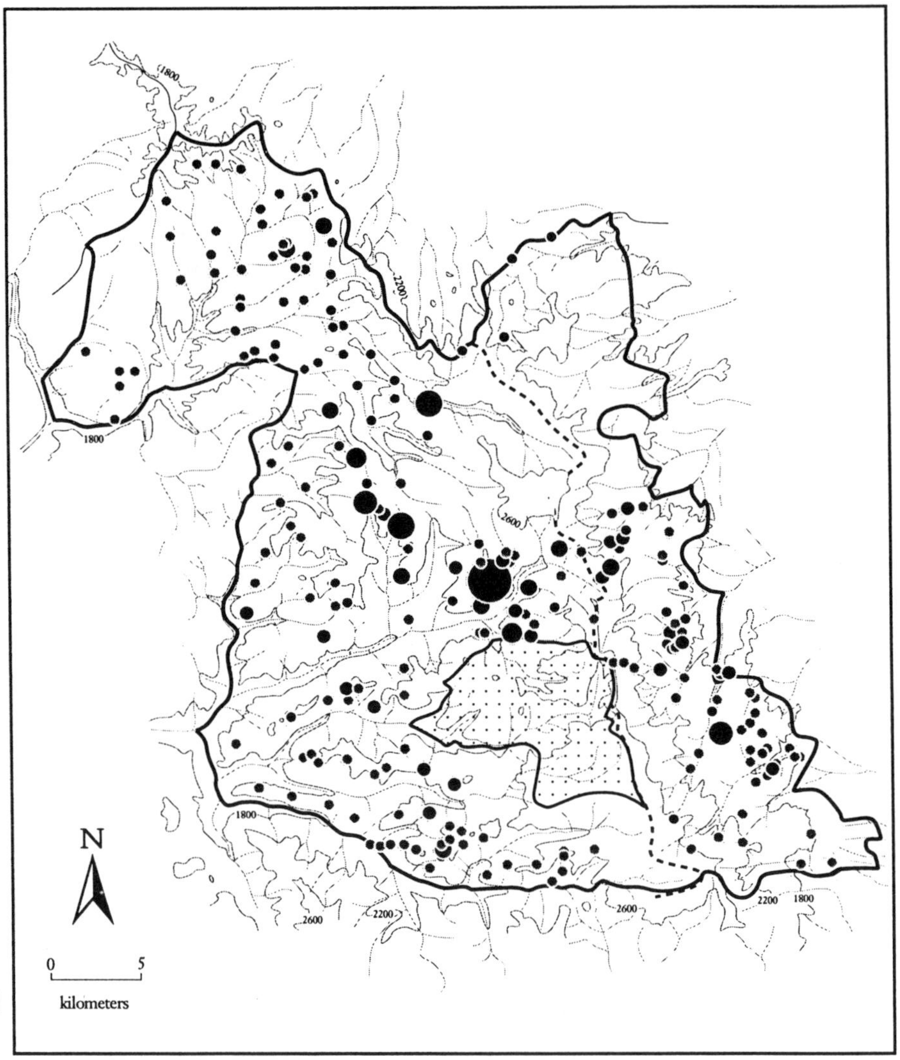

Figure 7.13 Peñoles Project area distribution of G-3M low, differentially-fired bowl (darkened locations).

as abundant over a wide area as it tended to be at Valley of Oaxaca sites. Thus, delineation of the spatial extent of components is not as straightforward at well-preserved mountain sites as it is in areas that have a history of recent agriculture. Reference here is to the presence or absence of Formative and Classic period occupations, and site sizes refer to overall settlement size, not to the extent of individual components.

3. "Length" or "extension" is an unusual means by which to express site size, but it is an accurate one for the Peñoles Project Area. Sites follow the topography, extending along ridgetops and rarely spilling more than very short distances downslope because of the steepness of mountainsides. As a result, large sites invariably have a linear configuration: they are very long, but not very wide.

4. Limitations of space require that this discussion be kept to a bare minimum. Many additional ceramic types, some lithic distributional data, and a great deal more architectural data could also be marshaled in support of the following argument.

5. For discussion of Monte Albán's ceramic types see Caso, Bernal and Acosta (1967) and Kowalewski, Spencer and Redmond (1978).

6. The apparent boundary marked by settlement falloff to the southwest and northwest of the Peñoles Project Area may be, in part, an artifice of survey area boundaries, but we think that most, if not all, of the sixteenth century Peñoles polity is contained within the project area.

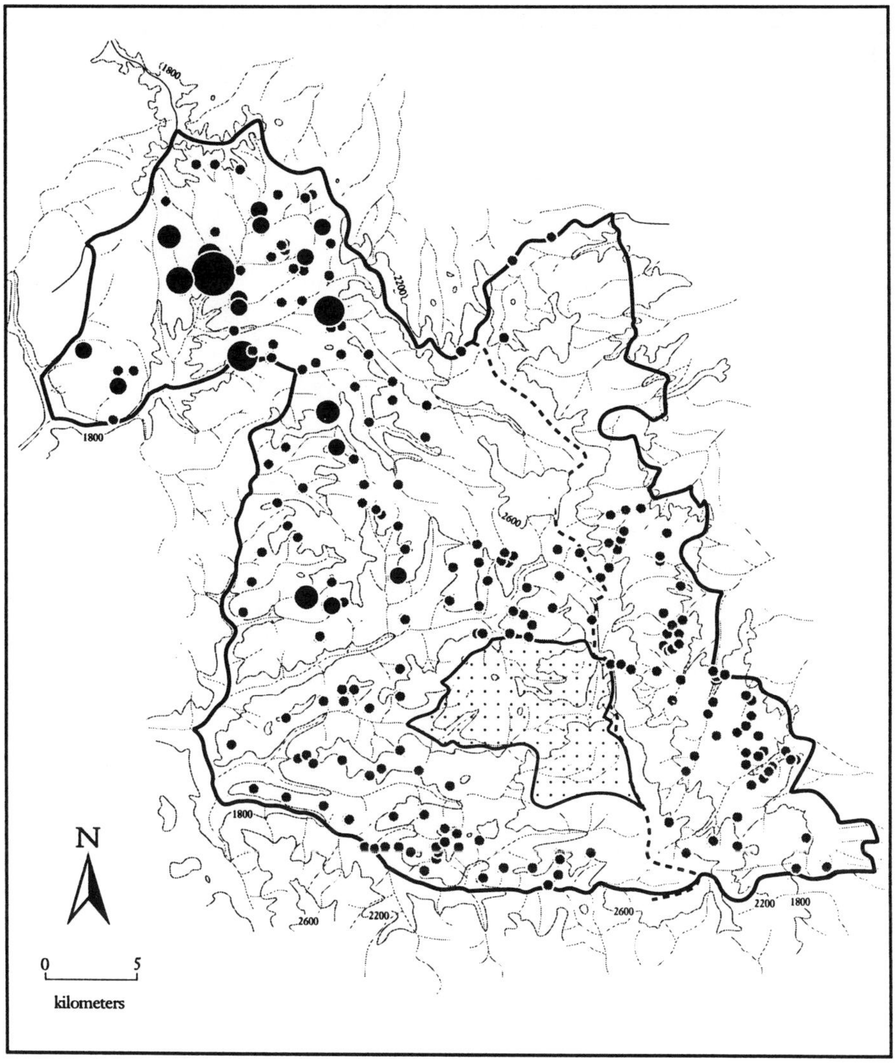

Figure 7.14. Zaragosa bowls in the Peñoles Project area (darkened locations).

References Cited

Acuña, René

1984 *Relaciones Geográficas del Siglo XVI: Antequera*. 3 volumes. Instituto de Investigaciones Antropológicas, Serie Antropológica, 58. Universidad Nacional Autónoma de México, Mexico City.

Blanton, Richard E.

1985 A Comparison of Early Market Systems. In *Markets and Marketing*, edited by Stuart Plattner, pp. 399-416. Monographs in Economic Anthropology, No.4. Society for Economic Anthropology and University Press of America, Lanham, MD.

Blanton, Richard E., Stephen Kowalewski, Gary Feinman and Jill Appel

1982 *Monte Alban's Hinterland, Part I: The Prehispanic Settlement Patterns of the Central and Southern Parts of the Valley of Oaxaca, Mexico.* Memoirs of the Museum of Anthropology, University of Michigan, Number 15. Ann Arbor.

Brito de Marti, Esperanza

1982 *Almanaque de Oaxaca*. México,D.F.: Almanaque de México.

Byland, Bruce E. and John M.D. Pohl
1987 The Marriage of Twelve-Wind and Three-Flint at White Hill: Pictures, Ruins, and Folklore Reveal a Tenth-Century Mexican Alliance. *Thesis: The Magazine of the Graduate School and University Center, CUNY* 2(1):10-17.

Caso, Alfonso, Ignacio Bernal y Jorge Acosta
1967 *La Cerámica de Monte Albán*. México, D.F.: Instituto Nacional de Antropologia e Historia.

Chase-Dunn, Christopher and Thomas D. Hall
1991 Conceptualizing Core/Periphery Hierarchies for Comparative Study. In *Core/Periphery Relations in Precapitalist Worlds*, edited by C. Chase-Dunn and T.D. Hall, pp. 5-44. Westview Press, Boulder.
1993 Comparing World-Systems: Concepts and Working Hypotheses. *Social Forces* 71:851-886.

de Herrera y Tordesillas, Antonio
1947 *Historia General de los Hechos de los Castellanos en las Islas y Tierrafirme del Mar Oceano.* 15 volumes. Madrid: Academia de la Historia. (Original 1601-1615).

Drennan , Robert D.
1989 The Mountains North of the Valley. In *Monte Alban's Hinterland, Part II: Prehispanic Settlement Patterns in Tlacolula, Etla, and Ocotlan, The Valley of Oaxaca, Mexico,* by S. Kowalewski, G. Feinman, L. Finsten, R. Blanton and L. Nicholas, pp. 367-384. Memoirs of the Museum of Anthropology, University of Michigan, Number 23. Ann Arbor.

Elam, J. Michael
1989 Defensible and Fortified Sites. In *Monte Albán's Hinterland Part II: Pre-Columbian Settlement Patterns in Tlacolula, Etla and Ocotlán, the Valley of Oaxaca, Mexico,* edited by S. Kowalewski, G. Feinman, L. Finsten, R.E. Blanton, and L.M. Nicholas, pp. 385-407. Memoirs of the Museum of Anthropology, University of Michigan, Number 23. Ann Arbor.

Feinman, Gary M. and Linda M. Nicholas
1990 At the Margins of the Monte Albán State: Settlement Patterns in the Ejutla Valley, Oaxaca, Mexico. *Latin American Antiquity* 1:216-246.
1992 Pre-Hispanic Interregional Interaction in Southern Mexico: The Valley of Oaxaca and the Ejutla Valley. In *Resources, Power, and Interregional Interaction*, edited by Edward Schortmann and Patricia Urban, pp. 75-116. Plenum, New York

Finsten, Laura
1995 Cultural Frontiers and System Boundaries in Pre-Columbian Oaxaca. *Chacmool 1992 Conference Proceedings*.

Finsten, Laura, Stephen A. Kowalewski, Charlotte A. Smith, Richard D. Garvin, and Mark D. Borland
n.d. Circular Architecture and Symbolic Boundaries in the Mixtec Sierra, Oaxaca. Manuscript in possession of the author.

Garvin, Richard D.
1994 *Modern and Prehispanic Agriculture in the Sierra Mixteca, Oaxaca, Mexico*. Ph.D. dissertation, Dept. of Archaeology, University of Calgary. Calgary, Alberta.

Gerhard, Peter
1993 *A Guide to the Historical Geography of New Spain* [Revised edition]. University of Oklahoma Press, Norman.

Hodge, Mary G.
1984 *Aztec City-States.* Memoirs of the Museum of Anthropology, University of Michigan, Number 18. Ann Arbor.

Kowalewski, Stephen
1982 Population and Agricultural Potential. In *Monte Albán's Hinterland, Part I: The Pre-Columbian Settlement Patterns of the Central and Southern Parts of the Valley of Oaxaca, Mexico,* edited by R. Blanton, S. Kowalewski, G. Feinman and J. Appel, pp. 149-180. Memoirs of the Museum of Anthropology, University of Michigan, Number 15. Ann Arbor.

Kowalewski, Stephen A., Gary Feinman, Laura Finsten, Richard E. Blanton, and Linda M. Nicholas
1989 *Monte Albán's Hinterland Part II: Pre-Columbian Settlement Patterns in Tlacolula, Etla and Ocotlán, the Valley of Oaxaca, Mexico.* Memoirs of the Museum of Anthropology, University of Michigan, Number 23. Ann Arbor.

Kowalewski, Stephen A., Charles S. Spencer and Elsa Redmond
1978 Description of Ceramic Categories. In *Monte Albán: Settlement Patterns at the Ancient Zapotec Capital* edited by Richard E. Blanton, pp. 167-194. Academic Press, New York.

Marcus, Joyce
1976 The Iconography of Militarism at Monte Albán and Neighboring Sites in the Valley of Oaxaca. In *The Origins of Religious Art and Iconography in Preclassic Mesoamerica*, edited by H.B. Nicholson, pp. 123-39. University of California at Los Angeles, Latin American Center.
1983 The Conquest Slabs of Building J, Monte Albán. In *The Cloud People: Divergent Evolution of the Zapotec and Mixtec Civilizations*, edited by K.V. Flannery and J. Marcus, pp. 106-108. Academic Press, New York.

Pohl, John D. and Bruce E. Byland
1994 *In the Realm of 8 Deer: The Archaeology of the Mixtec Codices.* University of Oklahoma Press, Norman.

Redmond, Elsa M.
1981 *A Fuego y Sangre: Early Zapotec Imperialism in the Cuicatlán Cañada, Oaxaca*. Memiors of the Museum of Anthropology, University of Michigan, Number 16. Ann Arbor.

Sanders, William T., Jeffrey R. Parsons, and Robert S. Santley
1979 *The Basin of Mexico: Ecological Processes in the Evolution of a Civilization.* Academic Press, New York.

Skinner, G. William
1963 Marketing and Social Structure in Rural China: Part I. *Journal of Asian Studies* XXIII:3-43.

Spencer, Charles S.
1982 *The Cuicatlán Cañada and Monte Albán.* Academic Press, New York.

Spores, Ronald
1972 *An Archaeological Settlement Survey of the Nochixtlán Valley, Oaxaca.* Vanderbilt University Publications in Anthropology, Number 1. Nashville.
1974 *Stratigraphic Excavations in the Nochixtlán Valley, Oaxaca.* Vanderbilt University Publications in Anthropology, Number 11. Nashville.

Wallerstein, Immanuel
1974 *The Modern World-System I.* Academic Press, New York.

Chapter 8

Actions at a Distance, Impacts at Home: Prestige Good Theory and a Pre-Columbian Polity in Southeastern Mesoamerica

Edward M. Schortman
Patricia A. Urban
Kenyon College

This chapter examines how economic and political processes operating at macroregional scales may have affected developments within the Late Classic (AD 600-950) polity that encompassed the Naco valley, northwestern Honduras. As Peregrine aptly points out in the introduction to this volume, world-systems theory encourages recognition of the multi-layered texture of reality (also see Feinman, Nicholas, and Upham, this volume). Economic, social, political, and ideological transactions occurring at different scales are all ultimately interrelated through the actions of individuals who participate in those processes. People are members of families, societies, and intersocietal networks and it is through their goal-directed behaviors in these arenas that processes operating over varied spatial extents are articulated. Modeling relations among these diverse processes in any one case and searching for cross-cultural regularities in their conjunctions remains a major challenge for archaeologists (see also Hall and Chase-Dunn, this volume).

We have examined Late Classic Naco data and behavior patterns from a macroregional perspective in an earlier essay, using this material as a stimulus for consideration of core-periphery relations in non-capitalist economic formations (Schortman and Urban 1994b). Here we want to turn our attention to issues pertinent to other analytical levels. A central question dealt with here is how would-be rulers' participation in intersocietal interaction networks translates into enhanced power within specific societies. Also considered is the manner in which non-elite households, basic units of residence and cooperation, are affected by these strategies and act to protect their interests in the face of elite encroachments. We hope that consideration of Naco data, as schematic and tentative as that presentation is, will encourage discussion of the possible ways political and economic formations within particular societies are significantly related to transactions operating on larger, macroregional scales.

World-Systems Theory and Modeling Intersocietal Ties

Interest in the effects of intersocietal interaction on trajectories of prehistoric sociopolitical change has increased dramatically over the past two decades. This concern, long dormant in the archaeological literature, has given rise to a number of different perspectives designed to model interaction processes (see Schortman and Urban 1987 for a review). One of the most promising emergent viewpoints is based on efforts to adapt Wallerstein's macroregional world-systems perspective (1974, 1980) on the development and spread of capitalism to precapitalist situations (e.g., Blanton and Feinman 1984; Ekholm and Friedman 1979; Pailes and Whitecotton 1979; Schneider 1977; Upham 1982). This transference has led to considerable reworking of Wallerstein's original formulation and heated debate concerning the appropriateness of applying even a modified version of world systems theory to prehistoric contexts (see Hall and Chase-Dunn, this volume; Schortman and Urban 1994b).

Nevertheless, certain basic assumptions underlying world-systems theory have carried over into archaeological considerations of prehistoric exchange relations (the points discussed below add to those outlined by Peregrine in the volume introduction). Use of Wallerstein's model has led us to question the viability, economic and otherwise, of individual societies. Their reproduction over generations is now assumed to have required significant inputs derived from beyond societal boundaries, the cessation or alteration of which could lead to significant sociopolitical shifts (e.g., Frankenstein and Rowlands 1978; Kohl 1987). The unit of analysis in studying sociopolitical change must, therefore, be the network of interacting polities and not the isolated society.

Another important notion inspired by world-systems theory is that intersocietal contacts are not necessarily adaptive, promoting equilibrium among all interaction partners. Weakly organized peripheries are exploited by and for the benefit of large, complex core states thereby creating durable patterns of development and underdevelopment. There is some skepticism concerning the degree to which intersocietal inequality characterizes all interaction networks (e.g., Kohl 1987, 1992; Schortman and Urban 1994b). Nevertheless, most researchers inspired by world-systems theory seem to agree that competition more often than cooperation guides human behavior. Elites within different societies move to advance their own interests at the expense of others and employ extrasocietal contacts as resources in these efforts (see the discussion of prestige good theory below). The last is hardly a novel viewpoint to those working from a Marxist perspective, as Wallerstein does. These assumptions, however, contrast markedly with traditional archaeological precepts stressing adaptation to the physical environment as the primary cause of sociopolitical form and change (e.g., Binford 1965; Sanders 1956; Sanders and Price 1968; Steward 1972 [1955]).

World-systems theory, as noted earlier, also leads to a consideration of relations among events and processes operating on different scales. Interactions occurring across broad areas affect developments within particular societies through the actions of individuals who partake in those exchanges. Central questions in this regard include: How did those involved in intersocietal transactions use the exotics they acquired to establish and maintain positions of power and prestige within their particular societies? In what ways did subordinates react to these efforts at political centralization?

Attempts to deal with the relationship between imports and competition for power have been most fully expressed in what is variably called "prestige good" (Ekholm 1972, 1978; Frankenstein and Rowlands 1978; Friedman 1982; Friedman and Rowlands 1978:224-232; Haselgrove 1982; McGuire 1987; Peregrine 1991, 1992) or "wealth finance" theory (Brumfiel 1987; Brumfiel and Earle 1987; D'Altroy and Earle 1985; Earle 1987; Gilman 1987). This framework is derived to a significant degree from recent French Marxist work, especially that concerning the "lineage mode of production" (Dupre and Rey 1973; Meillassoux 1960, 1981), as well as from ethnographic studies of "Big Man" societies in the Pacific (e.g., Keesing 1983; Strathern 1971). The focus is on how and under what conditions individuals can use control over imported social valuables within a society to create and maintain sociopolitical hierarchies with the monopolists ensconced at the apex. Some recent reworkings of world systems theory dealing with the sociopolitical significance of so-called luxury goods exchanges also explore this theme (e.g., Blanton and Feinman 1984; Kohl 1987; Schneider 1977). We will summarize here the general thrust of these arguments as they relate to the study of prehistoric exchange systems and their sociopolitical consequences.

Prestige Good Theory

Conceptual Structure

A basic problem faced by would-be rulers of kinship-based societies is how to control labor and, thus, extract surpluses and services from their followers while maintaining the *simulacrum* of a reciprocal relationship among people at different social levels (Ekholm 1978:128-130; Renfrew 1982:269, 286, 289; Spencer 1982; G. Webster 1990; Wells 1980:97-98; see also the discussion of labor mobilization and surplus accumulation in Hall and Chase-Dunn, this volume). To ensure effective control, followers must be made dependent on their new leaders so that they cannot easily refuse to comply with elite requests. A common solution involves elite monopolization of locally rare but generally needed and valued items (herein termed "prestige goods") which they pass down the hierarchy in "exchange" for subsistence products, services, and objects destined for subsequent export. The exotics may figure prominently in processes of production and/or social reproduction important to all individuals regardless of rank. They may also serve as status markers the display of which legitimizes the rights of lesser notables to receive support from their followers (Ekholm 1972, 1978; D'Altroy and Earle 1985:203; Earle 1987:72-75; Frankenstein and Rowlands 1978:76-77; Myers 1987:200; Strathern 1971:196, 225; Wells 1988:211-213).

Such goods maintain their value, and their local distribution is monopolizable, because they are rare within the society. This rarity follows from their acquisition through inter-elite exchanges, the considerable skill needed to make them, and/or their protection by sumptuary laws (Brumfiel 1987:114; Clark 1987; Dupre and Rey 1973:150; Frankenstein and Rowlands 1978:77-78; Friedman 1982:183-184; Haselgrove 1982:81-82; McGuire 1987:130; Shennan 1982). Regular removal of social valuables from circulation, as when they are buried with their owners, also ensures scarcity (Dupre and Rey 1973:149-150; Halstead and Shea 1982:93-94; Haselgrove 1982:82; 1987:115). The faction that exclusively controls the acquisition and/or manufacture of such socially critical resources also monopolizes political power. The rest of the population, elite and non-elite, is dependent on the monopolists for goods that ensure survival and create social status.

Prestige good systems, such as those outlined above, emphasize vertical ties of dependence; recipients of paramount largesse have a vested interest in preserving the system and compete with each other for favors from the paramount. Horizontal ties conducive to revolt or usurpation are discouraged (Brumfiel 1987:114; D'Altroy and Earle 1985:196; Frankenstein and Rowlands 1978:83; Earle 1987:69; Rowlands 1987:60; Schneider 1977). Prestige good systems are also dynamic. Aspiring elites initially compete with each other for control of exotic social valuables with which to "capture" dependents. The more successful scions exploit their supporters for exchangeable surpluses which can be used to acquire larger quantities of exotic valuables and so snare additional clients. The more prestige goods the elite control the more dependents they can attract and so the cycle continues until some limit on population growth and nucleation, such as the ability of supporters to continue generating increased quantities of surpluses, is reached (Kristiansen 1979; Haselgrove 1982:81; Sawyer 1979:157; Schortman and Urban 1987).

Continued functioning of prestige good systems depends on the ability of local rulers to maintain their monopoly over: acquisition of valuables via external elite interaction networks; local distribution of items obtained from afar; and/or production of prestige goods through artisans attached to elite patrons (Braithwaite 1984:105-107; Brumfiel and Earle 1987; Ekholm 1972, 1978; Frankenstein and Rowlands 1978:77-78, 82; Friedman 1982; Friedman and Rowlands 1978:224-232; Gilman 1987; Schortman 1989; Schortman and Urban 1987). Given the political power invested in prestige goods, their acquisition outside established, hierarchical channels opens the way for increased competition and, at least in some cases, social fragmentation (Ekholm 1972; 1978:131; Frankenstein and Rowlands 1978:79; Friedman 1982; Kipp and Schortman 1989; Strathern 1971:227). In fact, any effort made by subordinates to protect or regain their economic autonomy is a threat to the dependency relations undergirding prestige good systems. Political and economic processes on local and extralocal scales are interrelated resulting in structures that are rarely stable.

Prestige good formulations translate the concepts of exploitation and competition so obvious on an interregional scale in world-systems theory to the societal level. Similarly, the assumption that individual societies are not viable but depend for their reproduction on external inputs is further emphasized and specified here. The perspective outlined above, therefore, provides a means of relating processes operating on macroregional and local levels by outlining how political actors employ foreign assets and connections in strategies of intrasocietal advancement.

Archaeological Applicability

But how useful is this approach in understanding actual cases of prehistoric economic and political development? Kowalewski in this volume rightly points out that there has been a tendency to see prestige goods as sources of power without examining the ways in which valuables are employed in political strategies. A prestige good, like any item, derives its behavioral significance in part from the manner in which it is used by people attempting to accomplish specific objectives. One of those goals, we argue, is the acquisition of power, and social valuables can have a role to play in such machinations. This is not to say that prestige goods structure economies or political systems. Such structures are created by people who may well use social valuables in the manner described above as *resources* in their contests for ascendancy (e.g., Runciman 1982; Yoffee 1985, 1991). It is up to the investigator to identify how prestige goods might have been deployed in power contests.

Another difficulty is that most work based on this viewpoint focuses on cases where an abundance of ethnographic or ethnohistoric data permits tracing the complex exchange networks that underpin sociopolitical hierarchies. Transference of prestige good theory to purely prehistoric contexts has faced significant problems tending to discourage such efforts. Salient among these difficulties are: (1) recognizing prestige goods; (2) identifying high status individuals apart from their possession of an abundance of valuables as burial furniture (Kowalewski 1989, and this volume); (3) reconstructing patterns of consumption, exchange, and production *within* societies; (4) determining to what extent there was elite control over social valuables. The second problem is a significant one in archaeology where we commonly identify a person interred with a sizable quantity of exotic items as a high ranking member of society and then cheerfully use this data to infer elite control of social valuables (Kowalewski, this volume). It is difficult to break free of this sort of circular reasoning without written documents that permit the identification of notables independent of their material possessions.

The first problem is frequently dealt with archaeologically by assuming that items which must be imported and/or require considerable skill and time to manufacture functioned as social valuables. This is, of course, only a rough approximation of ancient esteem but in the absence of written records it is frequently the best we can do. As noted above, prestige goods must be monopolizable by only a small segment of the population. The criteria of foreignness and/or difficulty of manufacture are directly related to this crucial aspect of social valuables and therefore provide at least one means of identifying them.

The third and fourth obstacles to the prehistoric application of prestige good theory require that detailed information be obtained on the organization of exchange, consumption, and production within entire polities (Marcus 1992). To a certain extent the intrasocietal distribution of prestige goods can be reconstructed through the study of their imperishable residues. Except in those cases where local populations surrendered distinctive, durable objects to their rulers in return for social valuables (e.g., Ekholm 1972), it is very hard to specify archaeologically what and how much in the way of goods or services flowed back up the hierarchy. Frequently we are left to infer, from the size of the elite population and their constructions, that both food and labor were part of this "exchange." Given the importance of elite control over the fabrication of social valuables from imported or local raw materials, information on how these manufacturing activities were organized and where they were located is of critical significance (Stark 1985:159; Tosi 1984:22; Wells 1988:207). Equally important is data pertaining to the consumption of prestige goods, including measuring their ubiquity in assemblages from different settlement tiers and inferring the manner in which valuables were used by varied social segments.

In order to apply prestige good theory prehistorically, therefore, we need information gathered from contemporary settlements of all sizes within a political unit, from large portions of those sites, and data on the organization and location of socially valuable production. This is a tall order to fill, requiring considerable investments of time and money to succeed. The study of politico-economic processes within the large, long-occupied polities and their capitals on which archaeologists traditionally focus poses significant difficulties (e.g., Ashmore 1988:153-154; D. Webster 1980). Simply studying, through survey and/or excavation, sufficiently large portions of such extensive political units to allow behavioral inferences can pose severe logistical problems (Cowgill et al. 1984). Distortions in the relationship between material and activity patterns following from prolonged, increasingly congested, occupation at major centers is also an obstacle to reconstructing ancient behavior patterns (e.g., Fletcher 1984; Gnivecki 1987:227; Oswald 1987). Until data derived from investigations of entire ancient polities (Marcus 1992) are available and used to evaluate hypotheses based on prestige good theory, however, we cannot be certain how applicable these precepts are to understanding prehistoric trajectories of sociopolitical change. We are left with the suspicion that prestige good theory best accounts for the effects of expanding capitalist states or world empires on less complexly organized peripheries, those described in the relatively recent ethnohistoric and ethnographic documents we have relied so heavily on to date. In more remote prehistoric periods different principles of interaction and hierarchy building might have been in operation.

The Naco Valley

Recent (1975-1979, 1988, 1990-1992, 1995) investigations in the Naco valley, northwestern Honduras (Figure 8.1) provide an opportunity to evaluate the role of political valuables within a prehistoric context. The valley encompasses 96 square kilometers of flat to gently rolling terrain watered by the Rio Chamelecon and bounded by the high, steep slopes of the Sierra de Omoa (Figure 8.2). Naco is situated at a potentially strategic point in several prehistoric interaction networks, following the Rio Chamelecon and mountain passes southwestward for 120 kilometers to the major lowland Maya center of Copan and north for 15 kilometers to the massive north coastal plain. The culturally complex lower Motagua valley lies approximately 30 kilometers northwest across the rugged Sierra de Omoa.

Research conducted by the Naco Valley Archaeological Project, directed by Henderson (Cornell University) from 1975-1977 and by the authors thereafter, defined a regional occupation sequence stretching from the Middle Preclassic (ca. 800 BC) to the Spanish Conquest in the early 16th century AD. During this long interval there were several oscillations in the centralization of regional political control (Henderson et al.

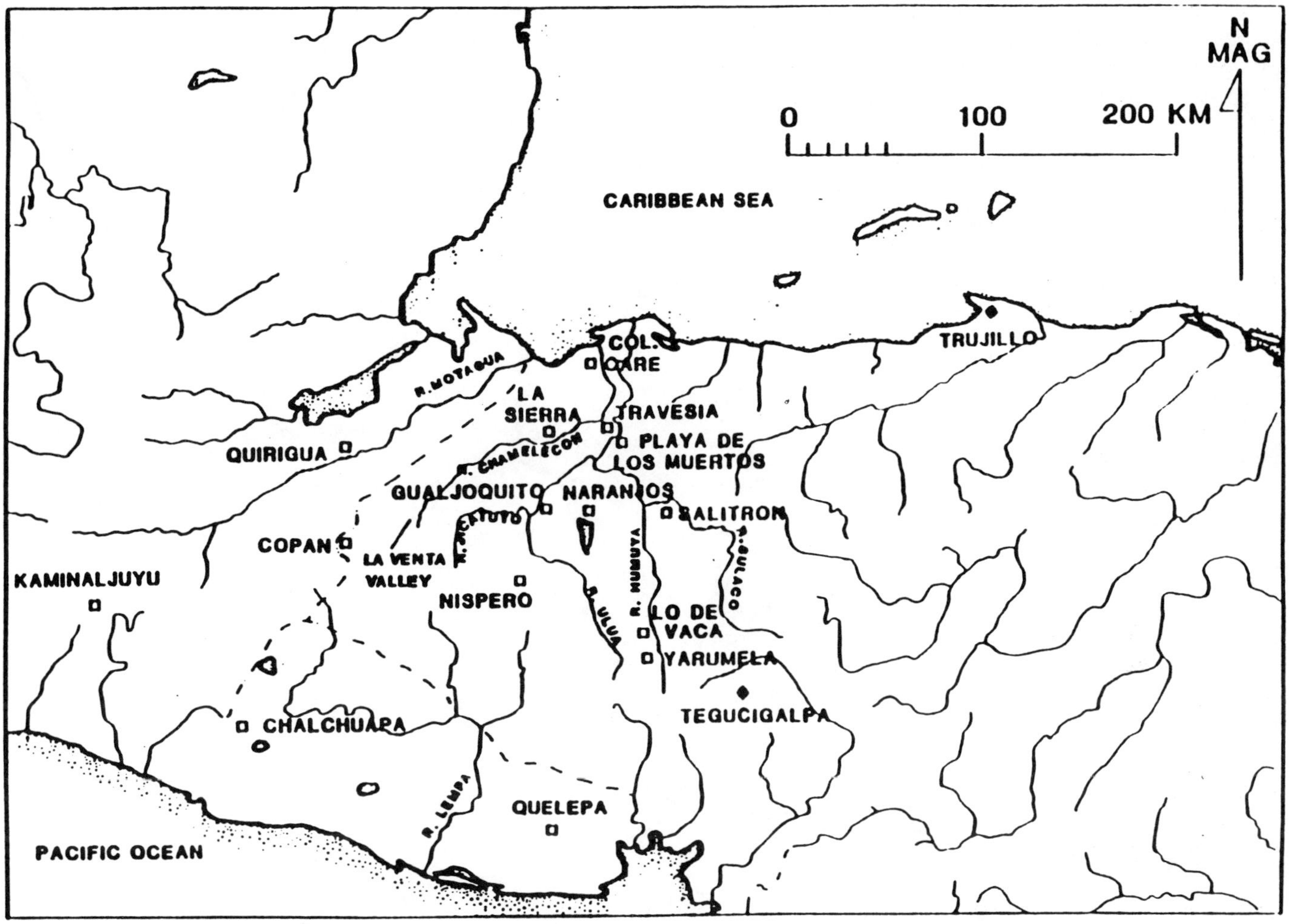

Figure 8.1 Map of the Southeast Mesoamerican Periphery, showing La Sierra.

1979; Urban 1986a, 1986b; Schortman and Urban 1991a, 1991b, 1994a, 1994b; Urban et al. 1988; Wonderley 1981, 1986). One of these maxima falls within the Late Classic period (AD 600-950) when the centrally located site of La Sierra served as regional capital (Figure 8.2). Comparable sociopolitical flouresences were experienced throughout southeastern Mesoamerica during the Late Classic, including societies classed as "lowland Maya" and non-Maya (see papers in Boone 1988; Robinson 1987; and Urban and Schortman 1986 for summaries).

La Sierra Polity Settlement Data

La Sierra contains 468 surface-visible Late Classic constructions within seven tenths of a square kilometer and dominates a five-tier settlement hierarchy defined by variations in numbers of structures and numbers, sizes, and elaboration of monumental buildings (platforms standing 1.5 meters high or taller). A site's categorization, therefore, crudely reflects the relative importance of its residents (i.e., the labor they could commission to build platforms and the number of people attracted to the site [Hendon 1992; Montmollin 1987, 1989]). Monumental constructions were concentrated at La Sierra where 38 of them form a large, "D"-shaped plaza, comprising the site core. The next two settlement strata contain sites with far fewer buildings: Tier 2 loci have 41-44 structures, including 6-8 monumental platforms (2 examples), Tier 3 settlements, 16-30 platforms of which 4-9 are monumental edifices (8 examples). The large platforms at these loci are formally grouped around a patio (Figures 8.3 and 8.4). Tier 4 sites have 13-18 structures including 2-4 monumental platforms but lack clear plaza arrangements (7 examples). The recovery of large-scale constructions at Tier 2-4 centers indicates that they were residences of elites subordinate to the valley paramounts at La Sierra. Tier 5 includes the bulk of recovered Late Classic loci with generally lesser numbers of structures and no more than one monumental platform. A total of 135 sites supporting Late Classic occupations have been identified within the valley containing 2,047 structures

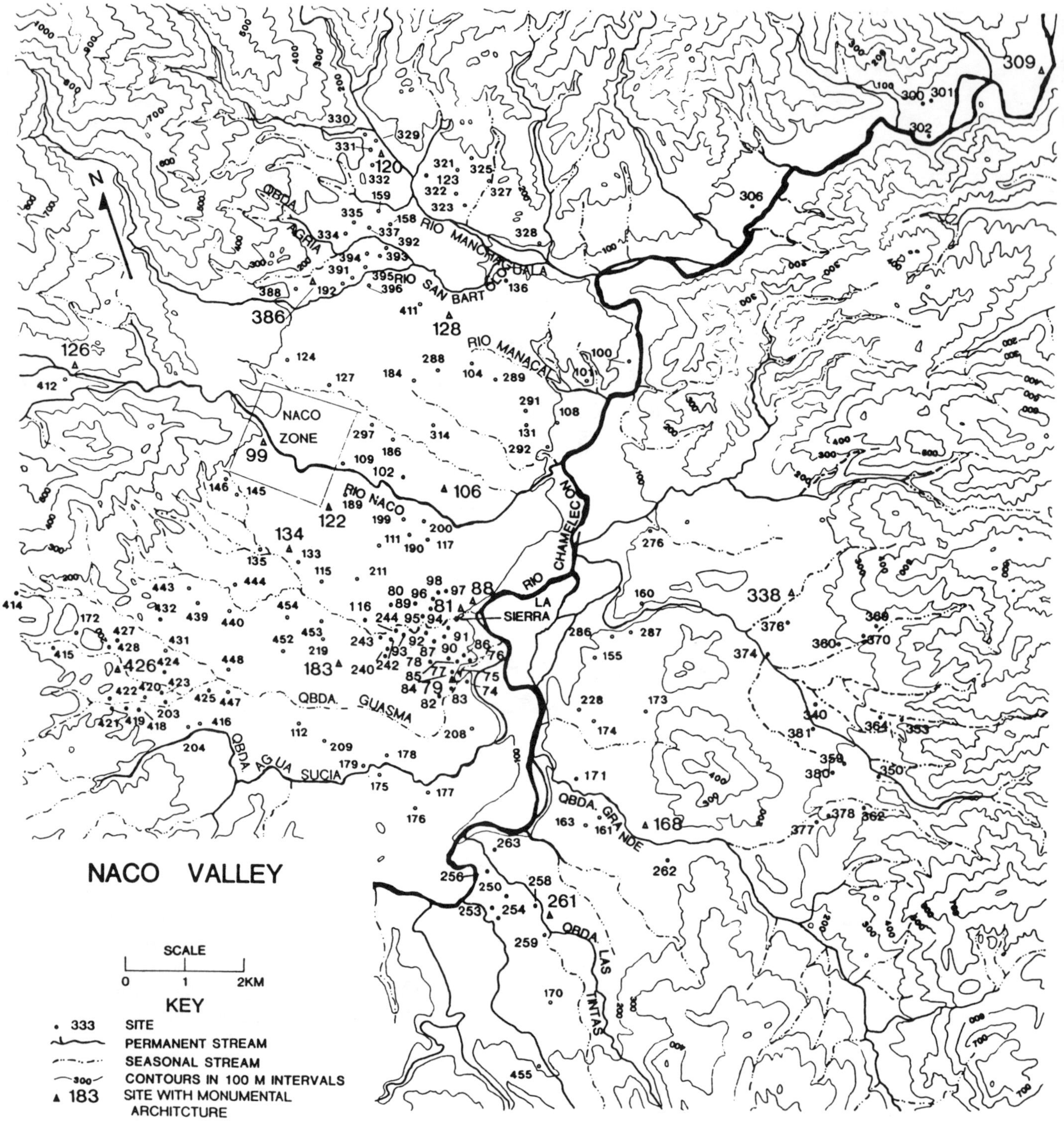

Figure 8.2 Distribution of settlement in the Late Classic Naco valley.

overall. A full 23% of these platforms are found within La Sierra itself while 35% are located at the center and in a one kilometer radius of it (the densely settled area immediately surrounding the capital is referred to here as La Sierra's "near periphery"). Not only was there a general nucleation of population in and around La Sierra but there was a locally high concentration of large Tier 3 sites within the near periphery (three examples).

Settlement data suggests that La Sierra was the capital of a sizable polity administered through a complex sociopolitical hierarchy reflected in the five-tier settlement system (Johnson 1978, 1983; Wright 1977;

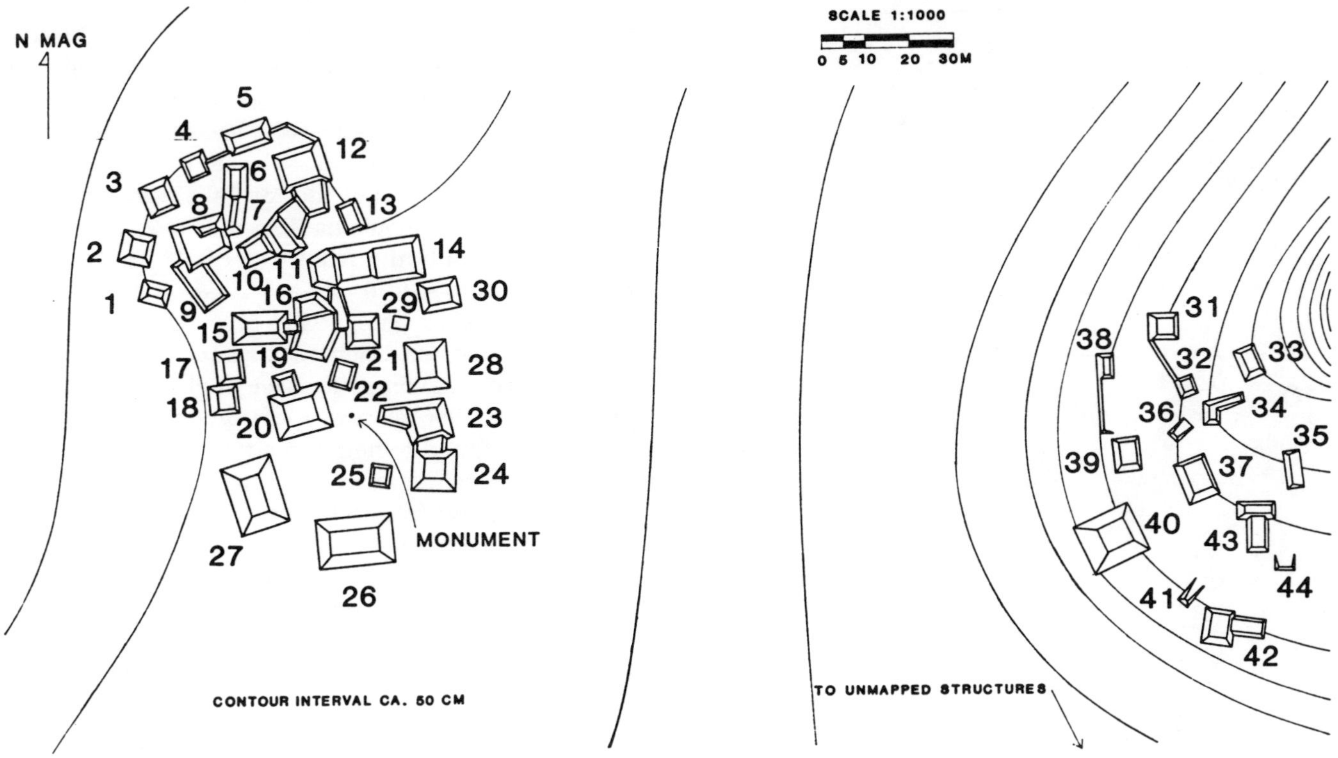

Figure 8.3 Site 168, a Level 2 center in the Late Classic Naco valley site hierarchy.

Wright and Johnson 1975). That La Sierra's rulers dominated the region is indicated by the concentration of monumental constructions and people at and near their capital. La Sierra's site core dwarfs comparable building efforts elsewhere in Naco, suggesting that valley paramounts enjoyed privileged control over local labor. This impression of political centralization is further supported by the degree of nucleation evident in the valley at large. It has been argued elsewhere that rulers of preindustrial polities strive to aggregate physically as many of their subordinates of all ranks as close to their capitals as possible. Such a strategy maximizes control and minimizes costs in collecting tribute as well as dispensing goods and services (Montmollin 1987, 1989; Roscoe 1993). There should be, therefore, a direct correlation between the degree of population nucleation around a primate center and the power of that polity's paramount elite. Similar patterns of presumed elite-sponsored nucleation on a larger scale (e.g., Tzacualli phase [AD 1-100] Teotihuacan in the Valley of Mexico [Parsons 1974; Sanders et al. 1979], and Monte Alban Early I phase [500-250 BC] in the Oaxaca valley [Blanton et al. 1981:70-71]) have been taken to indicate the existence of highly centralized political units. Aggregation of population and monumental construction at La Sierra, therefore, implies that the Late Classic witnessed a period of profound political centralization within the Naco valley which distinguishes that era from the political fragmentation of the preceding and succeeding intervals (the Early Classic, AD 200-600, and Early Postclassic, AD 1100-1300, Urban 1986a, 1986b; Urban et al. 1988). Identifying the exercise of power is one thing; specifying how that power was obtained and preserved another. It was in an effort to address the latter issue that we came to examine the Late Classic Naco political economy using insights derived from prestige good theory.

The Late Classic Naco valley is a particularly apt laboratory in which to study the operation of a prehistoric political economy. The area supported a complexly organized administrative system the capital of which was still relatively small. In part this is because significant occupation at La Sierra was short-lived, beginning in the late part of the Early Classic (ca. AD 400-650) and largely terminating by AD 1100. The total size of the polity also facilitates the study of its structure and organization. Finally, post-Late Classic occupation at La Sierra seems to have been minimal and not disruptive of most Late Classic architectural or artifactual patterns. Naco provides an opportunity to study relations among political hierarchy and interregional interaction that would not be as accessible in larger, more impressive, settings.

The study of prestige-good political economies, as noted earlier, depends heavily on reconstructing patterns of production, consumption, and distribution on a polity-wide scale. Intensive excavations at regional capitals may well yield large quantities of valuables but

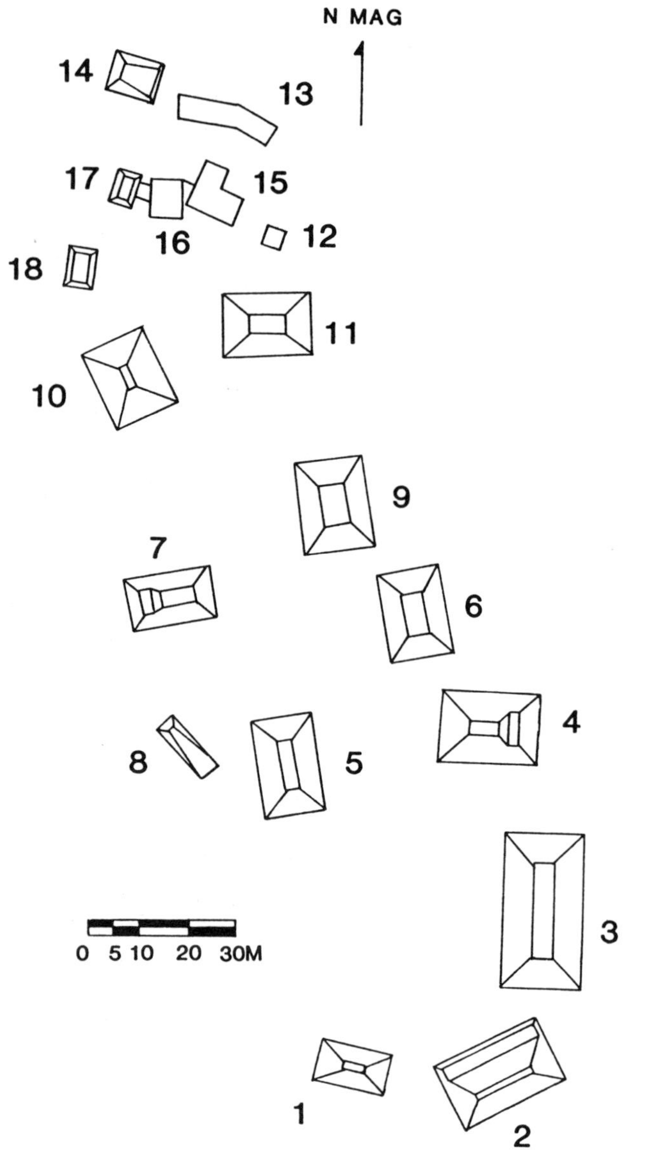

Figure 8.4 Site 261, a Level 3 center in the Late Classic Naco valley site hierarchy.

unless comparable investigations are carried out at all site hierarchy levels we cannot be certain to what extent these items were actually monopolized by the paramount rulers or how significant they were in the daily lives of all polity residents. These are difficult criteria to meet and we can never be absolutely sure that excavated samples from any site or region are truly "representative" (Kent 1987:8-11). Nevertheless, it is important to convey some sense of the extent of Naco research on the Late Classic so that the reader is in a better position to evaluate the statements that follow.

The Naco valley has been thoroughly surveyed on foot, less than one square kilometer remaining unexamined. Extensive investigations have been conducted at Late Classic settlements from all levels of the contemporary site hierarchy. A total of 339 Late Classic buildings have been excavated resulting in the exposure of approximately 10,760 square meters of deposits dating to this interval; 146 edifices dug within La Sierra (31% of the Late Classic buildings found here), 33 investigated in the capital's near periphery, and 160 from rural contexts (13% of known Late Classic structures from both areas). Over half a million artifacts relevant to studies of Late Classic material distributions have been analyzed to date, of which the vast majority are pottery sherds. The Late Classic regional database is not as complete as we might wish and work planned for 1996 in rural portions of the La Sierra polity is designed to help remedy imbalances in excavated samples. Nevertheless, information in hand provides a point from which some preliminary inferences can be advanced concerning the range of prestige goods present within Late Classic La Sierra society and their distribution among all social segments. The following discussion will be based, therefore, on data in which we have some confidence, if not blind faith.

Strategies of Hierarchy Maintenance

We turn then to a consideration of what role(s), if any, centralized control of social valuables played in strategies designed to maintain Late Classic elite power within the La Sierra polity. The focus is on two data classes that have been consistently identified as social valuables within Mesoamerica based on their rarity throughout much of the area and/or the skill required in manufacture: prismatic obsidian blades and carved marine shell ornaments (e.g., Rice 1987:80, 82; Spence 1983:434). Manufacture and distribution of fired clay effigies (figurines, whistles, and ocarinas) will also be discussed as study of this industry provides insights into non-elite reactions to elite domination efforts.

Obsidian

Prismatic obsidian blades, prized throughout Mesoamerica for their sharp working edges, are commonly represented in Late Classic Naco lithic assemblage from all sites. These blades were knapped from carefully prepared polyhedral cores that had to be imported. Source characterization studies of 58 excavated Late Classic examples indicate that most (69%) derive from Ixtepeque, Guatemala, approximately 175 kilometers to the southwest (the remainder come from El Chayal in south-central Guatemala [5%] and an unknown source [28%])(Bouey 1991, 1994). Not only were obsidian blades made from exotic raw materials but considerable skill was needed to produce them (Clark 1987; Sheets 1983). These implements, therefore, represent the paradigmatic prestige good within the Naco valley: they were imported, required special abilities to manufacture, and were needed by households at all levels of the sociopolitical hierarchy where they served in basic production processes. Exclusive paramount elite control of this commodity would help guarantee compliance from subordinates.

The evidence in hand suggests that La Sierra's rulers tried to monopolize the production and distribution of finished obsidian blades. This tool type was used by all Naco residents but manufacturing locales, identified by the presence of polyhedral cores and/or core fragments as well as debitage, are largely concentrated at La Sierra and in its near periphery (all figures are based on analyses of materials unearthed between 1979-1995; studies of lithics recovered during 1995 are still ongoing and results of this and the anticipated 1996 work may modify the patterns outlined below). Five patio-focused structure groups, the domestic loci of ancient households, provided evidence of intense involvement in blade production by residents of the capital. Two groups yielded 58 and 14 core and core fragments while seven to eleven cores and core fragments were found at three more structure aggregates. The remaining excavated groups had between one and four core/core fragments implying widespread but low-level participation in blade manufacture throughout the capital and its environs. It appears at present that all households in La Sierra and its near periphery were involved in blade production to some extent.

Diagnostics of blade knapping are found sporadically in rural Late Classic contexts suggesting occasional, low-level involvement in this craft (a total of eight cores/core fragments have been recovered from four sites beyond the immediate La Sierra area to date while other indicators of blade production were unearthed from one additional settlement).

Present evidence suggests that prismatic obsidian blade manufacture was largely, if not exclusively, carried out by artisans who resided at La Sierra and likely operated under the auspices of elite patrons. Polyhedral cores were probably acquired by valley paramounts and supplied to attached specialists who engaged in this craft to varying degrees. Occupants of at least five patio groups (those with 7-58 recovered nuclei) fashioned blades far in excess of their immediate needs. That signs of blade manufacture were found at every structure aggregate excavated in La Sierra and its near periphery implies that these surpluses were not destined for consumption within the center and its immediate surroundings. Instead, most implements probably found their way to rural contexts. Recovery of a few blade production diagnostics from the latter area suggests that dependence on centralized manufacture was not absolute; some people were capable of supplementing the output of La Sierra's workshops with their own efforts. Even in these cases, however, economic autonomy may have been tightly circumscribed. Clustering of blade manufacturing markers at rural administrative centers (Tier 2-4 sites) hints at an intraregional distribution system in which blade nuclei as well as finished products reached consumers through political intermediaries and not by "free" exchange. La Sierra's paramounts, therefore, may have monopolized blade production through a combination of direct supervision over workshops at the capital and indirect control of rural manufacture through centralized distribution of essential cores.

Imported polyhedral nuclei were not the only source for chipped stone tools in the Late Classic valley, nor was the prismatic blade the only form in which these implements appeared.[1] A percussion flake industry was contemporary with the prismatic blade tradition. The former involved hard-hammer removal of irregular flakes from small perlite nodules which apparently derive from volcanic deposits on the southern valley margins.[2] The skill and raw material requirements for prismatic blade production made this industry dependent on imported, prepared cores and restricted participation to those few artisans with the appropriate skills and access to essential raw materials. Manufacturing flakes was a more casual affair, the needed abilities and resources being generally available to most Naco residents (see also Clark 1987; Sheets 1983). Flake cores, in fact, are widely distributed at sites of all sizes throughout the Late Classic Naco valley. Wear studies of the Naco chipped stone assemblage are still in progress and it is not clear whether blades and flakes were used in complementary or overlapping tasks. It is obvious, however, that Late Classic households, especially in rural areas, were not completely dependent for chipped stone tools on centrally produced blades. They could augment this supply using widely available materials and skills (we are indebted to N. Ross, currently working with the Naco lithics, for much of the data on stone tool manufacture outlined above).

Marine Shell

Ornaments carved of marine shell are not nearly as ubiquitous within Mesoamerica in general, nor the Naco valley in particular, as obsidian. Nevertheless, they fit our definition of a prestige good in that they required considerable skill to produce (e.g., Flannery and Winters 1976) and were not available from local sources within the valley (the north coast littoral is 35 kilometers distant [straight-line measurement] at its closest point). A marine shell workshop was recognized during excavations of a small, patio-focused structure group ca. 45m north of the La Sierra site core. These investigations unearthed 1,256 marine shell fragments (preliminarily identified as conch) and 12 coral pieces. Associated with these objects was a distinctive chert tool form with a carefully fashioned, narrow point showing unidirectional and alternate/opposite wear (Schafer 1990). The sturdy working ends of these tools would have been well-suited to shell engraving and/or cutting (see Flannery and Winters 1976:Fig. 2.14a-e for an illustration of a very similar tool type used to work shell in the Early Formative Oaxaca valley). Shell and coral fragments are rarely found elsewhere at La Sierra, then only in minuscule amounts, and the same can be said for the distinctive chert tool type associated with them (Schortman and Urban 1991a, 1991b). Marine shell and the "engraving/cutting" tools described above are not found outside the Late Classic capital. At the very least, this distribution suggests that working marine shell was more highly centralized than the production of obsidian blades.

We would surmise, therefore, that imported marine shell and the skills (as well as tools) needed to fashion artifacts from it were under the strict control of La Sierra's paramounts. Unlike obsidian, however, shell jewelry was not essential for the performance of domestic tasks. Also, only one finished shell ornament has been recovered from a Late Classic context in the valley (at La Sierra). These items may have been disposed of in deposits about which we know very little, e.g., elite burials. Alternatively, most shell artifacts could have been exported and not kept for local circulation. In the latter case shell jewelry would not constitute a prestige good as defined here because it was not needed by Naco households at all hierarchical levels. An elite monopoly over shell-working would not create bonds of dependence linking rulers and subjects. Such a monopoly, however, might still have been crucial to the operation of the Late Classic Naco political economy and to the paramountcy of the La Sierra elite.

Marine shell artifacts, valued by rulers throughout most of Mesoamerica, likely served as important currency in interpolity transactions. One possible recipient for the goods fashioned at La Sierra is Copan where items made from conch are found and were invested with considerable symbolic significance associated with rulership (Baudez 1986). The single shell workshop known from the Late Classic Copan valley yielded only small quantities of shell debitage, including some conch. In addition, no tools suitable for the heavy cutting tasks by which raw shell could be transformed into finished artifacts were found (R. Widemer personal communication, 1992). The Copan data suggests that conch shell had already undergone significant shaping before its arrival in the valley, Copan artisans carrying out small-scale modifications of the imports. The large amounts of conch debris, including sizable fragments, found at the contemporary Naco workshop in association with stone tools arguably used in shell working tentatively indicate that some of this initial shaping occurred in the La Sierra polity. Shell may, therefore, have moved southwest in return for other materials, particularly polyhedral obsidian cores. As noted above, the majority of sourced, Late Classic Naco obsidian artifacts derive from the Ixtepeque flows. It is generally agreed that access to this source in Late Classic southeastern Mesoamerica was controlled by Copan (Sheets 1986:236). Shell artifact manufacture, therefore, might well have provided the essential "currency" needed to acquire important elements of the Late Classic Naco political economy. Exclusive elite control over the fashioning of exports would have been crucial to paramount domination strategies. Only those with access to goods appropriate for interregional, especially inter-elite, exchanges could participate in such transactions. By concentrating shell artifact manufacture at one La Sierra locale, valley rulers guaranteed that they alone successfully engaged in interpolity contacts through which imports central to the functioning of all Naco households were acquired. It is for these reasons, we argue, that marine shell working is even more restricted in its distribution than prismatic obsidian blade production.

Figurines

Fired clay figurines are ubiquitous within the Late Classic Naco valley and are believed to have been important in ritual behaviors throughout Mesoamerica (Bell's continuing, analysis of figurine form, style, and manufacture is the basis of the following discussion). This data class most likely served in ideological transactions no less significant to all Naco inhabitants than the predominately maintenance chores in which obsidian blades functioned. The political significance of figurine and blade manufacture differs, however, in that both raw materials and skills crucial to the former industry were widely distributed and easily acquired within Late Classic Naco (participation in ocarina fabrication may have required specialized skills, a point that is still under study). Difficult to monopolize from the center, figurine production could be incorporated into the strategies of rural households seeking to preserve some level of economic independence.

The distinctive marker of figurine manufacture is the hollow, fired clay mold, of which 79 have been identified so far in Late Classic collections (counts from 1995 are incomplete as study is ongoing). Twelve come from La Sierra, four from that center's near periphery, and the remainder were unearthed at rural settlements of all sizes (Table 8.1). Roughly 80% of these distinctive artifacts, therefore, derive from rural contexts. Insofar as frequency of molds recovered from a site reflects the intensity of figurine production at that locus, it appears

Table 8.1. Distribution of Figurine Molds among Late Classic Naco Loci

Site	*Site Tier*	*#Figurine Molds*	*%Late Classic Collection*
La Sierra	1	12	15%
81	3	3	4%
101	4	1	1%
120	4	1	1%
123	4	1	1%
426	4	12	15%
96	5	1	1%
108	5	1	1%
337	5	29	37%
386	5	5	6%
423	5	7	9%
428	5	2	3%
444	5	1	1%
470	5	3	4%

that figurine manufacture was not an elite monopoly. The uneven distribution of molds further hints at the existence of rural household specialization in figurine working (compare Sites 337 and 426 with other excavated loci in Table 8.1). Whether this variation follows from the differential availability of appropriate clays or some other set of factors is not known (a recently completed survey of Naco clay deposits does not suggest that variable access to raw materials accounts for discrepancies in levels of figurine manufacture among sites [Connell 1991]).

Data on figurine production reveal a portrait of the Late Classic Naco political economy at odds with that provided by studies of obsidian blade and marine shell fabrication. We are presented here with a glimpse of the actions people might take to preserve some measure of economic autonomy and thereby resist absolute domination by powerful elites. Fashioning figurines for immediate use would have helped households meet some of their own needs, freeing them at least partly from dependence on the output of centralized workshops. Those social units that, for one reason or another, intensively engaged in this craft could further enhance their material statuses through intravalley exchanges with people engaged in other specializations. Craft production might, therefore, have been a double-edged sword used by different social segments to both advance and frustrate domination strategies. Prestige good monopolies, in this scenario, were countered by rural investment in craft activities employing resources and techniques beyond the control of valley rulers. These moves and countermoves together contributed to the creation of a heterogenous polity divided along lines of occupation and power.[3]

Discussion

Workshops of varying sizes involved in the production of incense burners, textiles, pottery vessels, and ground stone implements have been identified in the Late Classic La Sierra polity (Schortman and Urban 1994b: Table 1; Schortman and Urban 1994a). It is still unclear how these were integrated within the ancient political economy and contributed, if at all, to strategies of elite domination and/or subordinate resistance. The three production, consumption, and distribution systems discussed above, however, convey some idea of how complex even a relatively small-scale, nonindustrial political economy can be. On the one hand there is good evidence for paramount control over the acquisition, production, and dissemination of a generally needed commodity (prismatic obsidian blades). This monopoly fits the general expectations of a prestige good model and almost certainly played an important role in maintaining the preeminence of the La Sierra elite. Supporting this intraregional system of domination was a strategy of centralized control over the fabrication of marine shell jewelry, much of the output arguably reserved for export. Excluding all other polity residents, elite and non-elite, from the manufacture of this commodity ensured that La Sierra's scions alone successfully participated in interregional transactions through which locally valued goods, such as polyhedral obsidian cores, were acquired.

Running parallel, and perhaps contrary, to these elite-dominated economic systems were the maneuverings of lower status individuals to retain some measure of household autonomy. Small perlite nodules were acquired locally and used as the source of simple flakes. The latter did not replace prismatic obsidian blades in rural assemblages but augmented them. Figurines, while not apparently fashioned in every household, were made throughout the valley. Access to these ideologically potent objects was not dependent on elite largesse. Relatively large-scale production of figurines may, in fact, have provided some rural households with a means of securing an enhanced position within the political economy. Production processes not easily controlled from the center, because of the general availability of raw materials and simple skill requirements, seem particularly appropriate components of resistance strategies (Clark 1987).

The data summarized above suggest that insights into elite domination efforts provided by prestige good theory can be fruitfully applied to purely prehistoric, noncapitalist situations (see also Braithwaite 1984; Kristiansen 1979, 1987a, 1987b; McGuire 1987; Shennan 1982, 1986; Spencer 1982). Prestige good formulations provide an effective way of understanding how macroregional and local politico-economic processes were articulated through the goal-oriented behavior of political actors. The Naco experience has also made us more sensitive about assuming the passivity of non-elites within ancient political economies. Allowance must be made for the active manipulation by *all* polity members of economic and political processes in efforts to dominate and resist subjugation, to create dependence and maintain autonomy. The dynamics of this struggle shape a political economy and determine the relative power of rulers. The resultant structure is never static or in equilibrium but contains within it tensions which, as circumstances shift, contribute to and channel further change.

Notes

1. Chipped stone tools were also made using hard-hammer percussion techniques from chert and, more rarely, quartz in the Late Classic Naco valley. Both raw materials are locally available. Interestingly, chert and quartz cores and flakes generally comprise a very small minority of Naco valley lithic assemblages in all time periods. Local chert in particular seems suitable for tool manufacture as indicated by replicative studies (Schafer 1991). We are at a loss, therefore, to account for the overwhelming preference exhibited by Late Classic Naco dwellers for imported obsidian over indigenous chert and quartz.

2. The percussion-flake industry employing apparent perlite nodules has a long history in Naco, stretching from at least the Middle Preclassic (ca. 800-400 BC) through to the Spanish Conquest in the 16th century AD. Tools made in this tradition dominate the earliest valley assemblage (800-400 BC) and are common in later deposits as well (AD 950-1530). During the Late Classic, however, products of this industry are generally swamped by prismatic blades knapped from imported polyhedral cores.

3. We continue to assume that figurines were produced solely for consumption within the Naco valley. The economic picture becomes more complex if they were also exported. Stylistic comparisons and chemical/mineralogical assays of figurines from Naco and surrounding areas will, we trust, shed some light on this important question.

Acknowledgements

A great many people played key roles in obtaining and interpreting the data on which this chapter is based. Among these individuals we would especially like to single out for thanks, Lic. V. Cruz Reyes, Arq. J. Maria Casco, and Dra. Olga Joya Gerentes (1988, 1990/1991, and 1994 to present respectively), and Lic. V. Veliz R., Lic. F. Cruz S., Dra. G. Lara, Lic. R. Agurcia, Lic. G. Hasemann, Sr. I. Orellano, and Sr. J. A. Duron, all of or formerly of the Instituto Hondureno de Antropologia e Historia, for their consistent support of our work. Many people contributed their time, skill, and good humor to the Naco researches over the years of whom we would like to mention M. Ausec, K. Anderson, E. Bell, V. Clark, L. Collins, S. Connell, J. Douglass, J. Miller, L. Neff, N. Ross, D. Schafer, S. Smith, L. True, M. Turek, and S. Yates for particular thanks. Archaeological investigations succeed or fail on the strength of their work crews and we were and are very fortunate to have the services of excellent laborers from the towns of Naco, Cofradia, La Aceguia, San Antonio, and San Jose in the Naco valley. Further, we are very grateful to the owners of all the sites we excavated in the valley, especially to Sr. Francisco Sunseri who has cordially welcomed us back over many years to La Sierra and done everything in his power to make the work progress smoothly. To all of these individuals we want to extend our most heartfelt thanks. Naco research has been and is generously funded by grants from the National Science Foundation (BBS-8712979, DIR-8900360, DIR-9100569, SBR-9322330; BNS-8919272, BNS-9022247, BNS-9121386, and SBR-9407751) National Endowment for the Humanities (RO-21897-89), National Geographic Society (4208-89), Fulbright Foundation, Wenner-Gren Foundation, Margaret Cullinan Wray program of the American Anthropological Association, and Kenyon College. Needless to say, we are very grateful for the support of these agencies. All errors and seeming lapses of logic, not to mention good sense and taste, remain our sole responsibilities.

References Cited

Ashmore, Wendy
1988 Household and Community at Classic Quirigua. In *Household and Community in the Mesoamerican Past*, edited by R. Wilk and W. Ashmore, pp. 153-169. University of New Mexico Press, Albuquerque.

Baudez, Claude
1986 Iconography and History at Copan. In *The Southeast Maya Periphery*, edited by P. Urban and E. Schortman, pp. 17-26. University of Texas Press, Austin.

Binford, Lewis
1965 Archaeological Systematics and the Study of Culture Process. *American Antiquity* 31:203-210.

Blanton, Richard and Gary Feinman
1984 The Mesoamerican World System. *American Anthropologist* 86:673-682.

Blanton, Richard, Stephen Kowalewski, Gary Feinman, and Jill Appel
1981 *Ancient Mesoamerica: A Comparison of Change in Three Regions.* Cambridge University Press, Cambridge.

Boone, Elizabeth
1988 *The Southeast Classic Maya Zone*. Dumbarton Oaks, Washington, D.C.

Bouey, Paul
1991 Source Determination of Archaeological Obsidian Specimens, Naco Valley, Honduras. In *Sociopolitical Hierarchy and Craft Production: The Economic Bases of Elite Power in a Southeast Mesoamerican Polity*, edited by E. Schortman and P. Urban, Appendix IV. Anthropology/ Sociology Department, Kenyon College.
1994 Source Determination of Archaeological Obsidian Specimens, Naco Valley, Honduras. In *Sociopolitical Hierarchy and Craft Production: The Economic Bases of Elite Power in a Southeast Mesoamerican Polity—Part III*, edited by E. Schortman and P. Urban, Appendix I. Anthropology/ Sociology Department, Kenyon College.

Braithwaite, M.
1984 Ritual and Prestige in the Prehistory of Wessex, 2200-1400 BC: A New Dimension to the Archaeological Evidence. In *Ideology, Power and Prehistory*, edited by D. Miller and C. Tilley, pp. 93-110. Cambridge University Press, Cambridge.

Brumfiel, Elizabeth
1987 Elite and Utilitarian Crafts in the Aztec State. In *Specialization, Exchange, and Complex Societies*, edited by E. Brumfiel and T. Earle, pp. 102-118. Cambridge University Press, Cambridge.

Brumfiel, Elizabeth, and Timothy Earle
1987 Specialization, Exchange, and Complex Societies: An Introduction. In *Specialization, Exchange, and Complex Societies*, edited by E. Brumfiel and T. Earle, pp. 1-9. Cambridge University Press, Cambridge.

Clark, John
1987 Politics, Prismatic Blades, and Mesoamerican Civilization. In *The Organization of Core Technology*, edited by J. Johnson and C. Morrow, pp. 259-284. Westview Press, Boulder.

Connell, Samuel
1991 Ceramic Economy of the Naco Valley. In *Sociopolitical Hierarchy and Craft Production: The Economic Bases of Elite Power in a Southeast Mesoamerican Polity—Part II*, edited by E. Schortman and P. Urban, pp. 20-30. Anthropology/Sociology Department, Kenyon College.

Cowgill, George, J. Altschul, and R. Sload
1984 Spatial Analysis of Teotihuacan: A Mesoamerican Metropolis. In *Intrasite Spatial Analysis in Archaeology*, edited by H. Hietala, pp. 154-195. Cambridge University Press, Cambridge.

D'Altroy, Terrence, and Timothy Earle
1985 Staple Finance, Wealth Finance, and Storage in the Inka Political Economy. *Current Anthropology* 26:187-206.

Dupre, G. and P. Rey
1973 Reflections on the Pertinence of a Theory of the History of Exchange. *Economy and Society* 2:131-163.
Earle, Timothy
1987 Specialization and the Production of Wealth: Hawaiian Chiefdoms and the Inka Empire. In *Specialization, Exchange and Complex Societies,* edited by E. Brumfiel and T. Earle, pp. 64-75. Cambridge University Press, Cambridge.
Ekholm, Kasja
1972 *Power and Prestige: The Rise and Fall of the Kongo Kingdom.* Skriv Service, Uppsala.
1978 External Change and the Transformation of Central African Social Systems. In *The Evolution of Social Systems,* edited by J. Friedman and M. Rowlands, pp. 115-136. University of Pittsburgh Press, Pittsburgh.
Ekholm, Kasja and Jonathan Friedman
1979 "Capital" Imperialism and Exploitation in Ancient World Systems. In *Power and Propaganda: A Symposium on Ancient Empires,* edited by M. Larsen, pp. 41-58. Akademisk Forlag, Copenhagen.
Flannery, Kent, and Marcus Winters
1976 Analyzing Household Activities. In *The Early Mesoamerican Village,* edited by K. Flannery, pp. 34-47. Academic Press, New York.
Fletcher, R.
1984 Identifying Spatial Disorder: A Case Study of a Mongol Fort. In *Intrasite Spatial Analysis in Archaeology,* edited by H. Hietala, pp. 196-223. Cambridge University Press, Cambridge.
Frankenstein, Susan and Michael Rowlands
1978 The Internal Structure and Regional Context of Early Iron Age Society in Southwestern Germany. *Bulletin of the Institute of Archaeology* 15:73-112.
Friedman, Jonathan
1982 Catastrophe and Continuity in Social Evolution. In *Theory and Explanation in Archaeology: The Southampton Conference,* edited by C. Renfrew, M. Rowlands, and B. Segraves, pp. 175-196. Academic Press, New York.
Friedman, Jonathan, and Michael Rowlands
1978 Notes Toward an Epigenetic Model of the Evolution of Civilization. In *The Evolution of Social Systems,* edited by J. Friedman and M. Rowlands, pp. 201-276. University of Pittsburgh Press, Pittsburgh.
Gilman, Antonio
1987 Unequal Development in Copper Age Iberia. In *Specialization, Exchange, and Complex Societies,* edited by E. Brumfiel and T. Earle, pp. 22-29. Cambridge University Press, Cambridge.
Gnivecki, Perry
1987 On the Quantitative Derivation of Household Spatial Organization from Archaeological Residues in Ancient Mesopotamia. In *Method and Theory for Activity Area Research,* edited by S. Kent, pp. 176-235. Columbia University Press, New York.
Halstead, P., and J. O'Shea
1982 A Friend In Need is a Friend Indeed: Social Storage and the Origins of Social Ranking. In *Ranking, Resource, and Exchange,* edited by C. Renfrew and S. Shennan, pp. 92-99. Cambridge University Press, Cambridge.
Haselgrove, Colin
1982 Wealth, Prestige, and Power: The Dynamics of Late Iron Age Political Centralization in South-East England. In *Ranking, Resource, and Exchange,* edited by C. Renfrew and S. Shennan, pp. 79-88. Cambridge University Press, Cambridge.
1987 Culture Process on the Periphery: Belgic Gaul and Rome During the Late Republic and Early Empire. In *Centre and Periphery in the Ancient World,* edited by M. Rowlands, M. Larsen, and K. Kristiansen, pp. 104-124. Cambridge University Press, Cambridge.

Henderson, John, Ilene Wallace, Anthony Wonderley, and Patricia Urban

1979 Archaeological Investigations in the Valle de Naco, Northwestern Honduras: A Preliminary Report. *Journal of Field Archaeology* 6:169-192.

Hendon, Julia

1992 The Interpretation of Survey Data: Two Case Studies from the Maya Area. *Latin American Antiquity* 3:22-42.

Johnson, Gregory

1978 Information Sources and the Development of Decision-Making Organizations. In *Social Anthropology: Beyond Subsistence and Dating*, edited by C. Redman et al., pp. 87-112. Academic Press, New York.

1983 Organizational Structure and Scalar Stress. In *Theory and Explanation in Archaeology: The Southampton Conference*, edited by C. Renfrew, M. Rowlands, and B. Segraves, pp. 389-421. Academic Press, New York.

Keesing, R.

1983 *Elota's Story: The Life and Times of a Solomon Islands Big Man.* Holt, Rinehart, and Winston, New York.

Kent, Susan

1987 Understanding the Use of Space: An Ethnoarchaeological Approach. In *Method and Theory for Activity Area Research*, edited by S. Kent, pp. 1-60. Columbia University Press, New York.

Kipp, Rita, and Edward Schortman

1989 The Political Impact of Trade in Chiefdoms. *American Anthropologist* 91:370-385.

Kohl, Philip

1987 The Use and Abuse of World Systems Theory: The Case of the Prehistoric West Asian State. In *Advances in Archaeological Method and Theory*, Vol. 11, edited by M. Schiffer, pp. 1-35. Academic Press, Orlando.

1992 The Transcaucasian "Periphery" in the Bronze Age: A Preliminary Formulation. In *Resources, Power, and Interregional Interaction*, edited by E. Schortman and P. Urban, pp. 117-137. Plenum Press, New York.

Kowalewski, Stephen

1989 Review of Rowlands, Larsen, and Kristiansen, "Centre and Periphery in the Ancient World." *American Anthropologist* 91:481-482.

Kristiansen, Kristian

1979 The Consumption of Wealth in Bronze Age Denmark. A Study in the Dynamics of Economic Processes in Tribal Societies. In *New Directions in Scandinavian Archaeology*, edited by K. Kristiansen and C. Carsten-Paluden, pp. 158-190. The National Museum of Denmark, Copenhagen.

1987a From Stone to Bronze: The Evolution of Social Complexity in Northern Europe, 2300-1200 BC. In *Specialization, Exchange, and Complex Societies*, edited by E. Brumfiel and T. Earle, pp. 30-51. Cambridge University Press, Cambridge.

1987b Centre and Periphery in Bronze Age Scandinavia. In *Centre and Periphery in the Ancient World*, edited by M. Rowlands, M. Larsen, and K. Kristiansen, pp. 74-85. Cambridge University Press, Cambridge.

Marcus, Joyce

1992 Political Fluctuations in Mesoamerica. *National Geographic Research and Exploration* 8:392-411.

McGuire, Randall

1987 The Papaguerian Periphery: Uneven Development in the Prehistoric U.S. Southwest. In *Polities and Partitions*, edited by K. M. Trinkhaus, pp. 123-139. Anthropological Research Papers, No. 37. Arizona State University Press, Tempe.

Meillassoux, Claude

1960 Essai d'Interpretation des Phenomenes Economiques dans les Societes Traditionelles d'Autosubsistence. *Cahiers d'Etudes Africaines* 4.

1981 *Maidens, Meal, and Money*. Cambridge: Cambridge University Press.

Montmollin, Olivier de
1987 Forced Settlement and Political Centralization in a Classic Maya Polity. *Journal of Anthropological Archaeology* 6:220-262.
1989 *The Archaeology of Political Structure: Settlement Analysis in A Classic Maya Polity.* Cambridge University Press, Cambridge.
Myers, T.
1987 Comment on, "Staple Finance, Wealth Finance, and Storage in the Inka Political Economy," by T. D'Altroy and T. Earle. *Current Anthropology* 26:200.
Oswald, Dana
1987 The Organization of Space in Residential Buildings: A Cross-Cultural Perspective. In *Method and Theory for Activity Area Research*, edited by S. Kent, pp. 295-344. Columbia University Press, New York.
Pailes, Richard and Joseph Whitecotton
1979 The Greater Southwest and the Mesoamerican "World System": An Exploratory Model of Frontier Relationships. In *The Frontier* Volume 2, edited by W. Savage Jr. and S. Thompson, pp. 105-121. University of Oklahoma Press, Norman.
Parson, Jeffrey
1974 The Development of a Prehistoric Complex Society: A Regional Perspective from the Valley of Mexico. *Journal of Field Archaeology* 1:81-108.
Peregrine, Peter
1991 Prehistoric Chiefdoms on the American Midcontinent: A World-System Based on Prestige Goods. In *Core/Periphery Relations in Precapitalist Worlds*, edited by C. Chase-Dunn and T. Hall, pp. 193-211. Westview Press, Boulder.
1992 *Mississippian Evolution: A World-System Perspective.* Prehistory Press, Madison.
Renfrew, Colin
1982 Polity and Power: Interaction, Intensification, and Exploitation. In *An Island Polity: The Archaeology of Exploitation in Melos*, edited by C. Renfrew and M. Wagstaff, pp. 264-290. Cambridge University Press, Cambridge.
Rice, Prudence
1987 Economic Change in the Lowland Maya Late Classic Period. In *Specialization, Exchange, and Complex Societies*, edited by E. Brumfiel and T. Earle, pp. 76-85. Cambridge University Press, Cambridge.
Robinson, Eugenia
1987 *Interaction on the Southeast Mesoamerican Frontier.* British Archaeological Reports Series, Oxford.
Roscoe, Paul
1993 Practice and Political Centralization: A New Approach to Political Evolution. *Current Anthropology* 34:111-140.
Rowlands, Michael
1987 Power and Moral Order in Precolonial West-Central Africa. In *Specialization, Exchange, and Complex Societies*, edited by E. Brumfiel and T. Earle, pp. 52-63. Cambridge University Press, Cambridge.
Runciman, William
1982 Origins of States: The Case of Archaic Greece. *Comparative Studies in Society and History* 24:351-377.
Sanders, William
1956 The Central Mexican Symbiotic Region: A Study in Prehistoric Settlement Patterns. *Viking Fund Publications in Anthropology* 23:115-128.
Sanders, William, Jeffrey Parsons and Robert Santley
1979 *The Basin of Mexico: Ecological Processes in the Evolution of a Civilization.* Academic Press, New York.
Sanders, William, and Barabara Price
1968 *Mesoamerica: The Evolution of a Civilization.* Random House, New York.
Sawyer, P.
1979 Kings and Merchants. In *Early Medieval Kingship*, edited by P. Sawyer and D. Wood, pp. 139-158. The School of History, University of Leeds, Leeds (originally published in 1977).

Schafer, David

1990 *Procurement, Production, Distribution and Use: An Analysis of the Chipped Stone Artifacts from the Naco Valley, Honduras.* BA Honors Thesis, Anthropology, Albion College.

1991 A Microcrystalline Source in the Naco Valley, Honduras. In *Sociopolitical Hierarchy and Craft Production: The Economic Bases of Elite Power in a Southeast Mesoamerican Polity—Part II*, edited by E. Schortman and P. Urban, Appendix III. Anthropology/Sociology Department, Kenyon College.

Schneider, Jane

1977 Was there a Pre-Capitalist World System? *Peasant Studies* 6:20-29.

Schortman, Edward

1989 Interregional Interaction in Prehistory: The Need for a New Perspective. *American Antiquity* 54:52-65.

Schortman, Edward, and Patricia Urban

1987 Modeling Interregional Interaction in Prehistory. In *Advances in Archaeological Method and Theory*, Vol. 11, edited by M. Schiffer, pp. 37-95. Academic Press, San Diego.

1991a *Sociopolitical Hierarchy and Craft Production: The Economic Bases of Elite Power in a Late Classic Southeast Mesoamerican Polity.* Anthropology/Sociology Department, Kenyon College.

1991b *Sociopolitical Hierarchy and Craft Production: The Economic Bases of Elite Power in a Southeast Mesoamerican Polity—Part II.* Anthropology/Sociology Department, Kenyon College.

1994a *Sociopolitical Hierarchy and Craft Production: The Economic Bases of Elite Power in a Southeast Mesoamerican Polity—Part III.* Anthropology/Sociology Department, Kenyon College.

1994b Living on the Edge: Core/Periphery Relations in Ancient Southeastern Mesoamerica. *Current Anthropology* 35:401-430.

Sheets, Payson

1983 Guatemalan Obsidian: A Preliminary Study of Sources and Quirigua Artifacts. In *Quirigua Reports*, Volume 2, edited by E. Schortman and P. Urban, pp. 87-101. University Museum, University of Pennsylvania, Philadelphia.

1986 Natural Hazards, Natural Disasters, and Research in the Zapotitan Valley of El Salvador. In *The Southeast Maya Periphery*, edited by P. Urban and E. Schortman, pp. 224-238. University of Texas Press, Austin.

Shennan, Stephen

1982 Exchange and Ranking: The Role of Amber in the Early Bronze Age of Europe. In *Ranking, Resource, and Exchange*, edited by C. Renfrew and S. Shennan, pp. 33-45. Cambridge University Press, Cambridge.

1986 Interaction and Change in Third Millennium BC Western and Central Europe. In *Peer Polity Interaction and Socio-Political Change*, edited by C. Renfrew and J. Cherry, pp. 137-148. Cambridge University Press, Cambridge.

Spence, Michael

1983 Comment on, "The Economic System of Ancient Oaxaca: A Regional Perspective." *Current Anthropology* 24:433-434.

Spencer, Charles

1982 *The Cuicatlan de Canada and Monte Alban: A Study of Primary State Formation.* Academic Press, New York.

Stark, Barbara

1985 Archaeological Identification of Pottery Production Locations: Ethnoarchaeological and Archaeological Data in Mesoamerica. In *Decoding Prehistoric Ceramics*, edited by B. Nelson, pp. 155-194. Southern Illinois University Press, Carbondale.

Steward, Julian

1972 *Theory of Culture Change.* University of Illinois Press, Urbana.

Strathern, Andrew

1971 *The Rope of Moka.* Cambridge University Press, Cambridge (originally published in 1955).

Tosi, M.

1984 The Notion of Craft Specialization and its Representation in the Archaeological Record of Early States in the Turanian Basin. In *Marxist Perspectives in Archaeology*, edited by M. Spriggs, pp. 22-52. Cambridge University Press, Cambridge.

Upham, Steadman

1982 *Polities and Power*. Academic Press, New York.

1992 Interaction and Isolation: The Empty Spaces in Panregional Political and Economic Systems. In *Resources, Power, and Interregional Interaction*, edited by E. Schortman and P. Urban, pp. 139-152. Plenum Press, New York.

Urban, Patricia

1986a *Systems of Settlement in the Pre-Columbian Naco Valley, Northwestern Honduras*. Ph.D. dissertation, University of Pennsylvania. Ann Arbor: University Microfilms.

1986b Pre-Columbian Settlement in the Naco Valley, Northwestern Honduras. In *The Southeast Maya Periphery*, edited by P. Urban and E. Schortman, pp. 275-295. University of Texas Press, Austin.

Urban, Patricia, Edward Schortman, Sylvia Smith, Julia Miller, L. Theodore Neff, Lavinia True, Marne Ausec, Sonya Kane, Heather Mahan, Matthew Dall, Christopher Eaton, David Schafer, Lisa Collins, Patricia Reed, Patricia Whooley, Nancy Condon, and Richard Goebels

1988 *The Naco Valley Archaeological Project, 1988 Season Summary*. Ms. on file in the archives of the Instituto Hondureno de Antropologia e Historia, Tegucigalpa.

Urban, Patricia and Edward Schortman

1986 *The Southeast Maya Periphery*. University of Texas Press, Austin.

Wallerstein, Immanuel

1974 *The Modern World System I.* Academic Press, New York.

1980 *The Modern World System II.* Academic Press, New York.

Webster, David

1980 Spatial Bounding and Settlement History at Three Walled Northern Maya Centers. *American Antiquity* 45:834-844.

Webster, Gary

1990 Labor Control and Emergent Stratification in Prehistoric Europe. *Current Anthropology* 31:337-366.

Wells, Peter

1980 *Culture Contact and Culture Change*. Cambridge University Press, Cambridge.

1988 Industry and Society in Late Prehistoric Europe. In *Tribe and Polity in Late Prehistoric Europe*, edited by O.B. Gibson and M. Geselowitz, pp. 207-218. Plenum Press, New York.

Wonderley, Anthony

1981 *Late Postclassic Occupations at Naco, Honduras*. Latin American Studies Program Dissertation Series 86. Cornell University, Ithaca.

1986 Naco, Honduras—Some Aspects of a Late Pre-Columbian Community on the Eastern Maya Frontier. In *The Southeast Maya Periphery*, edited by P. Urban and E. Schortman, pp. 313-332. University of Texas Press, Austin.

Wright, Henry

1977 Recent Research on the Origins of the State. In *Annual Review of Anthropology*, edited by B. Siegel, A. Beals, and S. Tyler, pp. 379-397. Annual Reviews, Palo Alto.

Wright, Henry, and Gregory Johnson

1975 Population, Exchange, and Early State Formation in Southwestern Iran. *American Anthropologist* 77:267-289.

Yoffee, Norman

1985 Perspectives on, "Trends toward Social Complexity in Prehistoric Australia and Papua New Guinea." *Archaeology in Oceania* 20:41-49.

1991 Maya Elite Interaction: Through a Glass Sideways. In *Classic Maya Political History: Hieroglyphic and Archaeological Evidence*, edited by T. P. Culbert, pp. 285-310. Cambridge Universiy Press, Cambridge.

Chapter 9

Conclusions

Gary M. Feinman
University of Wisconsin-Madison

The papers in this volume provide a comprehensive overview of the current theoretical orientations, analytical applications, and practical debates that comprise contemporary world-systems approaches in archaeology. In this brief concluding essay, I highlight some of these debates and outline potentially productive directions for future world-systems research. Yet, before addressing present themes and future research prospects, it is worth taking a historical look back at the issue of scale in anthropological archaeology. By so doing, some of the reservations toward and alternatives to the world-system perspective are reviewed and addressed.

Historical Background

In 1961, Alexander Lesser critiqued current social evolutionary thought for the inadequate attention that it gave to large-scale spatial processes (what he called borrowing and diffusion). Lesser focused on such relations as marriage alliances and trade partnerships that frequently extended well beyond the bounds of single societies. Lesser (1952, 1961), an evolutionist himself, recognized the historical significance and universality of this macroregional interaction, which he reasoned was under-emphasized by the current evolutionary perspective that focused on change within social aggregates that were characterized as distinct and separate societies. By definition, the social evolutionists viewed larger-scale phenomena as external. From this perspective, extra-societal relations were considered the realm of historical accident, obscuring the system of linkages that constituted the true core or inner workings of a society.

Lesser (1961:41) argued that the interdependence between social aggregates was not only virtually universal, but that such interconnections were generally not the consequence of haphazard, incidental contacts. Lesser went on to propose that understanding such large-scale relations required the conceptualization of human social life and history along a broad time-space continuum of associations. It is important to note that Lesser did not advocate a return to a more culture-historical framework, as macro-scale processes were no more systematically interpreted from that theoretical vantage.

Lesser's thoughtful critique had relatively little immediate effect on social evolutionary theory, a body of theory that also provided the foundational underpinnings for the "New Archaeology" of the 1960s. Therefore, it is not surprising that one of the characteristics of early processual archaeology was that regions served as the "investigatory universe appropriate for most archaeological problems" (Dunnell 1985:297). Societies or cultures often were viewed as relatively tightly bounded social entities that largely could be studied independently of one another. These social entities were placed and compared along the trajectory that passed from bands to states. Although the greater emphasis on regional approaches and systematic survey procedures revolutionarily advanced archaeology's ability to tackle specific social evolutionary questions, little systematic rigor was given by processual archaeologists to the consideration or examination of extra-societal linkages (Trigger 1984:284-285).

By the mid-1980s, armed with the data from recent regional research efforts, many processual archaeologists were becoming increasingly uncomfortable with the modeling of ancient societies as bounded systems (e.g., Kowalewski et al. 1983). As a reaction to the predominantly local focus of processual archaeology, greater concern was devoted to questions of cultural frontiers and societal boundaries (e.g., De Atley and Findlow 1984; Green and Perlman 1985). Although papers along these lines expressed a greater awareness of spatial scale than had been exhibited in most earlier work, the clear lack of theoretical coherence illustrated the absence in archaeology of an overarching framework to model or investigate what used to be called diffusion (Trigger 1984:286).

The publication of *The Modern World System I* (Wallerstein 1974) had a rapid and significant impact in many social and historical disciplines. Yet, in archaeology, the initial effect of Wallerstein's work, which contained the basis for a systematic macroregional approach, was far more muted (cf., Pailes and Whitecotton 1979). In part, this limited immediate influence was a product of Wallerstein's own focus on the capitalist world, a system that he sees as radically different from any that had occurred before (Wallerstein 1993). Likewise, Wallerstein's explicit presentation of world-systems theory as an alternative to regionally focused evolutionary or developmentalist theory was problematic, as the latter theoretical approach (neo-evolutionism) had been the intellectual backbone for two decades of processual archaeology. Although Wallerstein's focus on the key importance of bulk goods conformed to the materially oriented perspective of most archaeologists, this emphasis on food and fuel hardly fostered macro-scale thinking in a discipline where most researchers study social settings in which bulk transport systems were rather limited.

More than two decades following the publication of Wallerstein's volume, world-systems theory has yet to penetrate the basic jargon of archaeology. Yet most, if not all, of the authors in this collection see at least an important germ in Wallerstein's work that can address the deficiencies in our theory noted by Lesser more than 30 years ago (see also Trigger 1984). As is evident from this collection, a neatly packaged, consensually accepted body of world-systems thought has not yet congealed. Nevertheless, the papers in this volume illustrate that a common and systematic language as well as a set of shared research questions are emerging. The broad world-systems perspective employed in this collection allows for the systematic analysis of macro-scale processes in archaeology, while facilitating cross-disciplinary discussions with other fields that also endeavor to understand long-term social processes and histories. Neither of these aims (a systematic language and agenda for the macro-scale that serves both inside and beyond archaeology) has been met by the pre-Wallerstein processual archaeology of the last decades or by traditional trait-based culture history (see Blanton and Feinman 1984; Kowalewski, Chapter 3).

Clarifying Misconceptions and Addressing Reservations

If the world-systems perspective is to take a key place in the theoretical toolbox of most archaeologists, a number of commonly held misconceptions and reservations about this body of thought must be clarified and addressed. Many of the problems, frequently raised by archaeologists, to ignore or dismiss world-systems approaches stem from a misunderstanding or misreading of Wallerstein's original treatise. As discussed by Peregrine (Chapter 1) and Hall and Chase-Dunn (Chapter 2; Chase-Dunn 1992; Chase-Dunn and Hall 1991), other commonly held reservations were based on legitimate limitations in the original incantation of world-systems theory. Yet, many of these have since been modified or re-thought in more recent world-systems perspectives, which are far more applicable to preindustrial, pre-capitalist societies. The remainder of this section confronts several of these oft-stated reservations to illustrate why it is no longer valid to throw out the "infant" world-systems approach along with the "bath water" of specific limitations that have been recognized in Wallerstein's seminal volume.

Core-periphery Relations

Some archaeologists reject the world-systems perspective because of superficial misunderstandings about its concepts and terminology. These problems have generally revolved around Wallerstein's use of the term 'world,' and misconceptions regarding core-periphery relations in the world-systems perspective. The first of these problems stems from Wallerstein's attribution of his 'world-systems' framework to the capitalist world, which truly is global in scale. Yet, most (although not all) preindustrial archaeologists would be uncomfortable with the notion that the past worlds they investigate were anywhere near global in size. Here, the problem is not merely the term 'world,' but Wallerstein's conjunction of that word with system, since a few chance or brief long-distance encounters do not constitute the basis for a truly interconnected socio-economic system.

Yet, Wallerstein's (1979) use of 'world' is not synonymous with global. By 'world,' Wallerstein (1979:156) refers to economic interconnections or divisions of labor that are large in scale, and thereby traverse cultural and, in some cases, political boundaries. Thus, the applicability of the world-systems perspective lies not in a claim for truly global pre-capitalist systems, but in the existence of important (or systemic) relations that transected regional, cultural, or political divisions. Subsequent world-systems thought recognizes that these supra-regional systemic linkages need not be economic (see Chase-Dunn and Hall 1991). In characterizing the preindustrial world, many more archaeologists would be comfortable with the existence of significant systemic linkages that crossed polity, cultural, or regional bounds than would recognize truly global pre-capitalist systems.

As with the word 'world,' some scholars have objected to the terms 'core' and 'periphery,' suggesting that they somehow describe an immutable or (for the latter) pejorative condition. Yet neither of these attributions is inferred nor necessary. For example, Chase-Dunn and Hall (1991:19-30) recognize two distinct classes of relationship (differentiation and hierarchy) between cores and peripheries. The latter entails domination and exploitation, while the former does not. The potential for change in these core-periphery relationships is recognized. Likewise, Blanton and Feinman (1984; see also Abu-Lughod 1989 for the Mediterranean) discuss significant shifts in the relative 'coreness' of specific Mesoamerican regions over time. Although scholars may not agree over which attributes (e.g., population density, architectural monumentality, access to resources, standard of living, military might) are central to 'coreness,' each of these concepts is subject to empirical examination. As these aforementioned attributes vary over time, so does core-periphery status (Finsten, Chapter 7).

The expressed criticism that world-systems approaches somehow necessarily depict people in peripheries as 'voiceless,' 'without agency,' or mere receptors for (emulators of) core customs is a false characterization that owes more to culture historical theory (diffusionism) than it does to Wallerstein or the world-systems perspective. For example, McGuire (Chapter 5; see also Schortman and Urban 1994) critiques the world-systems approach because he believes that in such systems peripheries would be expected to emulate the core. Yet, he finds that the possible peripheral areas surrounding the ancient Hohokam core in the Salt-Gila Basin in Arizona did not adopt traits from (or become culturally more similar to) that core region. Such an expression (cultural borrowing) of core-periphery dominance would certainly be predicted by the culture history paradigm. Yet, it would not be a necessary expectation from the world-systems perspective, which recognizes that significant differences can often be the product of intense contact (Paynter 1989:379; Wallerstein 1974:98).

In an expansion of Wallerstein's original framework, Chase-Dunn and Hall (1991:28) distinguish "spread" from the "backwash" effects of core-periphery relations. They propose that the former (borrowing, diffusion, increasing similarity) is more typical of early state world-systems, while the latter (increasing differentiation between core and periphery) is more likely in world-systems that were dominated by empires. Yet this hypothesis remains unsubstantiated, and the same core can have diverse relations with various peripheries (e.g., McGuire, Chapter 5). Clearly, understanding the nature of core-periphery relations requires careful investigation of both the core and the periphery. From this perspective, specific outcomes of core-periphery relations cannot be explained if a strong analytical 'voice' is not given to peripheries as well as cores (Wolf 1982:23).

Single Cores and Bulk Goods

Among the archaeologists who are familiar with Wallerstein are those who tend to equate his writings with the entire world-systems perspective. From this vantage, limitations in Wallerstein's original framework can be made a basis to discount or ignore world-systems perspectives more generally. Yet, many of the problems in the initial world-systems formulations have since been modified or critiqued in later world-systems perspectives.

Focused on the rise of the capitalist world, Wallerstein envisioned the early capitalist world-system as having a single core (Western Europe), which he argued was articulated in an inter-societal network primarily through the exchange of bulk goods. Even if we accept the accuracy of Wallerstein's specific sixteenth-century analysis (but see Schneider 1977), these characterizations clearly would not fit many archaeological cases. Ancient worlds often have multiple cores (and frequently lack a truly dominating polity) (Abu-Lughod 1989; Feinman et al., Chapter 6).

Given the nature of preindustrial transportation, systemic linkages between regions and polities were not always exclusively based on the long-distance movements of bulk products (Hall and Chase-Dunn

1993:125). The exchange of light-weight, prestige goods can help to define systemic interconnections (Adams 1974; Blanton and Feinman 1984; Schneider 1977); albeit their relative importance remains at issue in specific cases (Kowalewski, Chapter 3; Peregrine, Chapter 4; Schortman and Urban, Chapter 8). *Contra*-Wallerstein, recent world-systems thinking has illustrated that single core states and a reliance on the exchange of bulk goods certainly are not definitional of (all) world-systems. Likewise, archaeologists should not rule out the utility of world-systems perspectives for the investigation of multi-core worlds or for macro-regions in which luxury items had a definitional role.

Scales of Analysis

As noted above, Wallerstein proposed his original formulation (1974) in direct opposition to regionally based developmental theories. His world-systems analysis championed the macro-scale as the preferred alternative to the investigation of societies or regions (which was typical of developmental approaches). Although Chase-Dunn and Hall (Chase-Dunn 1992; Chase-Dunn and Hall 1991, 1993; Hall and Chase-Dunn 1993, Chapter 2) have broadened the world-systems perspective in many productive ways that make the overall approach more comparative and inter-disciplinary, they remain steadfast to Wallerstein's notion of macro-scalar imperative. For example, they (Chase-Dunn and Hall 1993:851; Chapter 2) flatly proclaim the world-system as the fundamental unit of social change.

Yet, as long as world-systems scholars proclaim the macro-scale to be the most important unit for socio-historical analysis, I do not see world-systems perspectives gaining their deserved attention in archaeology. The question of which scalar unit is most significant for human history is at least partially an empirical question (although not one easily resolved), and not an issue that can be decided by theoretical fiat. As Abu-Lughod (1993) recently has argued for thirteenth-century Eurasia, shifts in power and dominance at the macro-scale do not always coincide with the nature of change in the broader arena. Such scalar discordance certainly is not unique to the thirteenth century or Eurasia. Who is to say which scale is more important for understanding history? In the study of life more generally (Lewontin 1970; Mayr 1982), it is recognized that understanding only comes from the investigation of several analytical scales simultaneously, and then the integration of those findings.

In archaeology, claims for the privileging of the macro-scale (over local factors) find little support. Webster (1993:419) spoke for many in the discipline when he commented "that the most significant of the forces that stimulate the emergence of cultural complexity in preindustrial societies and thereafter maintain and reshape it are usually quite localized." Although I would give more weight to the broad-scale factors in history than Webster, I certainly can agree with him that local/regional political, economic, environmental, and demographic factors generally are critical for understanding long-term change in preindustrial societies. Yet a central point of this volume is that we cannot rely on those local and regional factors alone (as archaeologists in the past have too often done), and that a systematic approach to inter-regional relations must also be developed and employed. As illustrated in this collection, world-systems perspectives offer a promising avenue toward that conceptual growth; however, there is no reason to burden its acceptance and implementation in the field with unverifiable claims.

To explain long-term historical change, archaeology and its sister disciplines need theories at various scales. In other words, regional and macroregional theories are not mutually exclusive alternatives, and both are necessary (along with theories about cities, households, individuals, etc.) to understand major social transitions (see Lightfoot and Martinez 1995:477-478). To explain organic evolution, multi-scalar theories about chemicals, cells, populations, ecosystems, and more are essential. Why should we expect not to have to bootstrap (Blanton 1990) and juxtapose theories in similar fashion to investigate an equally complex diachronic process, the path of human history?

Future Directions

To this point, I have argued that a more systematic approach to scalar units larger than regions is needed in archaeology, and that the broadened world-systems perspective offers a promising pathway for this comparative analysis. I also have endeavored to remove many of the misconceptions and 'straw men' that have hindered a broader application of this framework. Although Wallerstein (1990:293) has recently suggested that "it may take 50 years by tens of thousands of scholars before...[the world-systems perspective] begins to pay off significantly," we need to ask ourselves what are the alternatives? Certainly, a backward reversal to normative and trait-focused culture history with its reliance on the non-behavioral diffusion concept is not a satisfactory option. Yet other archaeological paradigms have given even less thoughtful attention to the supra-regional scale.

Beyond being the best theoretical path available for analyzing sub-continental processes, the broad world-systems perspective offers critical debates and key questions for future comparative archaeological analysis. Some of these issues are embodied in the four hypotheses that conclude the paper by Hall and Chase-Dunn

(Chapter 2). Their first and second hypotheses, which concern the relationship between the degree of core complexity and the nature/degree of inter-societal domination, are considered in Chapters 3 through 7 of this volume. Hall and Chase-Dunn's third hypothesis concerning the relative importance of "spread" and "backwash effects" in different long-distance exchange contexts is addressed in Chapters 5 and 8. And, hypothesis four concerning the shifting role of semiperipheries is examined in Chapters 4 and 7. Yet as Hall and Chase-Dunn (Chapter 2) recognize, additional empirical case studies are clearly necessary if significant future progress is to be made on the examination of these hypotheses.

Another theme, central to this collection, but ripe for future archaeological analysis concerns the importance/role of prestige goods in inter-societal interaction. Peregrine (Chapter 4) and Schortman and Urban (Chapter 8) ascribe significant systemic implications to precious goods, while Kowalewski (Chapter 3) affords them lower importance. Although this debate is not new (e.g., Brumfiel 1987; Flannery 1968; Friedman and Rowlands 1977; Johnson 1989; Schneider 1977; Upham 1982; Wallerstein 1974), its importance in archaeology grows as greater attention is given to macro-scale research issues.

Nevertheless, the current impasse (between those who champion the role of preciosities and those who do not) owes much to the manner in which this debate is framed by macro-scale analysts on both sides of the question. The crux of the current debate is an argument over the cross-cultural importance of prestige goods. The issue is framed as if that importance is more or less uniform across all societies or, perhaps, a simple function of either transport efficiency or societal complexity. The stalemate may relate to the overly dichotomous nature of this argument, which has both sides searching for a general, cross-cultural 'answer' or pattern.

The time is here to dissect the variable role of such precious goods in different and specific societal settings. In some time-space contexts, portable wealth may be critical to faction-building and hence political power; in others, the exchange of wealth may have a far more minor import (Blanton et al. 1992; Blanton et al., 1996; Feinman 1995). The specific societal meaning and role of wealth or prestige goods would seem to be a key determinant of the importance of such goods in macro-scale interactions. This importance may vary over time, even within the same cultural region.

Clearly, this issue serves as an example in which detailed societal-scale interpretation and analysis must be boot-strapped to macroregional theory, if we are to extricate ourselves from the current conceptual logjam. Progress in that direction would contribute markedly to broader, cross-disciplinary world-systems issues. But more central to archaeology, it also would yield a more behavioral path toward the eventual understanding of horizon styles, interaction spheres, and the mechanisms of stylistic diversification, the explanations for which have long puzzled archaeologists (e.g., Willey 1991).

I conclude by making the presumption to speak for the volume's 11 authors. We offer our ideas in the spirit of Redman's (1991:303) plea for archaeologists "to look at the world from all angles, both the obvious and the less obvious; and to put forward interesting propositions, providing enough information for others to determine whether a dialogue should be pursued." We have provided the data to start a dialogue about pre-Columbian world-systems. We have presented the theory. We have advanced several points of contention, ideas, and hypotheses for future research. We hope this volume will be a starting point from which that dialogue will be pursued.

References

Abu-Lughod, Janet

1989 *Before European Hegemony: The World System A.D. 1250-1350.* Oxford University Press, New York.

1993 Discontinuities and Persistence: One World System or a Succession of Systems? In *The World System: Five Hundred Years or Five Thousand?* edited by Andre Gunder Frank and Barry K. Gills, pp. 278-291. Routledge, London.

Adams, R. M.

1974 Anthropological Perspectives on Ancient Trade. *Current Anthropology* 15:211-239.

Blanton, Richard E.

1990 Theory and Practice in Mesoamerican Archaeology: A Comparison of Two Modes of Scientific Inquiry. In *Debating Oaxaca Archaeology,* edited by Joyce Marcus, pp. 1-16. Anthropological Papers No. 84, Museum of Anthropology, University of Michigan, Ann Arbor.

Blanton, Richard, and Gary Feinman

1984 The Mesoamerican World System. *American Anthropologist* 86:673-682.

Blanton, Richard E., Gary M. Feinman, Stephen A. Kowalewski, and Peter N. Peregrine

1996 A Dual-Processual Theory for the Evolution of Mesoamerican Civilization. *Current Anthropology* 37(1).

Blanton, Richard, Stephen Kowalewski, and Gary Feinman

1992 The Mesoamerican World-System. *Review* 15:419-426.

Brumfiel, Elizabeth M.

1987 Elite and Utilitarian Crafts in the Aztec State. In *Specialization, Exchange, and Complex Societies,* edited by Elizabeth M. Brumfiel and Timothy K. Earle, pp. 102-118. Cambridge University Press, Cambridge.

Chase-Dunn, Christopher

1992 The Comparative Study of World-Systems. *Review* 15:313-333.

Chase-Dunn, Christopher, and Thomas D. Hall

1991 Conceptualizing Core/Periphery Hierarchies for Comparative Study. In *Core/Periphery Relations in Precapitalist Worlds,* edited by Christopher Chase-Dunn and Thomas D. Hall, pp. 5-44. Westview, Boulder.

De Atley, Suzanne P., and Frank J. Findlow

1984 *Exploring the Limits: Frontiers and Boundaries in Prehistory.* BAR International Series 223. Oxford, England.

Dunnell, Robert C.

1985 Archaeological Survey in the Lower Mississippi Alluvial Valley, 1940-1947: A Landmark Study in American Archaeology. *American Antiquity* 50:297-300.

Feinman, Gary M.

1995 The Emergence of Inequality: A Focus on Strategies and Processes. In *Foundations of Social Inequality,* edited by T. Douglas Price and Gary M. Feinman, pp. 255-279. Plenum Press, New York.

Flannery, Kent V.

1968 The Olmec and the Valley of Oaxaca: A Model for Inter-Regional Interaction in Formative Times. In *Dumbarton Oaks Conference on the Olmec,* edited by Elizabeth P. Benson, pp. 79-110. Dumbarton Oaks Research Library and Collection, Washington, D.C.

Friedman, Jonathan and Michael Rowlands

1977 Notes Towards an Epigenetic Model of the Evolution of 'Civilization'. In *The Evolution of Social Systems,* edited by Jonathan Friedman and Michael Rowlands, pp. 201-278. Duckworth, London.

Green, Stanton W., and Stephen M. Perlman

1985 *The Archaeology of Frontiers and Boundaries.* Academic Press, New York.

Hall, Thomas D., and Christopher Chase-Dunn

1993 The World-Systems Perspective and Archaeology: Forward into the Past. *Journal of Archaeological Research* 1:121-143.

Kowalewski, Stephen A., Richard E. Blanton, Gary Feinman, and Laura Finsten
1984 Boundaries, Scale, and Internal Organization. *Journal of Anthropological Archaeology* 2:32-56.
Johnson, Gregory A.
1989 Dynamics of Southwestern Prehistory: Far Outside—Looking In. In *Dynamics of Southwestern Prehistory*, edited by Linda S. Cordell and George J. Gumerman, pp. 371-389. Smithsonian Institution Press, Washington D.C.
Lesser, Alexander
1952 Evolution in Social Anthropology. *Southwestern Journal of Anthropology* 8:134-146.
1961 Social Fields and the Evolution of Society. *Southwestern Journal of Anthropology* 17:40-48.
Lewontin, R. C.
1970 The Units of Selection. *Annual Review of Ecology and Systematics* 1:1-18.
Lightfoot, Kent G., and Antoinette Martinez
1995 Frontiers and Boundaries in Archaeological Perspective. *Annual Review of Anthropology* 24:471-492.
Mayr, Enrst
1982 *The Growth of Biological Thought: Diversity, Evolution, and Inheritance.* Harvard University Press, Cambridge.
Pailes, Richard, and Joseph Whitecotton
1979 The Greater Southwest and Mesoamerican "World" System: An Exploratory Model of Frontier Relationships. In *The Frontier: Comparative Studies,* Vol. 2, edited by William Savage and Stephen Thompson, pp. 105-121. University of Oklahoma Press, Norman.
Paynter, Robert
1989 The Archaeology of Equality and Inequality. *Annual Review of Anthropology* 18:369-399.
Redman, Charles
1991 In Defense of the Seventies—The Adolescence of the New Archaeology. *American Anthropologist* 93:295-307.
Schneider, Jane
1970 Was There a Precapitalist World-System? *Peasant Studies* 6:20-29.
Schortman, Edward M., and Patricia A. Urban
1994 Living on the Edge: Core/Periphery Relations in Ancient Southern Mesoamerica. *Current Anthropology* 35:401-430.
Trigger, Bruce G.
1984 Archaeology at the Crossroads: What's New. *Annual Review of Anthropology* 13:275-300.
Upham, Steadman
1982 *Polities and Power: An Economic and Political History of the Western Pueblo.* Academic Press.
Wallerstein, Immanuel
1974 *The Modern World-System I: Capitalist Agriculture and the Origins of European World-Economy in the Sixteenth Century.* Academic Press, New York.
1979 *The Capitalist World-Economy.* Cambridge University Press, Cambridge.
1990 World-Systems Analysis: The Second Phase. *Review* 13:287-293.
1993 World Systems versus World-Systems. In *The World System: Five Hundred Years or Five Thousand?* edited by Andre Gunder Frank and Barry K. Gills, pp. 292-296. Routledge, London.
Webster, David
1994 Comment on "Living on the Edge: Core/Periphery Relations in Ancient Southeastern Mesoamerica," by Edward M. Schortman and Patricia A. Urban. *Current Anthropology* 35:419-420.
Willey, Gordon R.
1991 Horizontal Integration and Regional Diversity: An Alternating Process in the Rise of Civilizations. *American Antiquity* 56:197-215.
Wolf, Eric R.
1982 *Europe and the People Without History.* University of California Press, Berkeley.

List of Contributors

Christopher Chase-Dunn
Dept. of Sociology
Johns Hopkins University
Baltimore, MD 21218

Thomas D. Hall
Dept. of Sociology and Anthropology
DePauw University
Greencastle, IN 46135

Stephen A. Kowalewski
Dept. of Anthropology
University of Georgia
Athens, GA 30602

Gary M. Feinman
Dept. of Anthropology
University of Wisconsin
5240 Social Science
1180 Observatory Drive
Madison, WI 53706

Laura Finsten
Dept. of Anthropology
McMaster University
Hamilton, Ontario
Canada L8S 4L9

Randall McGuire
Dept. of Anthropology
State University of New York at Binghampton
P.O. Box 6000
Binghampton, NY 13902-6000

Linda M. Nicholas
Dept. of Anthropology
University of Wisconsin
5240 Social Science
1180 Observatory Drive
Madison, WI 53706

Peter N. Peregrine
Dept. of Anthropology
Lawrence University
Appleton, WI 54912-0599

Edward Schortman
Dept. of Anthropology and Sociology
Kenyon College
Gambier, OH 43022-9623

Steadman Upham
The Graduate School
125 Chapman Hall
University of Oregon
Eugene, OR 97403

Patricia Urban
Dept. of Anthropology and Sociology
Kenyon College
Gambier, OH 43022-9623